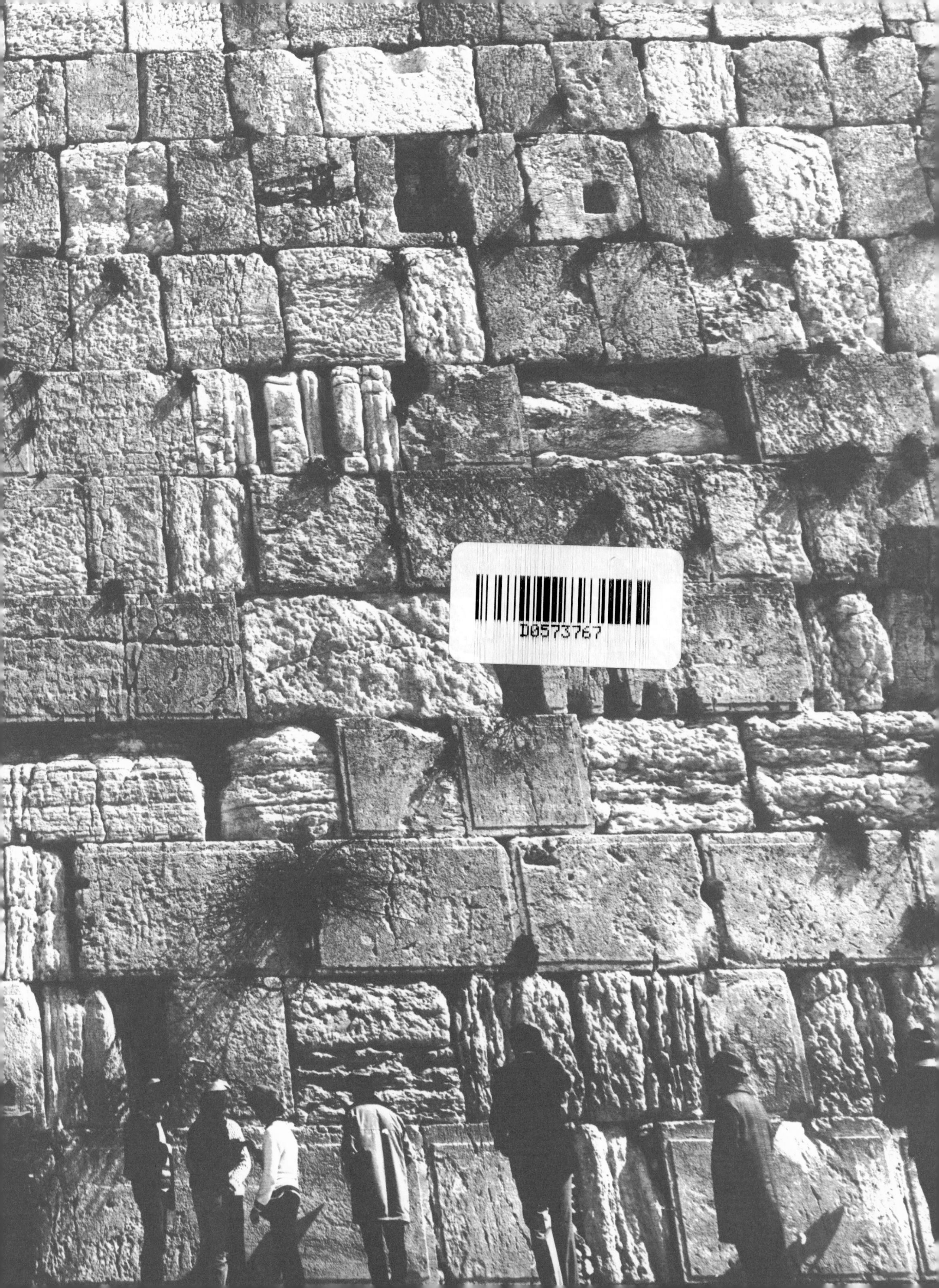

The
Western Wall

The Western Wall

Meir Ben-Dov, Mordechai Naor
Zeev Aner

Translated by Raphael Posner

ADAMA BOOKS
NEW YORK

הכותל

מאיר בן־דב, מרדכי נאור, זאב ענר

Designed by: Yoav Ben-Zur.
Yoav Graphics Ltd.

Library of Congress Catalog Card No. 86-70788
ISBN 965-05-0055-3

Adama Books, 306 West 38th Street
New York, N.Y. 10018

Printed in Israel

FOREWORD

What is the secret of the Western Wall? The usual answer is that the Wall is the only remnant of the Second Temple, destroyed by Titus, and considered a monument to Israel's days of religious and national glory. Some say the Wall is a symbol of the Jewish people, which has survived for thousands of years. Some stand awestruck in front of the Wall's massive masonry; others relate to the Wall as the holiest place in Judaism. The Western Wall is undoubtedly one of the cornerstones of Jewish existence. The Western Wall is mentioned in thousands of volumes. These books contain material on all the many aspects of the Wall: Jewish religious law, memoirs, evaluations, philosophical contemplation, poems, stories, and research. Until now, however, there has been very little discussion of how the historical, religious, and national monument in the heart of Jerusalem has been the focus of Jewish attention for centuries.

The preparation of this volume took two years. During this period, we examined hundreds of sources, exploring libraries, museums, archives, and private collections. We studies thousands of pictures and photographs. Much of the material was written by us; the rest is the work of some of the finest scholars and rabbis.

We have no illusions that the work is complete. Only after we immersed ourselves in the sea of material — historical, legal, archaeological, and literary — did we realize how central the Western Wall is to the life of Jews in Israel.

Many people helped us in all stages of our work. Our gratitude is extended to all of them.

The Authors

Jerusalem, Israel

CONTENTS

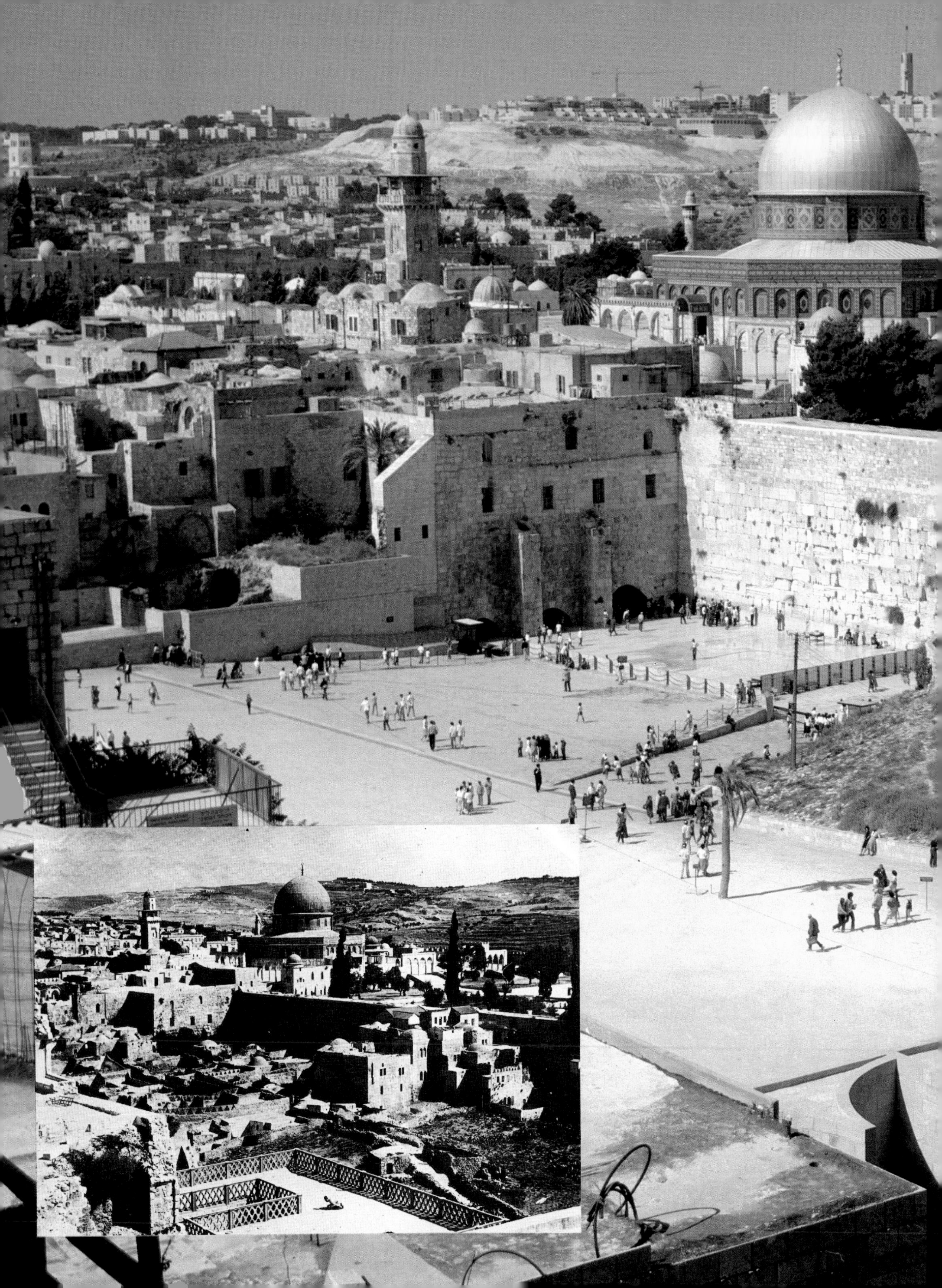

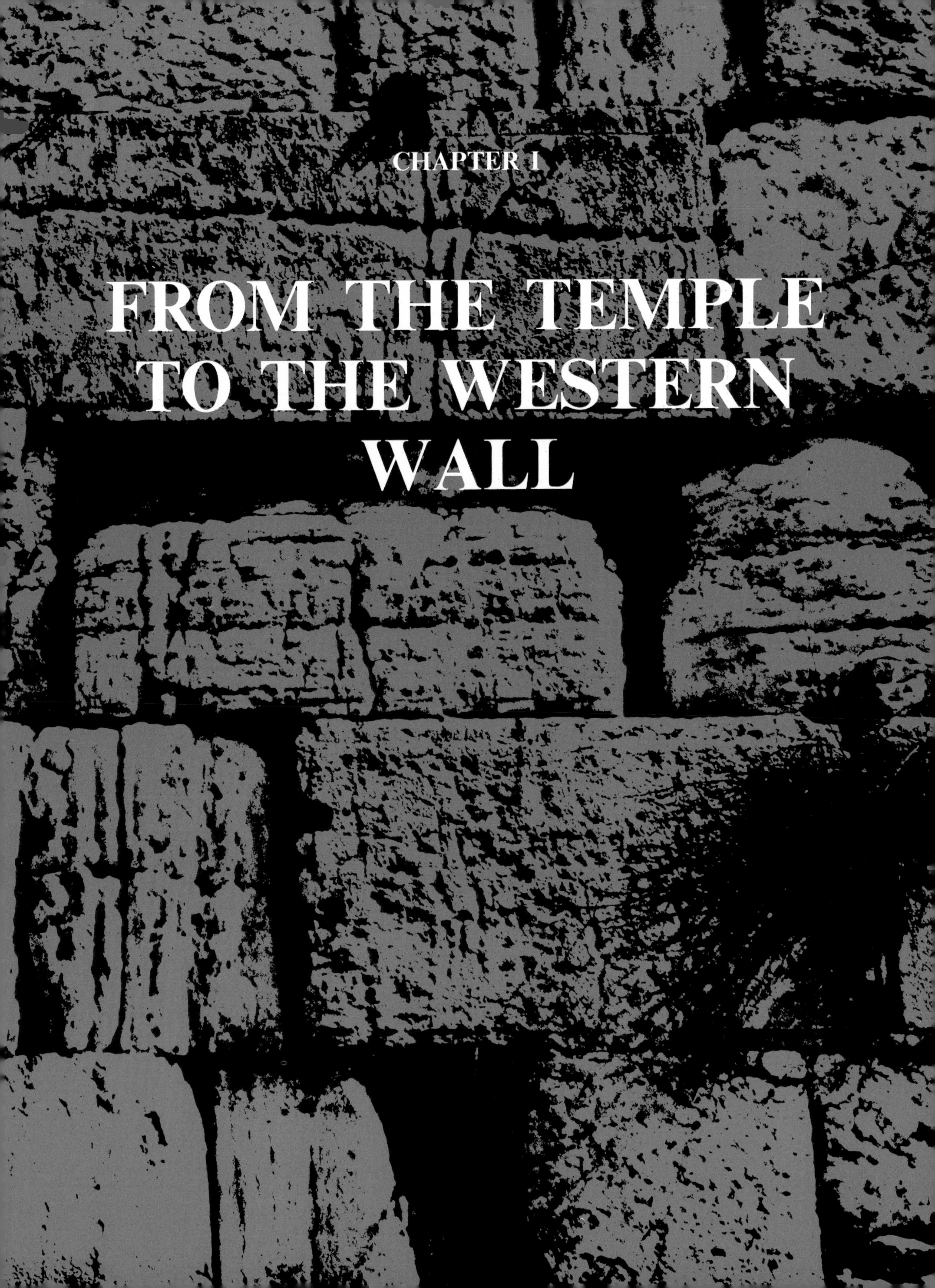

CHAPTER I

FROM THE TEMPLE TO THE WESTERN WALL

"Behold I have decided to build a house for the Lord as the Lord spoke to my father David."

"And Gad came that day to David and said to him, 'Arise, set up an altar for God in the theresing-floor of Araunah, the Jebusite.' And David went up according to the word of Gad which God had commanded him... So David bought the threshing-floor and the cattle for fifty silver shekels. And David built an altar for the Lord there..."
(II Samuel 24:18-25).

The Old City of Jerusalem, an etching, 1844.

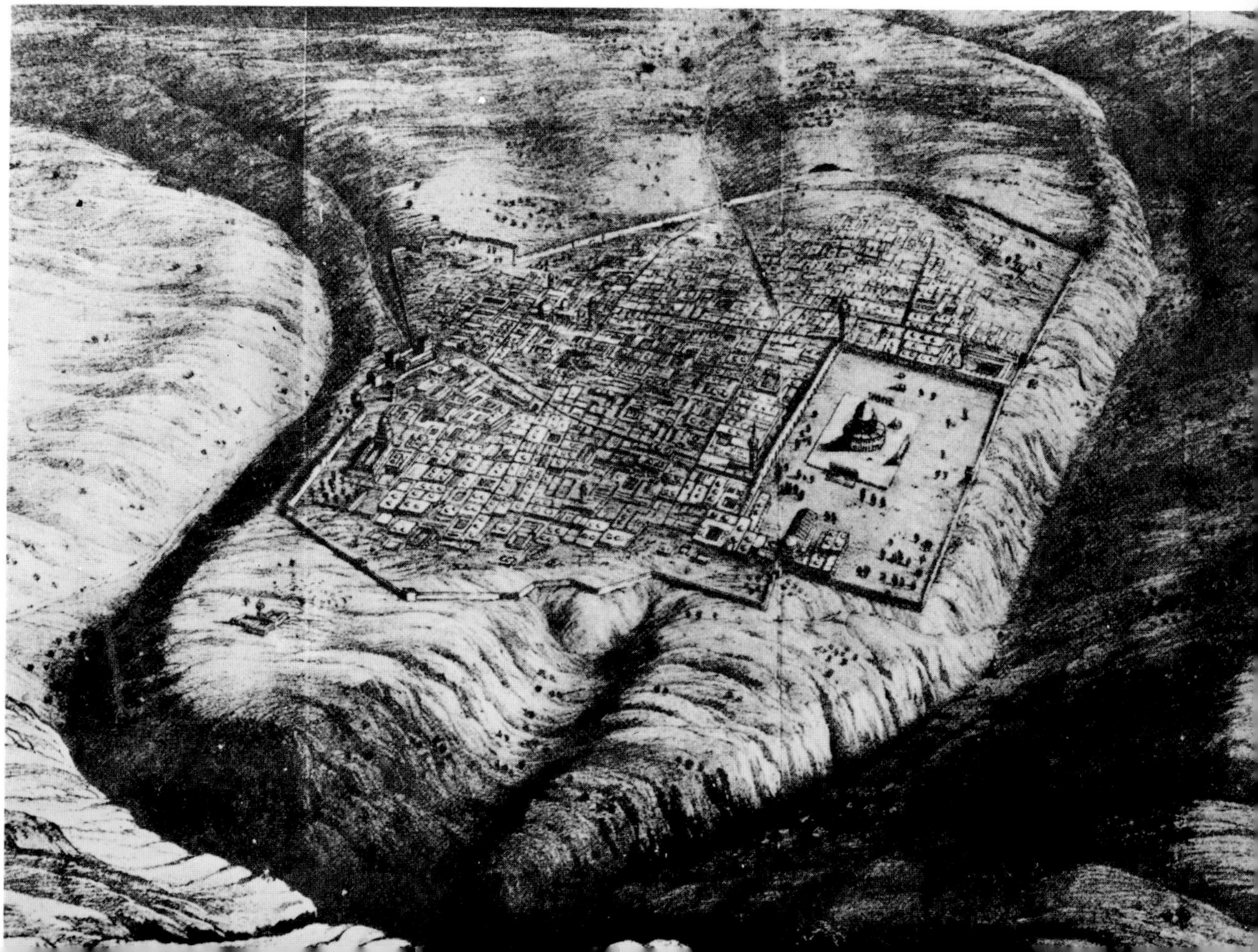

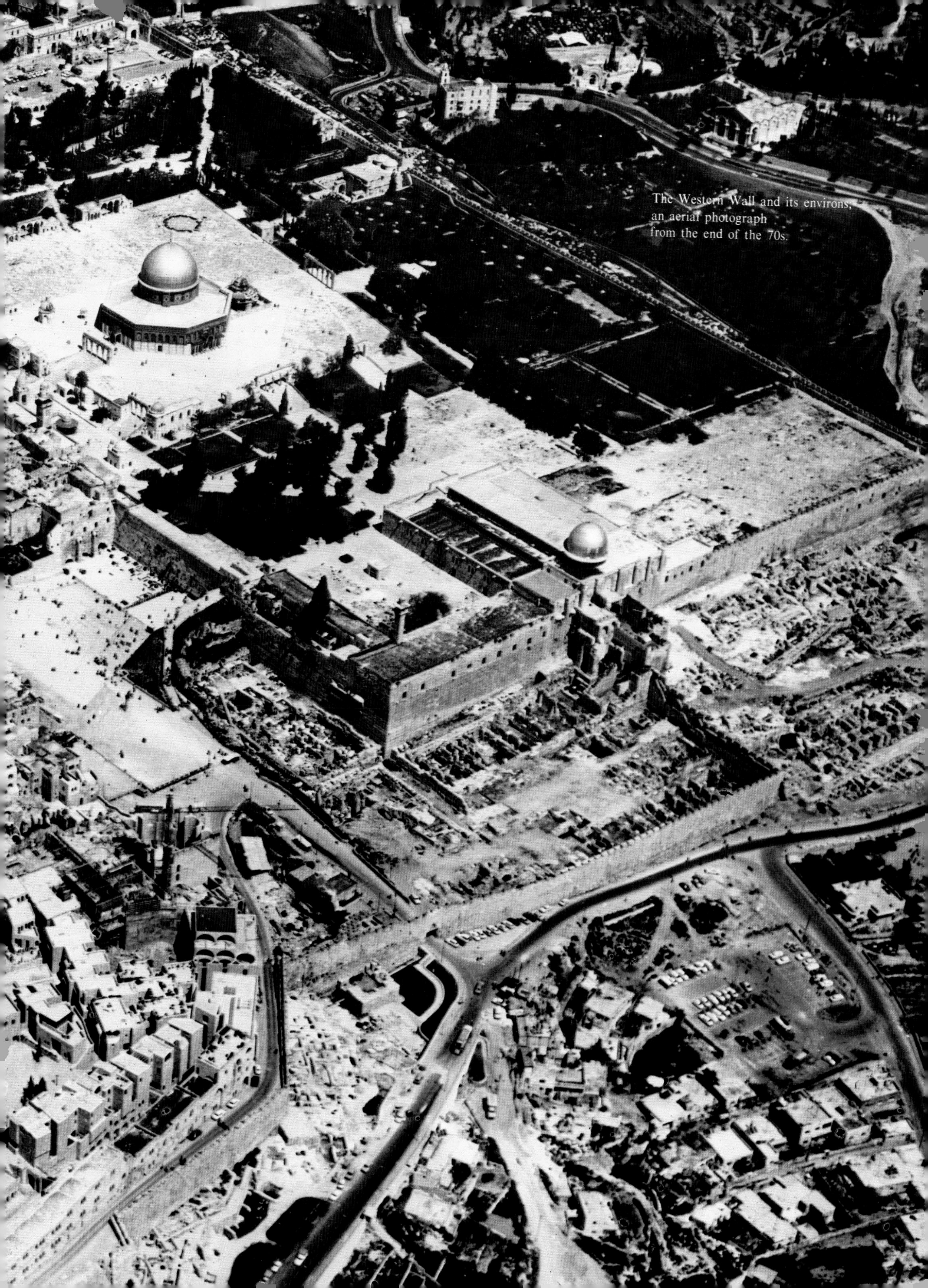

The Western Wall and its environs,
an aerial photograph
from the end of the 70s.

The Western Wall area. In the center: the excavations at the southern wall.

This place, according to ancient Israelite traditions, had been the stage on which the most significant and dramatic incident in the lives of the Patriarchs was played out – the Binding of Isaac, *Akedat Yitzhak*. And indeed, the erection of that altar brought an end to the epidemic that plagued the Israelites towards the end of David's reign. Already at that time, David considered building a temple next to the altar to replace the Tent of Assembly as the place in which the most sacred and symbolic of Israel's cultic objects, the Ark of the Covenant, would be deposited. This temple would be the focus of Israel's cultural and religious life and the center of judicial and legal activity. Its unblemished operation in honesty and uprightness would fix the spiritual level of the whole nation; it would act as a beacon, by the light of which the moral life of the people would be navigated to find the right path to a perfect society. The prophets of Israel, preaching in the shadow of the Temple, understood that concept to mean social justice, economic equality, and mutual respect and love.

It seemed to David that at that time, in the autumn of his life, Israel was established as a nation. The wanderings and the process of settlement which had started with the exodus from Egypt were over. It was, therefore, fitting now to bring the Ark of the Covenant, the symbol of God's presence in Israel, to a permanent abode. The Tent of Assembly, identified with Israel's wanderings, was no longer appropriate – a permanent temple was required. David started planning the building and even began to gather the necessary materials; but it was not to be. Our sources tell us that this was providential because David's hands were "full of blood." The blood of Israelites which had been spilt in his violent struggle to unify the tribes and establish his rule over them and the blood of the peoples he had conquered. Building the Temple, the house of peace, required cleaner hands than his.

A seal from First Temple times found near the Wall.

The inscription reads: "To King Zif."

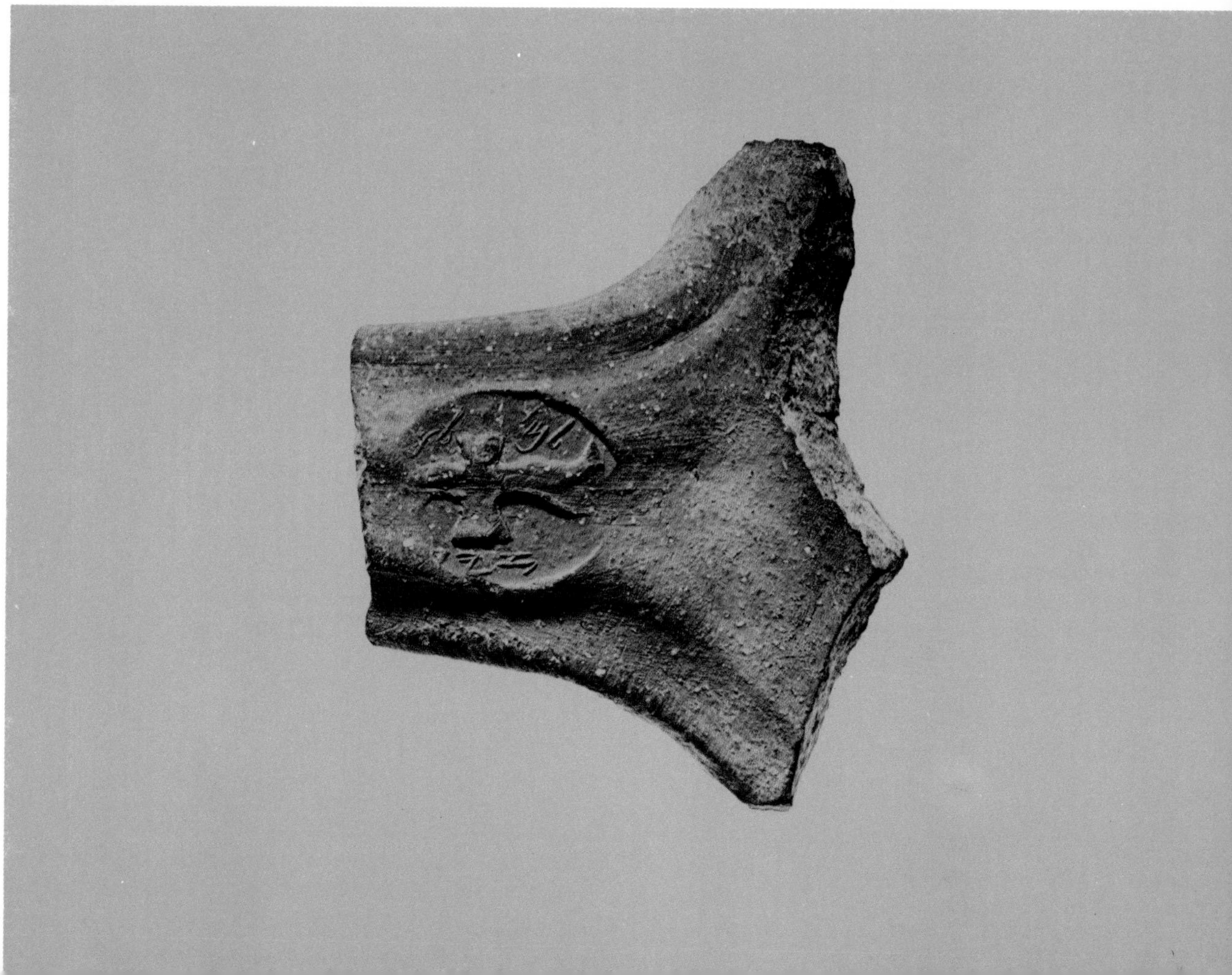

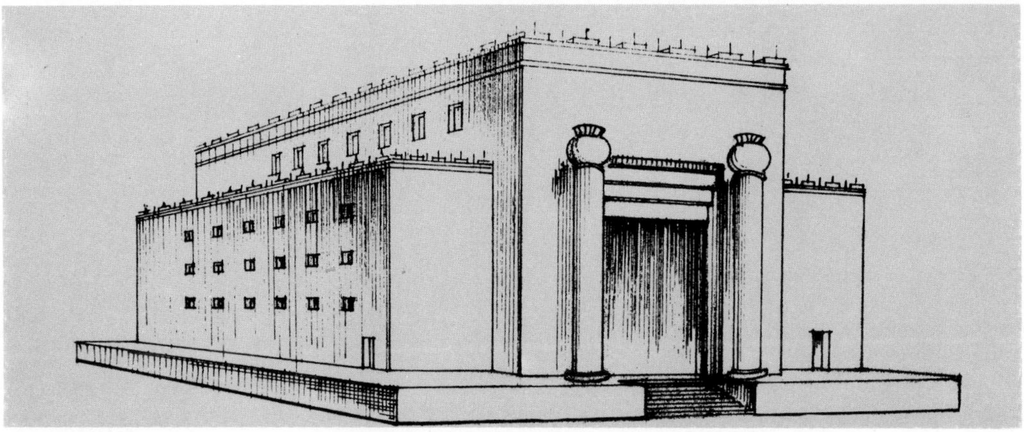

The First Temple, a schematic reconstruction. The two pillars in the facade were called *Yakhin* and *Boaz.*

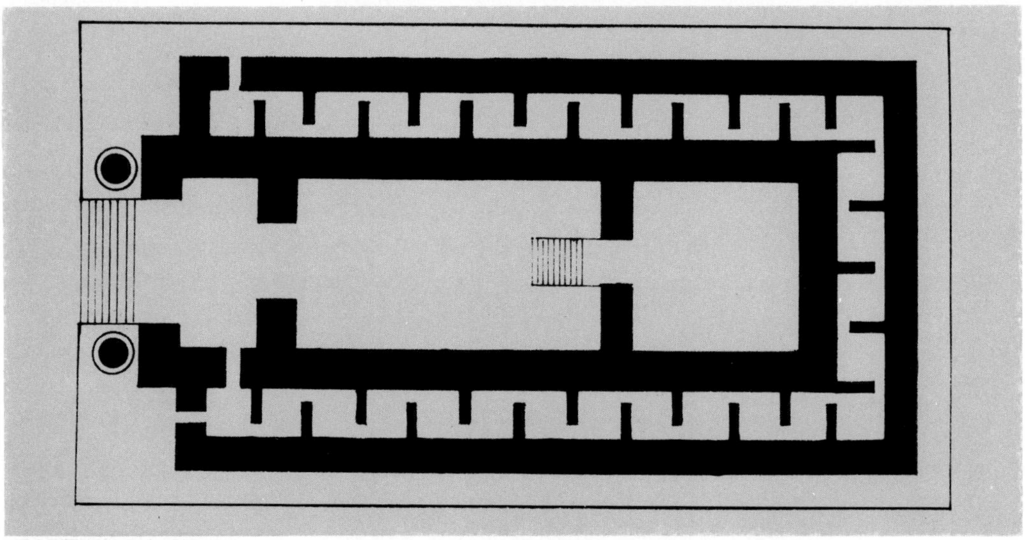

Plan of the First Temple.

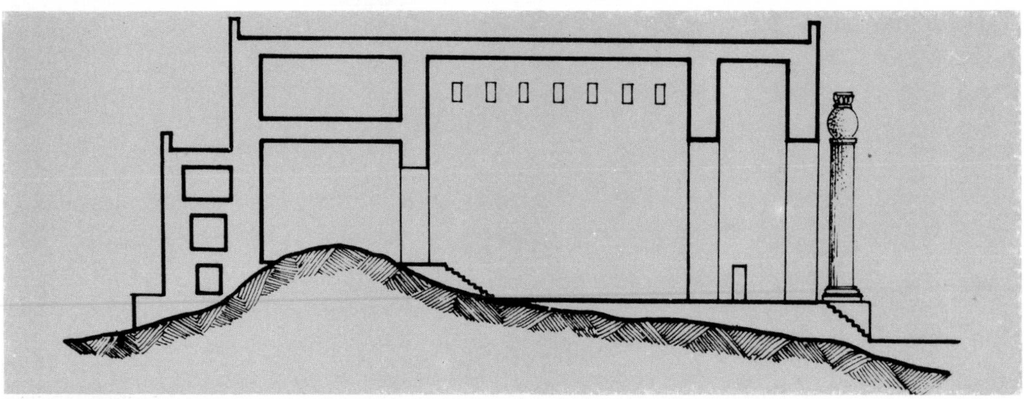

The First Temple, a side view.

The Temple was built by Solomon, his youngest son who succeeded him to the throne. As soon as he felt that his grip on the throne was firm, he set about the task of building the Temple, the pinnacle of his father's dreams. "And it came to pass in the four hundred and eightieth year after the exodus of the Israelites from Egypt, in the fourth year of the reign of Solomon, in the second month, that is the month of Ziv, that he built the house of the Lord." (I Kings 6:1). After seven years of intensive work, the Temple was ready. In the construction artisans and builders from Tyre and Sidon cooperated with the Israelites. The building that resulted was one of the most impressive in the kingdom and its fame even spread into the neighboring countries. But far more important than its architectural beauty and its dimensions was its influence on the life of the nation. It became the core of Israel's spiritual life and inspired lofty ideas which shaped the life of the nation for generations.

"So, because of you Zion will be ploughed as a field"

The Temple stood some four hundred years until it was destroyed by Nebuchadnezzar, the king of Babylon. The quality of these years was not uniform neither with regard to the nation's history nor to that of the temple; some of them were sombre and others exalted. Just a few years after Solomon's death, his son, Rehoboam, had to hand over the contents of the Temple treasury to Shishak, the king of Egypt, in order to persuade him to lift his siege of

The First Temple according to Ezekiel's vision; a reconstruction according to Ch.Chipier, 1887.

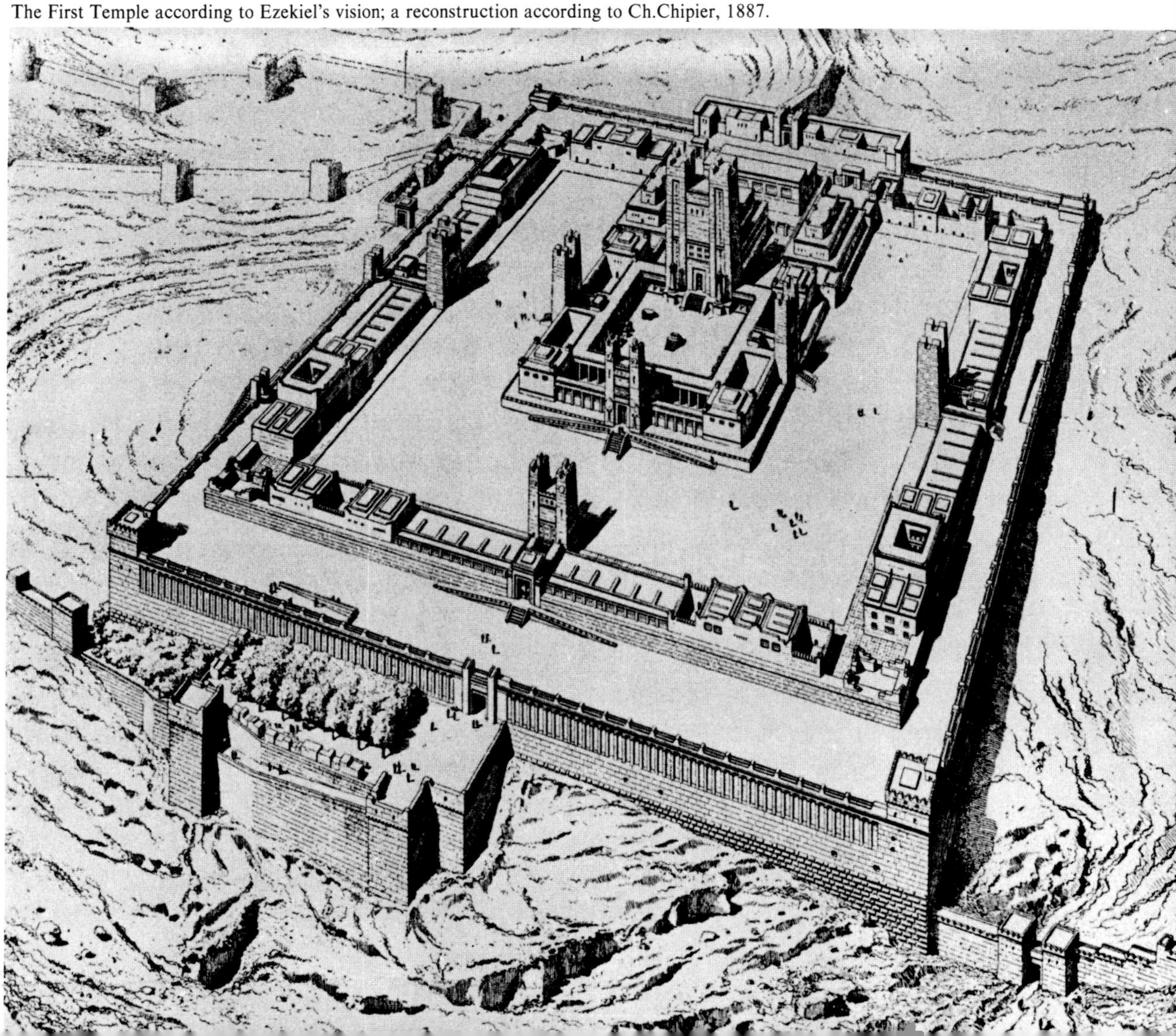

Jerusalem and spare the city. The years even witnessed Israelite kings who abandoned Israel's traditional ways and instituted pagan worship into the Temple. Ataliah, the daughter of Jezebel, who ruled in Judah, was the most extreme of these and her downfall brought about a revival of Jewish worship, and an effort to renew the ancient traditions in the spirit of God's Torah. Temple activity reached a peak in the seventh century B.C.E., in the reign of Josiah (Josiahu) when the Temple was purified and significant and far reaching reforms were instituted in the cult forms and, indeed, in Jewish religious philosophy. It seemed at that time as though Israel had once again found the right path with the Temple as its guide. But Josiah's successors were unable to meet the challenge and could not steer the ship of state aright through the storms of socio-economic problems on the one hand and those of foreign policy and diplomacy on the other. The result was that the Temple became a royal instrument to further the narrow temporal interests of the court which were often mistaken. The contemporary prophets realized what was happening and raised an anguished, public outcry against this perversion of the sacred. The more extreme among the prophets, with Jeremiah and Micah at their head, went so far as to prophecy that this behavior would only lead to catastrophe and even to the destruction of the Temple itself. At the end of the period, in the beginning of the sixth century B.C.E., Jerusalem was conquered by the Babylonian hosts and the Temple was indeed destroyed. Our traditions have it that this took place on the ninth of the month of Av, on which selfsame day, the Second Temple would also be destroyed. The echoes of that terrible day have reverberated throughout Jewish history till this day.

"The glory of this, the latter house will be greater than that of the former"

The political upheaval in the East at the end of the sixth century B.C.E. and the rise of Persia led by Cyrus, remade the political map of the area and inaugurated a new era. Cyrus was trying to rule the world by dividing it in small and comparatively independent states. Because of their size, these states would be weak and Cyrus would be able to control them with limited forces. Furthermore, the independence these states enjoyed – and particularly the freedom of religion – would have a calming effect and reduce, if not eliminate, the desire to rebel.

At Cyrus' instigation, therefore, a call went out to the exiled Jews in Babylon to return to their homeland and rebuild their capital, Jerusalem and the Temple in it. The valuable Temple artifacts, which Nebuchadnezzar had plundered and which were stored in the Babylonian treasury, were returned to the Jews. The Jews answered the call and so started the Return to Zion.

Under the leadership of Zerubabel and Joshua, the work got under way and the altar service was renewed. But the returnees soon ran into difficulties in the form of determined opposition on the part of the strangers who had been settled in the country and who united against the returning Jews. It was only some decades later, when Ezra and Nehemia came under the auspices of the Persian king, that it was possible to undertake the rebuilding of the Temple itself and the rehabilitation of Jerusalem, including the reconstruction of its walls.

The new Temple was designed according to the *Halakhah*, Jewish law, and was built on the foundations of Solomon's Temple on the plateau of the Temple Mount. The ruins of the old Temple were still *in situ*, and old men who had seen that Temple helped the builders in their task. Thus, the Second Temple arose. True, it was more modest than its predecessor, but it gave forth a ray of hope for a more exalted spiritual life on the basis of which the returnees would be able to establish a state that would last forever. Under Persian rule and with the guidance of the high-priesthood, the Temple slowly assumed its position at the head of the political and spiritual leadership of Israel renewing itself in its own land.

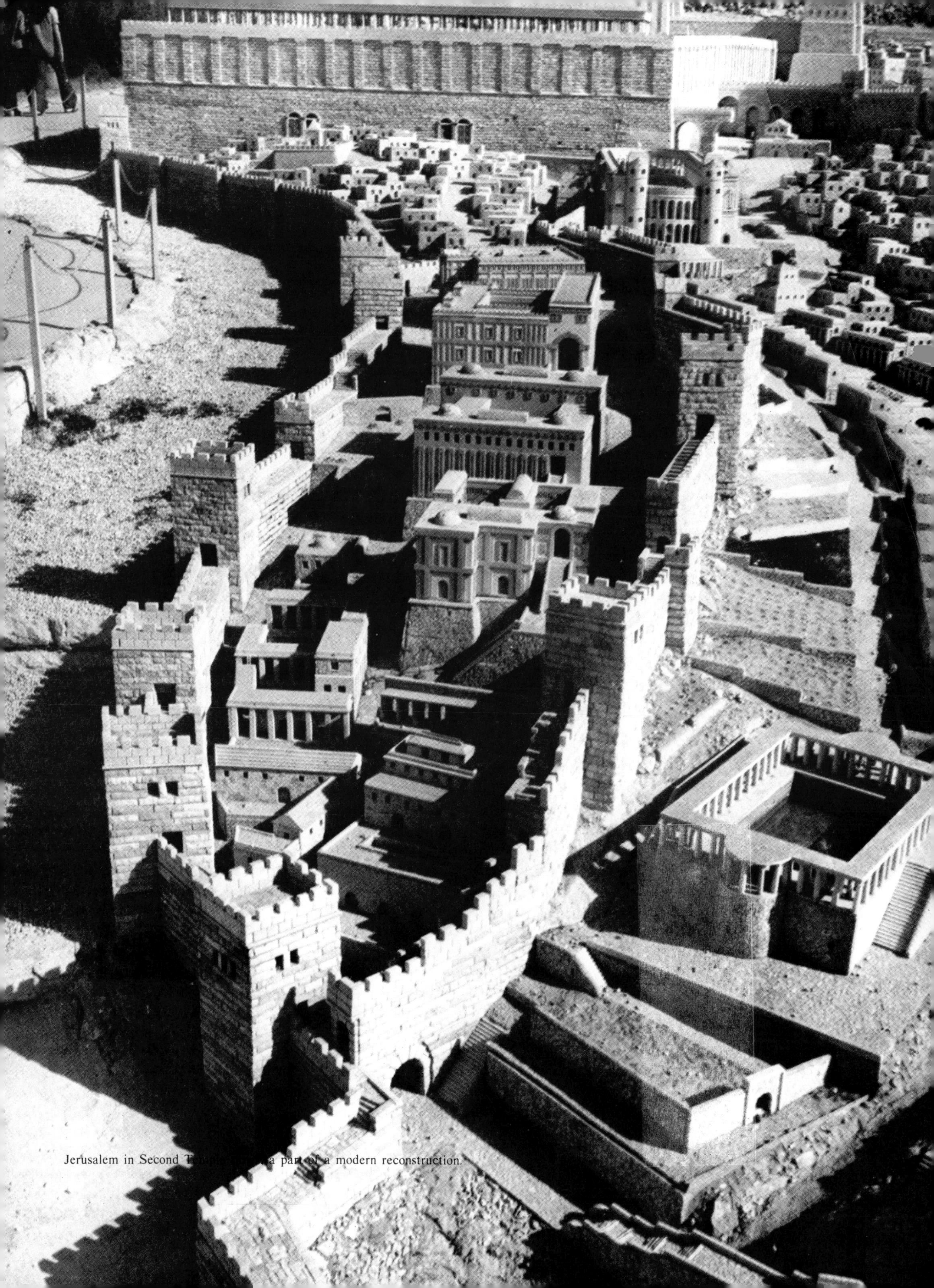

Jerusalem in Second Temple times: a part of a modern reconstruction.

Persian rule came to an end, and the East was conquered by Alexander the Great and his Greeks. His successors, the Diadochi, created two major powers in the area, one ruled by Ptolemy and the other by Seleucus. In the third century B.C.E., the land of Israel was under the rule of the Ptolemaic dynasty, which was based in Egypt, and in the second century it came under the rule of the Seleucids who ruled Greater Syria.

Generally speaking, the Jews enjoyed freedom of religion and, to a degree, even political independence. They used these years well to rehabilitate the nation and strengthen themselves. A unique leadership developed which gave new expression to ancient life styles and instituted new trends of thought based on the prophetic philosophies which were at the very foundations of the Jewish people. But harder times were at hand. The end of the first half of the second century B.C.E. was particularly turbulent. Antiochus IV Epiphanes ascended the Seleucid throne and with the help of those Jews who had already been beguiled by Hellenism, strove to bring the whole Jewish people into the alien culture. Antiochus believed that if he could unify the religion and life-style of all the countries in his empire, he would be able to face the new awesome world power that was starting to turn its attention to the East – Rome.

Once again the Temple stood in the center of the stage of world events. Statues of the king were set up within the Temple precincts and Greek pagan cultic rites were practiced there. The result was that the Jews revolted under the leadership of Mattathias the Hasmonean and his sons. The success of this revolt restored to the Temple its ancient glory. It was purified of the pagan worship and once again became the focus of the Jewish people in Jerusalem, their capital. The Hasmonean kings exploited to the full the country's position at the cross-roads of the world and integrated it into the international economic system. The national coffers were filled with treasure and a part of it was allocated to building Jerusalem and the Temple. When Eretz Israel had been under foreign rule, further building had not been allowed at the

The Temple in Jerusalem; an imaginary painting.

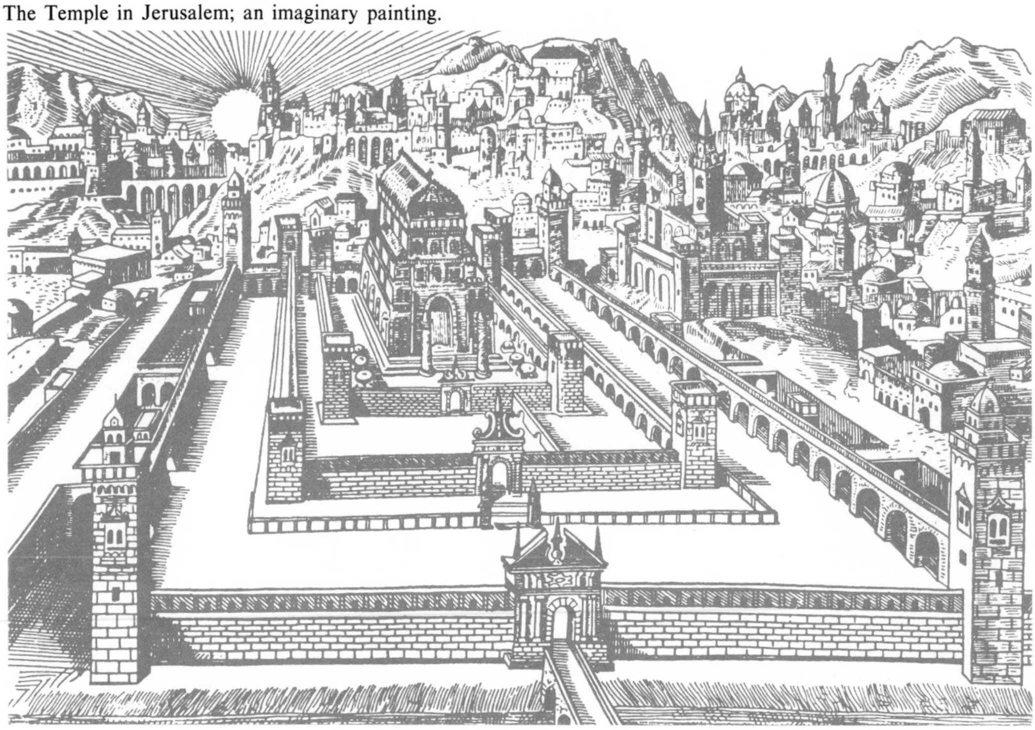

The Second Temple; a sketch and a schematic reconstruction.

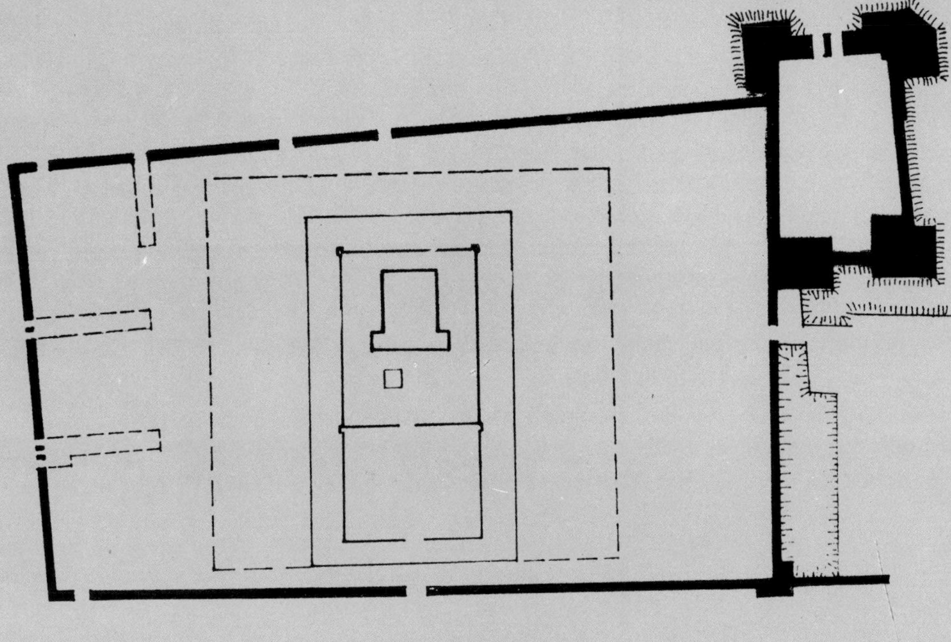

Temple site. The rulers had been apprehensive lest too much monumental-style building in one area be converted into a stronghold for the purpose of rebellion and so had forbidden any extension of the existing Temple edifice. Now, under the Hasmonean kings, the Jews could – and did glorify and exalt the House of God and the mountain on which it stood. The Temple Mount area was rehabilitated and reconstructed most firmly. Vestiges of this activity exist today in the eastern wall of the Temple Mount.

"He who has not seen Herod's building has not seen a beautiful building in his life"

Herod usurped the Hasmonean throne and although he continued the former economic and internal policies, he instituted major changes in the country's foreign policy. He appreciated the might of Rome and, foreseeing what would happen in his area of the world, developed a very close relationship with that power in order to further his own interests and the good of his people. His efforts brought unprecedented prosperity to the country. Herod had been deeply impressed by the buildings in Rome and Greece and by Egyptian architecture and this, the most solid of the plastic arts, became his passion. His dream was that his country be known throughout the world as the home of inspiring edifices, and he reached the pinnacle of success in his reconstruction of the Temple. In fact, he built the Third Temple, but since the rebuilding had not been the result of the destruction of the Second Temple and the internal parts of the edifice were preserved and only the external sections rebuilt, we still call it the Second Temple.

The sanctuary itself, which, in the course of time, was destined to be destroyed by Titus' legions, was made up of three areas: the *Ulam* (a vestibule or hall); the *Hekhal* (the main room for divine service) and the *Kodesh Ha-Kodoshim* (the Holy of Holies), which were joined by doorways. The doorway between the *Hekhal* and the Holy of Holies was covered by two heavy cloth curtains, each of which covered the whole space thus ensuring that the Holy of Holies was completely isolated from the *Hekhal*. The main Temple artifacts, such as the *Menorah* (Candelabrum) and the Golden Table, stood in the *Hekhal* whereas the Holy of Holies contained only the *Even Ha-Shetiyah*, which according to the Temple traditions, was the foundation stone on which the world was created. Only the high priest was allowed to enter the Holy of Holies, and that only once a year on Yom Kippur, the Day of Atonement. The Ark of the Covenant, which had stood in the Holy of Holies in the First Temple, had disappeared with its destruction at the hands of Nebuchadnezzar. The Temple traditions in Jerusalem claimed that it was stored in a hidden place and would reappear when the time was right. The Holy of Holies was, therefore, a small area endowed with unique sanctity; as its name implies, nothing was more sacred.

In the First Temple the Ark of the Covenant had stood at the western wall of the Holy of Holies, perhaps in a special niche created to house it. It is possible, that the location of the

Ornamentation from Second Temple times, from the eastern Huldah Gate in the southern wall.

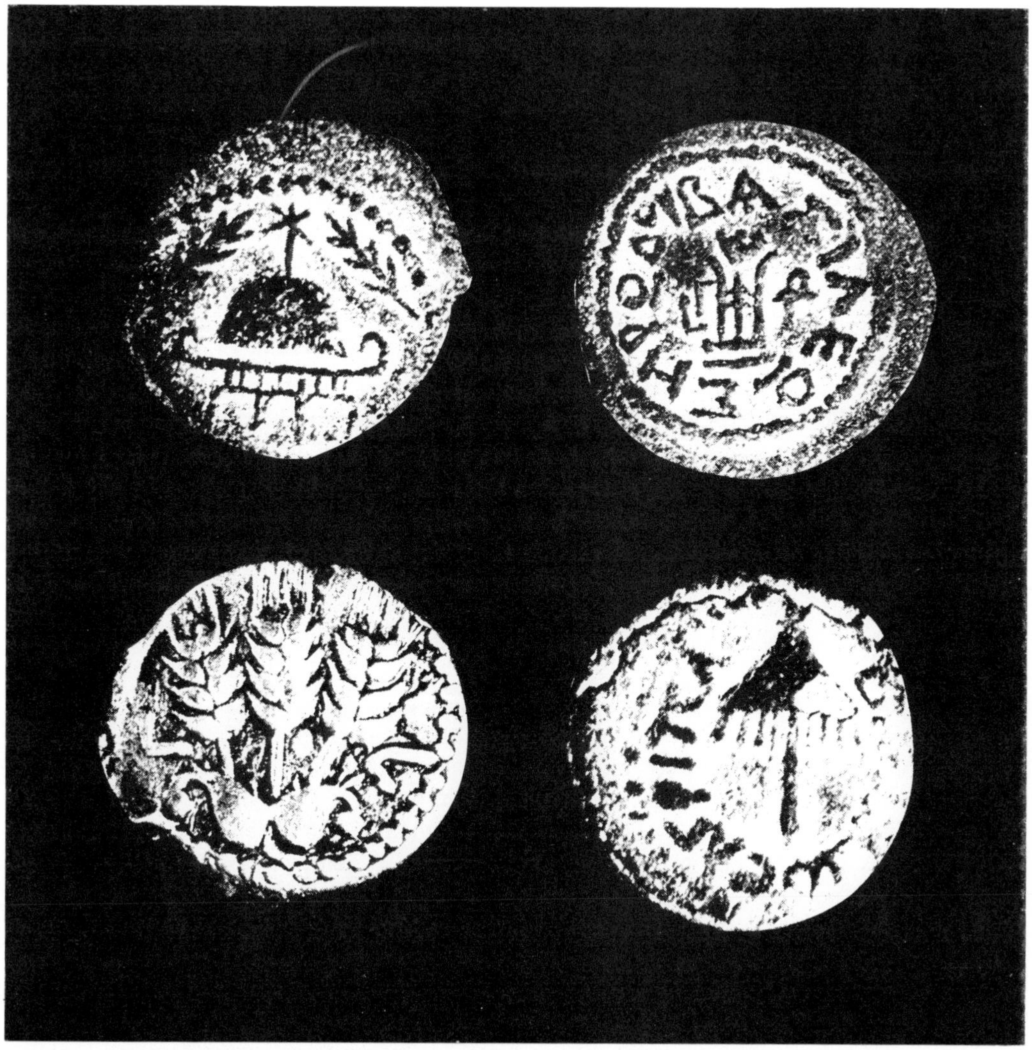

Coins from the periods of Herod (above) and Agrippa I.

Even Ha-Shetiyah evoked memories of the Ark of the Covenant. At any event, according to the Temple traditions, of the four walls of the Holy of Holies the western was the choicest and the most sacred, because it was the resting place of the Divine Presence and, perhaps, because it was there that the Ark of the Covenant had stood.

From the outside, Herod's Temple was magnificent. Its outer walls were as high as fifty metres and they were so thick that their width was utilized in the form of small casemate rooms with a corridor joining them. The walls thus protected the actual Temple, and also provided storage space for its treasures. The walls had no doors or windows facing outward except one, the main entrance to the *Ulam*. The building was of the highest quality and the artistic capitals that surrounded the sanctuary were faced with gold. A barbed metal lattice-work structure was located on the roof to prevent birds from alighting there and befouling it.

The Temple building stood in the center of an enormous stone-paved piazza, which was designed to hold tens of thousands of visitors. This space was supported by four buttress walls of tremendous proportions. These are the walls of the Temple Mount and must not be confused with the walls of the Temple itself. The Temple Mount area was square – or, to be more correct, trapezoid – and orientated from north to south, thus it had a northern wall, an eastern wall, a southern wall and a western wall.

As long as the Temple existed, no sanctity attached itself to any of the Temple Mount walls because all the holiness was inside the Temple and in the sacred precincts around it. Even so, the southern wall was more honored than the other three because in it the two main gates (entry and exit) to the Temple Mount were located – the Huldah Gates, and thus the southern wall constituted the facade of the Temple Mount. At its foot, throngs of pilgrims gathered and slowly made their way up onto the Temple Mount. It was by this wall that they stood to listen to the preachers with their exhortations to honesty and morality. Beggars used to sit around the gates calling on the generosity of the pious pilgrims, and magicians and fortune-tellers used to display their talents there. Nevertheless, notwithstanding all this activity and notwithstanding its impressive architecture, the southern wall was only a buttress wall supporting the Temple Mount as were the other three walls, including the western one.

The second Temple period, from the time that its spacious piazzas were constructed on the support walls in the days of Herod and until it was destroyed at the hands of Titus, were the most glorious days the Temple Mount had ever known. Tens of thousands visited it on the major pilgrim festivals, and it also served as the site of Jerusalem's courts, including the Sanhedrin, the supreme court of the land. Generations of sages and teachers received their education on the Temple Mount, and they established Israel's Torah as the main core of its cultural life.

Notwithstanding Roman rule, the nation's leaders succeeded in maintaining peace and prosperity although often Rome's representatives, the procurators, were men of small and mean spiritual stature. Compared to other peoples conquered by Rome, Jerusalem and the Temple enjoyed a great measure of religious freedom. Even the Romans displayed great consideration when it came to the Jewish religion with its many – and to them, strange – prohibitions. This was because they realized that Judaism and its philosophical-theological system were unique in the world of those times. All these conditions contributed to an exceedingly rich spiritual life at the center of which stood the Temple radiating its influence throughout the whole Jewish people, in Eretz Israel and outside it.

However, with the passage of time the influence of the fanatics increased, and a rebellion was proclaimed against Rome. The rebels failed to read the political picture of the times correctly, and their revolt was doomed to failure. To this must be added the fact that the zealot factions were divided even among themselves and spent a great deal of time and energy on internal factional fighting as well as conducting a struggle against the more moderate elements in the population. The result was an absymal failure paid for by untold numbers of victims, tens of thousands of whom died in vain, and by the destruction of the Jewish people's religious and spiritual symbol – the Temple.

"The western wall of the Temple will never be destroyed – because the Divine Presence is in the west"

The Second Temple was destroyed on the ninth of Av in the year of 70 C.E. This was the culmination of a three-year long war which sapped the strength of the Jewish population of Eretz Israel and Jerusalem – and not only because of the struggle against the Romans but mainly because of the civil war that raged among the Jews. Not for nothing do contemporary sources assign the blame for the downfall on gratuitous hatred and internecine conflict!

The Roman commanders, led by Titus, conferred on the Mount of Olives on the eve of the fall of Jerusalem. The main item on the agenda was a question, the answer to which would have been self-understood in a campaign in any other part of the world: Should they destroy the Temple or not? It was accepted Roman policy to destroy all the sources of power, including spiritual, of a rebellious province, and in this case the Temple was the focus of both temporal and spiritual Jewish independence. Titus, however, felt that it would not be wise to devastate this architectural gem – after all, the Romans are not barbarians! – and, after a bitter discussion, his opinion carried the day. In fact, however, the Temple was put to the torch and destroyed! How it happened is still a moot point among the historians. Some say that a simple Roman soldier just disobeyed orders and threw a flaming faggot into the Temple; others claim that indeed the Romans wanted to spare the Temple, but that the zealots forced their hand by carrying on their impossible struggle from the roof and from the very *Hekhal*. The Romans argued that the zealots had already desecrated and defiled the Temple by using it as a military stronghold so they, the Romans, were not destroying a holy Temple but merely razing a fortress!

Be that as it may, the Temple was destroyed, and Jerusalem laid waste. Its inhabitants, except for those who were killed or taken into captivity, were driven from the city to other towns and villages in Judah. Tragically, the Second Temple period in Jewish history had come to an end.

There is a tradition that the Temple's western wall remained standing. This is not a reference to the western wall of the Temple Mount – all its walls have survived to this day. The western wall about which it was prophesied that it would never be destroyed, is the western wall of the actual sanctuary, and in the course of time, it was razed to the ground completely. The tradition, which is in *Lamentations Rabbah* 1:30, goes (in paraphrase) as follows:

When the Romans conquered the Temple, Titus assigned its destruction to four of his commanders – one for each wall. All of them accomplished their tasks except for an Arabian count by the name of Pengar who had been assigned the western wall. When Titus asked him why he had not destroyed it, he said that he wanted to leave some vestige so that people would see how great, strong and impressive was the Temple, of which this wall was only a small part.

A Roman coin commemorating the fall of Jerusalem in 70 C.E.

According to Jewish tradition, the salvation of the western wall was providential because that is where the Divine Presence rests. We must again stress that the subject of these traditions is the western wall of the Temple building itself.

"Give us back our city; restore our Temple; show us our Holy of Holies"

The site of the Temple had become an enormous ruin, and severe restrictions had been placed on the Jews. They were not allowed to reside in Jerusalem or to visit the ruins there. The situation became even worse after the suppression of the Bar Kokhba rebellion in the year 135. At the Emperor Hadrian's orders, a temple to Jupiter, who was adored by the Romans and who had a temple on Capitol Hill in Rome, was built on the site of the Temple in Jerusalem. It was also decided to rehabilitate Jerusalem, but as a pagan city with its name changed to Aelia Capitolina – Aelia for the emperor whose full name was Publius Aelius Hadrianus and Capitolina for the Capitol in Rome. It is possible that at that time the western wall of the Temple was still standing and that it was integrated into the new pagan house of worship. However, Hadrian's project did not last and it too finally disappeared. During the entire Roman period in Eretz Israel, that is, the second and third centuries, Jerusalem was in ruins and the Temple Mount desolate. Jews, who wanted to view the ruins, could come to Jerusalem –

The Gates of Mercy (or The Golden Gate) in the eastern wall. In early times it was considered sacred.

A reconstruction of the entrance at Huldah's Gates. Above: a detail.

A capital in the Moslem style from an early period. It was found in the piazza at the Western Wall.

but only to the Mount of Olives and look at the Temple site from there. It was at that time that the eastern wall and the remains of its Shushan Gate became predominant.

When Christianity became the official religion of the Roman Empire at the beginning of the fourth century, maintaining Jerusalem and the Temple in ruins became an important policy of its emperors. Emperor Constantine and his successors saw the destruction of the Temple as a symbol of Judaism's demise and the growth of Christianity in its place. They therefore strictly enforced Hadrian's edicts; Jews were not allowed to settle in the city and, above all, the Temple Mount was to remain devastated as a memorial to the liquidation of Judaism in its previous form. Only on the ninth of Av were Jews allowed into Jerusalem to bewail the destruction of their Temple. We can assume that on that day Christian propagandists mingled with the mourners to preach their explanation of the Temple's destruction and what it signified.

Occasionally, during a long historical period, the idea of rebuilding the Temple and resettling Jerusalem as the capital of a sovereign Jewish state arose. Perhaps the most notable of these occasions was when Julian the Apostate became emperor of Rome in 362. Julian repudiated Christianity as the official religion of the empire and wanted to re-introduce paganism and emperor-worship, and he requested the Jews to offer sacrifices for the welfare of the emperor as they had done when the Temple existed. In their response, the Jews asked that Jerusalem be rehabilitated and the Temple and its altar rebuilt so that they would be able to comply with his request. The emperor, no doubt motivated by other political reasons as well, concurred and for the first time in nearly three hundred years practical steps were taken to rebuild the Temple. In 365, however, Julian was murdered and his successor was a devout Christian; the ante-Julian situation was restored. Furthermore, a major conflagration destroyed the stores of wood that had been prepared on the Temple Mount; the Jews claimed sabotage on the part of the Christians, and the Christians claimed that the raging fires was the hand of God.

Some two hundred and fifty years later, hope again stirred in the Jewish breast. In 614 Chosroes II, king of Persia, conquered Eretz Israel, Syria and portions of Asia Minor from the Byzantines. He was helped by the Jews and in appreciation made them the rulers of Jerusalem. The way was now open to restore the Temple Mount and rebuild the Temple. However, after only three years the Persian-Jewish alliance was abrogated because the Persians were afraid of the large Christian population of Jerusalem. Anyway, the Persians held their conquests for only a short time; in 628 the Byzantine Christians reconquered everything from the Persians, including Jerusalem.

The Christians now took bloody vengeance against the Jews for having helped the Persians and decided to destroy the Temple Mount area completely so that it should never again serve as a rallying point for Jewish national and religious aspirations. The remains of the Temple Mount that survived did so only because of their enormous size and the limited time the Byzantines had at their disposal – the latter because from the early 30s of the seventh century a new enemy, the Moslem Arabs, began to exert pressure on them. And indeed, in 638 Jerusalem fell into Moslem hands.

For the long years of the Roman and Byzantine occupation it was, with the exception of the two short episodes in the times of Julian and Chosroes, the eastern wall which was the focus of the Jews' attention when they came to look at the ruins of the Temple, for it is that wall which is visible from the Mount of Olives. The gate in the eastern wall had been used by the priests on ceremonial occasions and this added to its importance.

"Then he commanded them to sweep the site of the Temple and to clean it and Omar supervised them..."

The Arab conquest brought in its wake two major changes in the situation which had existed in Jerusalem for several centuries. Firstly, the Jews were allowed to live in the city, and some tens of families came from Tiberias to take advantage of this privilege. They took up residence at the south-west corner of the Temple Mount so as to be near the ruins of the Temple. The other change was with regard to the Temple Mount itself. For centuries, the Christians had insisted that it stand desolate and had made no attempt to use it for their own purposes. This policy was repudiated and in time the Moslems chose the Temple Mount as the site of a large mosque and so decided to rehabilitate the whole area. In order to give the site Islamic legitimacy, it was identified as the place from which the prophet Mohammed had ascended to heaven when he travelled from Mecca on his wondrous horse Al-Buraq. At the end of the seventh century and the beginning of the eighth, two mosques were built on the Temple Mount: the Dome of the Rock in the upper section and Al Akza at the southern end. In order to build these mosques, the walls supporting the area had first to be repaired for they had been severely damaged when the Byzantines had tried to destroy them a few decades earlier. Some of the original gates into the Temple Mount were also restored and incorporated into the overall plan as entrances, and new gates were opened to answer the specific Moslem needs.

From the great amount of evidence from the Arab period before the Crusader conquest, the following picture emerges. The Jews who lived in Jerusalem and those who came to visit it and the Temple Mount, used to pray at the eastern wall and western wall and at the gates to the Mount, particularly at the Huldah Gates at which site the Moslems had built two new gates. Curiously enough, although the Jews now had access to the Temple Mount walls and even to the Temple Mount itself which some Jews did visit, they still continued the tradition which had developed in Byzantine times of going up to the Mount of Olives. It seems that although the reason for this custom no longer existed, the Jews saw it as a time-honored custom and continued to respect it. In none of the sources we have is there any hint of the western wall as having any special sanctity.

The Jews who came to the walls often perpetuated the memory of their visit by inscribing their names on the stones. Several such inscriptions have been discovered, and they are all on the southern wall in the vicinity of the Huldah Gates.

The picture is thus fairly comprehensive. Islam had built its mosques on the Temple Mount. Jews had begun to resettle Jerusalem, and many Jews made pilgrimage to it. The places of pilgrimage were those about which a tradition of sanctity had developed. Some Jews even ventured to visit the Temple Mount itself.

"The remaining outstanding thing in the Holy City is the Western Wall"

At its beginning, the Crusader conquest of Jerusalem at the end of the eleventh century, brought untold suffering to the Jewish community. But, after the turmoil settled and the Crusaders began to rehabilitate Jerusalem as a Christian city, Jews and Moslems were permitted to live in it and visit it. The tumult of pilgrims was once again heard in Jerusalem's narrow alleys. The city was small; its walls followed the course of the Turkish wall that was later in history to be built by Suleiman the Magnificent. The Temple Mount was occupied by the knightly Order of Templars and served as their staff headquarters and for billeting their troops. The Dome of the Rock was converted into the Templum Domini church; this was the first time a church was established on the Temple Mount as indeed it was the first time that Christians had made any use of the Mount at all. The Al Akza mosque and its surrounding buildings became a Templar monastery, the actual mosque building becoming the church of the complex under the name Templum Solomonis. Solomon's name became attached to many of the area's installations under the influence of Jewish traditions.

For several centuries Jerusalem was successively under the rule of the Crusaders, the Ayyub Moslems, the Tatars, and the Mameluke sultans of Egypt. This period lasted from the Crusader conquest in 1099 until Jerusalem was taken by the Ottoman sultans in 1516. Travellers and residents have left us a great many reports about the holy places that were the foci of Jewish attention at the time. (For details, see Chapter III). Together with the already acknowledged sites such as the Gates of Mercy in the eastern wall, the Huldah Gates and the Temple Mount, we come across, for the first time, mention of the Temple Mount's western wall as an important sacred site. It would seem that the Western Wall's location inside the city and its easy accessibility from the Jewish quarter, transformed it into a favored place of prayer. At the beginning of this period the Western Wall is appended to the holy itinerary as another sacred place but towards its end, at the closing of the fifteenth century, the Western Wall already appears in the reports by itself. Travellers and visitors describe it as a place of prayer and go into detail as to its size and the dimensions of its stones. However, the Wall was not yet recognized by Jerusalem's civil authorities as a site holy to the Jewish Community. The impression gained from the sources is one of slow development. At first the Western Wall is appended to the accepted list of holy places and, with time, the new tradition takes a hold in the folk-consciousness. It is during this period that the traditions about the Divine Presence never leaving the western wall begins to attach themselves to this Western Wall, the western

Jerusalem and the Sanctuary in Second Temple times; a reconstruction.

Jerusalem and the Temple Mount; a painting by Reuven Rubin.

buttress wall of the Temple Mount instead of the western wall of the actual Temple itself for which they were originally intended. In order to magnify the Western Wall's importance, the new traditions ascribe to it special sanctity from the time of the destruction. These traditions about the Western Wall are, therefore, approximately eight hundred years old at the most, and they are the first Jewish traditions adressing themselves to this area of the Temple Mount. The Moslem religious tradition of the Western Wall as the site where Mohammed tethered his horse Al-Buraq is only a few decades old; it started when the Western Wall became the focus of modern Jewish national aspirations. Until that time, Al-Buraq had waited for his master at the eastern or southern wall.

"In the days of the sultan Suleiman the site of the Temple was not known, and he ordered that it be sought"

In 1516/17 Jerusalem, Eretz Israel and Egypt were conquered by the Ottomans led by the sultan Selim I. Selim succeeded his father Bayezid, the sultan who had begun to put Turkey on the political map of Europe at the end of the fifteenth century and the beginning of the sixteenth. At that time the Jews were expelled from Christian Spain, and Bayezid, whose empire sorely needed administrative talents and economic and trade expertise, opened its gates to the persecuted Jews and even encouraged them to come and settle in his domains. This Turkish policy was continued by his son Selim I, and his grandson, Suleiman who later came to be known by the appellation, "The Legislator" or "The Magnificent." Suleiman extended the borders of his empire and exerted military pressure on Europe to the extent of besieging Vienna. In order to relieve the pressure on Europe, Carl V of Spain spread the rumour that a crusade was in the process of organization to liberate Eretz Israel and Jerusalem. Carl also toyed with the illusion that he could actually conquer Eretz Israel which was the bottle-neck of the overland route to India. At that time it was clear that the continent which Columbus had discovered was not India but a new world and although seamen had learned to circumnavigate Africa and so reach India by way of the sea, there was still no cheap substitute for the overland route which passed through Eretz Israel and the Gulf of Elat. In order to meet the challenges posed by Europe and its rulers, Suleiman invested great efforts in developing Jerusalem and preparing it for a defensive war. The city's walls were rebuilt, and strong watchtowers were built in them; these are the existing walls of the Old City. Suleiman's Jerusalem policy had another purpose as well; he wanted to stress the fact that the city was a Moslem city, and he therefore had the Dome of the Rock covered with glazed ceramic bricks in place of the original glass covering which had deteriorated in the course of the centuries.

Notwithstanding these efforts, Turkish rule in Arab areas was still problematic although most of the inhabitants of those areas were also Sunnite Moslems. A revolt which erupted in Suleiman's time was put down with great cruelty. In order to strengthen his hold on Jerusalem which was surrounded by a wall and would therefore be very difficult to regain should it rebel, the Sultan followed a policy of populating it with as many different loyal nationalities as possible. It was at that time that the settlement of Magreb Arabs in the city was extended. These were mainly from Morocco and, before that, from southern Spain from which they had been driven out when the Christian reconquered that country. These people were Moslems but quite different from the indigenous Arab population. The Turkish government followed a

The two sections of the Gate of the Chain from the Crusader period.

similar policy in the nineteenth century when they settled tens of thousands of Moslem Circassian refugees from Russia throughout the rural areas of Syria and Eretz Israel.

As a part of their population policy, the Turks encouraged Jews to settle in the area, and Jewish refugees from Spain and Portugal were also welcomed. The result was a substantial increase in the Jewish population of Eretz Israel. Tiberias and Safed blossomed, and the Jews constituted a majority in both towns. Jerusalem and Hebron also received a welcome infusion of Jewish settlers. Suleiman, however, was not satisfied and, in order to encourage still more Jews to come, took an unprecedented step – he granted official recognition to the Western Wall as a Jewish holy place and commissioned the court architect to prepare it as a monumental site. Furthermore, the Jews were granted legal rights regarding the Wall and a firman was entered in the court archives of the Sultanate in Constantinople confirming the Jews' status in the area of the Western Wall. Many years later, when the Jews felt that their rights at the Wall had been curtailed, they appealed to the Turkish authorities on the grounds of this firman, the actual copy of which had, apparently, been lost. At any rate, the sultan Suleiman hoped that such an important holy place, a vestige of the ancient Temple itself, would attract great numbers of Jews from Europe and thus strengthen the Jewish population of Eretz Israel. Since the Jews would be completely dependent on the sultan's mercies, it could be expected that they would remain loyal to him and act as a counter-balance to the local Arabs and an obstacle to any possible rebellion.

It was in those days that religious traditions began to be woven around the Western Wall. Then, more than before, the existing traditions about the western wall of the Temple were transferred to the Western Wall of the Temple Mount, in order to endear it to the Jews and make it the foremost accepted Jewish holy place.

Since the Jews now had a sort of substitute for the Temple and close by it too and since they were not allowed to enter the Temple Mount itself, it having become a Moslem domain, the Jewish religious prohibitions against entry into the Temple site, were further developed and stressed. It seems that it is better and easier to refrain from entering the Temple Mount for your own internal religious reasons than to refrain because the temporal authorities forbid it. This approach also supplied a religious and philosophical solution to a serious problem. Which Jew could renounce Jewish rights to the Temple Mount? Now, no Jew had to. The Jewish attitude was: The Temple Mount belongs to us but because of the halakhic uncertainties regarding the exact location of the Holy of Holies, we will refrain completely from entering it so as not to defile it. It is clear that the religious prohibition against entering the Temple area is a product of the period under discussion; in Crusader times Jews had entered the Temple Mount and even Maimonides, who was one of the greatest codifiers of the *Halakhah*, Jewish law, did visit the site of the Temple although in his Code of Law he rules that even after the destruction of the Temple, sanctity is still attached to the site, and all the laws of ritual impurity still apply.

"There are men with hearts of stone and there are stones with human hearts"

In the four hundred years of Ottoman rule in Eretz Israel and Jerusalem the *status quo* concerning the Western Wall was preserved. The area which had been created in front of the Wall was reserved for Jewish prayer, and the Wall was classified as the most sacred place in the Jewish religion both for the community as a whole and for the individual Jew, standing, as it did, close to the source of Jewish sanctity, the Temple. The Wall was known throughout the world wherever there were Jews, and all Jewish pilgrims who came to Eretz Israel visited it. In the course of time, even non-Jewish pilgrims and ordinary tourists made it a point to visit this place of Jewish prayer and it became known as "The Wall of Tears" or "The Wailing Wall," because of the weeping and wailing that was heard there. Many are the reports extant written by Christian visitors in the last few centuries and a great number of them exhibit the traditional Christian attitude: the weeping at the Wall signifies the deserved calamity which came on the Jews because they rejected Jesus, who had prophesied the destruction of the Temple and who had seen in it the termination of the "old covenant" between God and Israel and the beginning of a "new covenant" with the followers of the new faith, Christianity.

With the start of the nationalistic stirrings among the Jews in the second half of the nineteenth century before the establishment of the Zionist movement, the Western Wall took on a new dimension – in addition to its religious significance it also became a symbol of the nationalistic aspirations of the Jewish people. Artistic representations of the Wall began to appear on documents acknowledging aid and contributions to Eretz Israel with the seal of both private and public bodies. In the past, the Wall had been a motif on religious objects such as *Haggadot* for the Passover *seder* ceremony, the *sukkah* of the Tabernacles festival, and candelabra for Hannukah; now the Wall acquired secular Jewish significance.

During the British mandate in Palestine, the Wall became a focus of the struggle between Jews and Arabs. The British authorities maintained the *status quo* of Turkish time meticulously. The sounding of the ram's horn, the *shofar*, at the Wall, particularly at the end of the Yom Kippur services, and the question as to whether it was permitted to put benches in the area at the Wall for the elderly became controversial issues over which the Jews and Arabs argued long and loudly; the echoes of these struggles reverberated outside the borders of the country.

When the Jewish Quarter of the Old City fell into Jordanian hands a short time after the establishment of the State of Israel in May 1948, the Western Wall passed into Jordanian control. For many years it stood desolate and only a few Jewish tourists who had foreign passports visited it, almost stealthily. The Jordanians did not damage the Wall, but they did not encourage tourists to visit it. They hoped that it would slowly be forgotten. Although the cease-fire agreements between Israel and Jordan called for the latter to permit Israelis to visit the Wall, the Jordanians never honored that part of the agreement.

Jordan joined in the Six-Day War against Israel and, as a result, Israeli forces conquered the whole of Jerusalem. The liberation of the Old City and the Western Wall was the emotional climax of a war which was not lacking in unforgettable events. In the great excitement following the war, the Magreb Quarter immediately adjacent to the Western Wall was cleared and the occupants relocated in the Old City. The decrepit half-ruined hovels that had made up the quarter were razed to the ground and a large piazza was formed in front of the Wall. A fitting and noble design for this area is one of the tasks that faces the generation which has had the good fortune to see the Wall restored to the Jewish people.

Rabbi Abraham Isaac Kook, a former chief rabbi of the Holy Land, once said: "There are men with hearts of stone and there are stones with human hearts." He was referring to the

Suleiman the Magnificent; he gave the Jews a firman for the Wall.

Jerusalem in the Mameluke period; a 14-century etching.

stones of the Western Wall and, indeed, with the liberation of the Wall after so many long years, his aphorism has become real to millions of Jews throughout the world.

The Temple Mount area.

CHAPTER II

ARCHITECTURE AND ARCHAEOLOGY

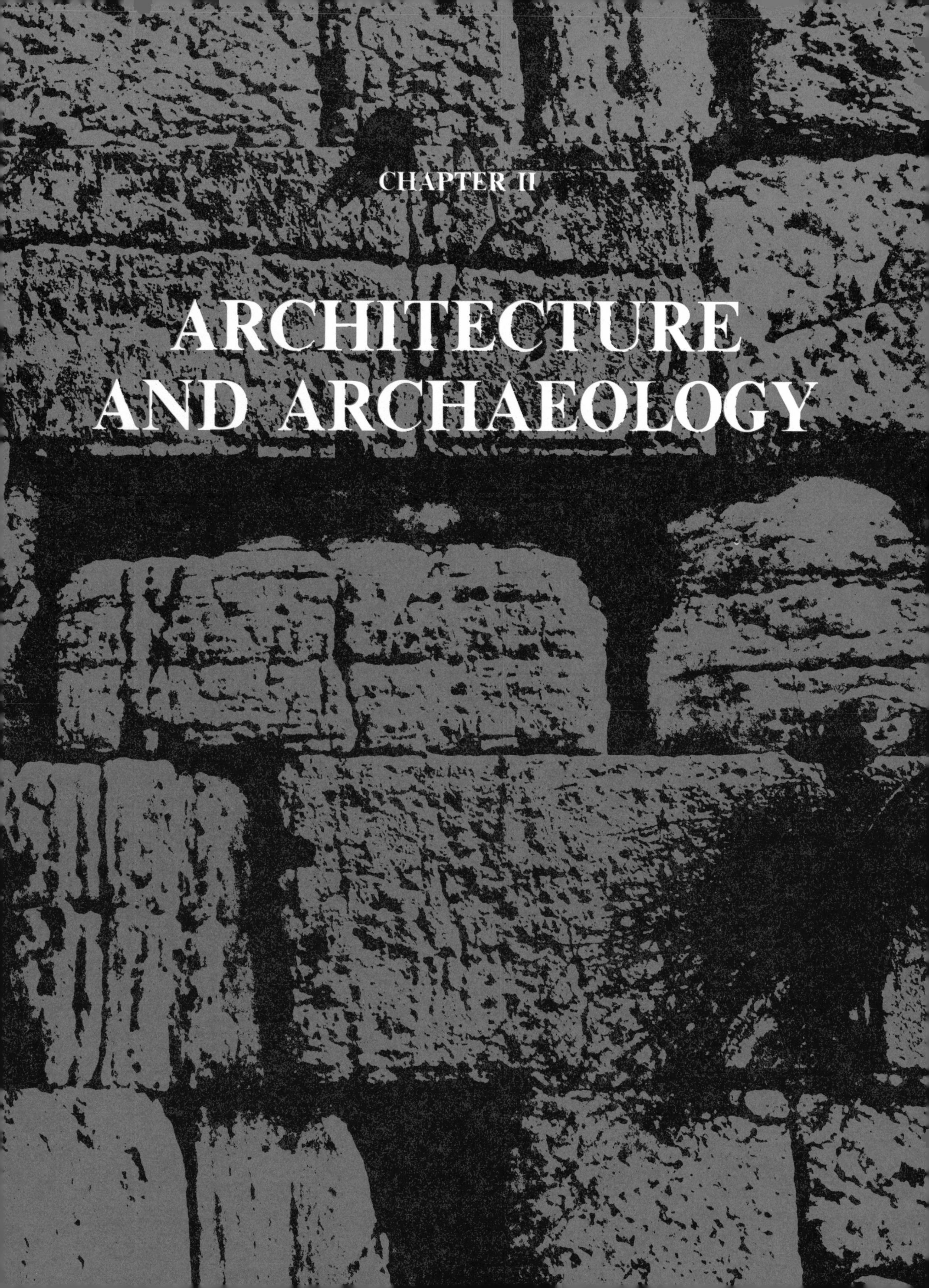

The Western Wall in the Second Temple Period.

Before Herod's time, the plateau on the Temple Mount was very limited in size and was inadequate for the vast throngs of pilgrims who came to the Temple. It must be said to Herod's credit that he succeeded in persuading both the Jewish people and the Roman authorities to allow him to redesign and reconstruct the whole area. The result was a much enlarged plateau and a Temple which was one of the most admired buildings in the ancient world. The plateau of the Temple Mount is so situated that it could have been extended in all directions but the planners chose the north, west and south sides although all of them presented difficulties. On the south and west sides there were dwelling houses that had to be considered and the north side posed a topographical challenge. We do not know why the planners ignored the east side of the plateau where any extension would have been outside the city and would have avoided the problems mentioned above. At any rate, the eastern wall was left as it was except for some additions to its northern and southern sections. In the Second Temple period this wall was known as the wall and colonnade which Solomon had built; it was already then recognized as being of great antiquity.

When the rebuilding was finished, an enormous flat space of 144,000 square metres had been created. To give a modern guide to its size, let us just say that it would have held more than twenty standard-sized soccer pitches! The area was paved and supported by monumental buttress walls. Underneath the floor of this area was a large empty cavity and the floor was held up by domed vaults. This method of construction, difficult though it was, was necessary because of the problem of ritual impurity. There was a possibility that graves might be located in the earth over which the plateau was extended. If the floor of the plateau had actually touched such earth, the whole Temple Mount plateau would be ritually unclean and the priests walking there would be unable to perform their duties. The elevation of the pavement of the plateau on domed vaults with a space between it and the earth and rock beneath solved this problem.

The longest of the buttress walls was the western wall; it measured 485 metres from its southern extremity to the Antonia citadel which stood at its northern end. At the foot of the wall, a road for pedestrians ran along its entire length. This road was paved with giant slabs of stone and was ten metres wide. Along both sides were rows of small shops attached to each other. The southern section of the western wall reared some thirty metres above the road; in the northern section the road followed the rising level of the bed-rock and in places the top of the wall was only twenty metres above it. In the southern section, the wall descended below the level of the road a further seven to nine metres until it hit the bed-rock. The "deep" spots were the foundations of wall and after it had been built, they were filled in with earth to the level of the road. Although they were in fact underground, the stones of those sections were dressed with the same care and artistry as those above ground.

The first twenty metres of the wall above the level of the paved road served as a buttress for the Temple Mount and was five metres thick. The thickness was made up of three huge stones adjacent to each other for the entire height. Thus the wall is three-stones deep. For its upper ten metres, the wall was approximately one metre thick and served as the outer wall of the double colonnade on the plateau. This upper section was decorated with pilasters, dummy pillars of stone attached to the outside surface. At the beginning of the seventh century, parts of the wall with the pilasters still existed; they were destroyed when the Byzantine emperor, Heraclius, reconquered Jerusalem from the Persians and their Jewish allies in 628. In vengeance and as a punishment, the new conquerors began to destroy the walls of the Temple Mount systematically. Many of the pilaster-stones have been discovered in the archaeological excavations at the foot of the wall; they were found in the stratum of the early seventh century.

Like the other walls, the Western Wall was built of enormous stones. Most of the stones weigh between two and eight tons each. Some stones weigh as much as ten tons and there are others – usually, but not always, at the corners – which weigh between forty and fifty tons and few of more than one hundred tons each. One extraordinary stone, in the section north of Wilson's Arch, is twelve metres long, three metres high and four metres thick – it weighs approximately four hundred tons!

All the stones of the Western Wall, as well as the other three, were dressed with fine chiselled borders. In the course of time, when the Wall was covered with earth and rubbish and water and sewage systems were dug in its close vicinity, some of the stones were badly damaged and it is impossible to distinguish the dressing on many of them. However, those parts of the Wall that were covered with earth alone are exceedingly well preserved and the artistry of Herod's masons at their best is clearly visible. The chiselled borders on the stones are not uniform; on some stones they are twenty centimetres wide and on others between five and seven centimetres wide. The depth of the borders is one and one half centimetres which is enough to create a play of light in which the Wall takes on a quilted appearance. Even from a distance, one can still see that the Wall is made of individual stones, an impression it would be impossible to achieve without the chiselled borders.

One advantage of the use of huge stones was the speed in which the work could be completed; had small, "normal-sized" stones been used, the task would have taken more than twice as long. After developing and practicing the necessary operative systems, the use of very large stones enabled the builders to proceed at an almost incredible speed. Working with small or unhewn stones requires a great deal of energy and time in fitting and cementing them. A large amount of plaster is also needed and its manufacture from burning chalk in ovens is a time-consuming process, which also requires great quantities of wood as fuel. Thus, the utilization of monumental stones saved time and money in addition to giving the walls, and thus the Temple Mount, a truly majestic appearance.

Incovering the past
t the southwest
orner of the Temple
lount.

The Gates in the Western Wall in Second Temple Times.

Archaeological surveys and excavations have revealed four gates in the Western Wall. Two of the gates were at the level of the paved pedestrian road at the foot of the Wall and the other two were built high in the Wall at the entry points of two huge overpass-staircases that were built against it. The first of these structures rested on what is known as Robinson's Arch and the other on Wilson's Arch. Flavius Josephus' description of the Temple Mount also talks of four gates in the Western Wall but the description in the Mishnah, Tractate Middot, tells of only one gate called Coponius' Gate. Some authorities have tried to reconcile the two sources by arguing that the Mishnah is earlier than Josephus and that the extra gates were added after the time of the Mishnah's description. This argument is, however, unacceptable, because the Mishnah brings its description in the name of Rabbi Eleazar bar Jacob who left Jerusalem for Jabneh at the time of the destruction and was thus contemporaneous with Josephus.

The contradiction between the Mishnah and Josephus is, however, only apparent, because they were referring to two different areas. The Temple Mount comprised two elements: the area which Herod extended and built and the area which is fixed in Jewish law as the sacred precincts, into which non-Jews and impure Jews were forbidden entry. This inner area, at which there were signs in Latin and Greek warning Gentiles not to enter on pain of death, was surrounded by a fence low enough for a person to look over, and was located inside the larger area which Herod had built. Herod's extension was nearly twice the area of the original sacred precinct. The Mishnah was describing the Temple Mount from the point of view of Jewish law. For non-Jews and impure Jews who were only permitted to enter the outer area, there was only one entrance to the Temple Mount – Coponius' Gate on the west side. The gate is named after the first Roman procurator at the beginning of the first century C.E., who was thus honored because he contributed to the gate's construction or, perhaps, gave the

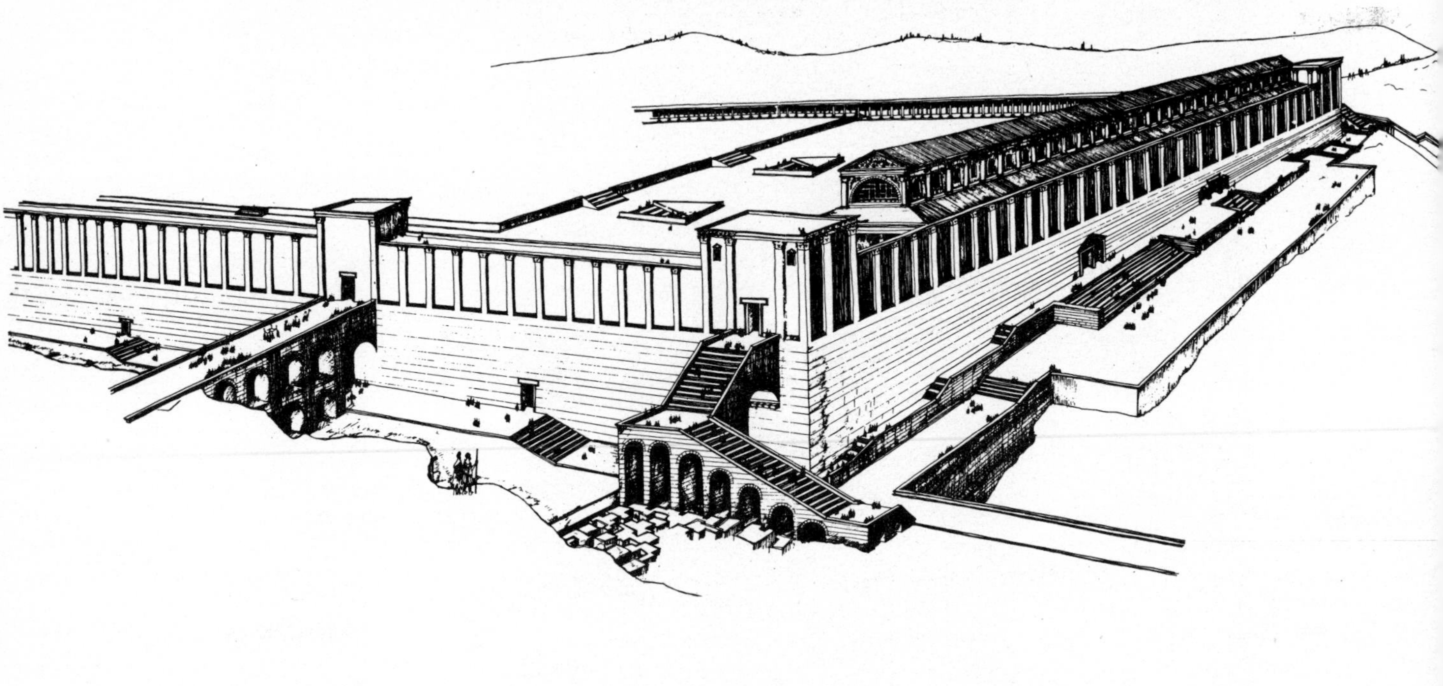

A sketch of the Temple Mount and the southern and western walls. In the forefront: the Western Wall and the two entrances into the Mount, today known as Robinson's Arch (to the right) and Wilson's Arch. Coponius' Gate is in the center of the Wall. (The exits of that gate and Huldah's Gates are not depicted correctly.)

Robinson's Arch (Stage 1) as it was before the excavations. An onion field conceals the treasures of the past.

necessary permission for it. Coponius' Gate thus led only into the outer area of the plateau from which there was no entrance into the sacred inner enclosure. Jews who were in a state of ritual purity, used the Huldah Gates in the southern wall which led directly into the inner sacred enclosure. There were two gates, situated approximately seventy metres apart; one was used for entrance and the other for exit. Coponius' Gate is to be identified with the gate which is nowadays known as Barclay's Gate, which was named after the American consul in Jerusalem in the nineteenth century and which was the first gate to be discovered from the eastern side, that is, from inside the Temple Mount. It is slightly to the north of the Magreb Gate, approximately 80 metres from the southwest corner of the wall. It leads directly into the western vaults of the Temple Mount on which the plateau rests. Nowadays, most of these vaults are in ruins and a few serve as water cisterns.

In time, the British expedition, led by Sir Charles Warren, examined the site and succeeded in identifying it. Since then, advances have been made and it is now known that Barclay's Gate is 5.6 metres wide from jamb to jamb and approximately 11 metres high from threshold to lintel. These measurements fit those given by the Mishnah for Coponius' Gate – 20 cubits high and 10 cubits wide. The important thing is the relationship of 1:2. Our measurements are at variance with those given by Barclay and Warren. They gave the height as 8.80 metres because they did not get down to the original threshold but to one which served the Arabs from the eighth to the tenth centuries. If this threshold, which its discoverers also agreed was

Robinson's Arch, stages 2 (opposite) and 3. The excavations are in full swing. The remains of the arch's pier were also uncovered (in the forefront).

secondary, is lowered to the level of the paved road which ran along the foot of the wall in Second Temple times, we arrive at a height of 11 metres. We may assume that in the Second Temple period, entrance was from the paved road.

There are another three entrances into the Temple Mount in the Western Wall. Another gate which led from the road into the vaults is located just north of Wilson's Arch. This gate is known as Warren's Gate after Sir Charles Warren who discovered it. This gate has been completely uncovered in the excavations along the foot of the Wall conducted by the Israel Ministry of Religions; it is 5.5 metres wide. The original lintel is missing and the existing lintel is an arch which was apparently an effort to rehabilitate the gate in the early Arab period after it had been destroyed when the Temple Mount was taken by Titus. This gate served the northwestern residential quarter of Jerusalem and led into the vaulted area under the plateau but not, it seems, into the plateau itself. It is possible that it was used as an entrance into the Temple Mount storage areas for cattle and goods.

The other two gates in the Western Wall were built at the entrance points of two overpass-

The southern colonade of the Temple Mount; a modern reconstruction.

structures into the wall, Robinson's Arch to the south and Wilson's Arch, north of it. The two structures led to impressive buildings which stood on the Temple Mount plateau but did not grant entry into the piazza itself. At the end of Robinson's Arch stood one of the largest and most impressive buildings on the Temple Mount – the royal colonnade or basilica, as it was known in the technical jargon of those days. This was a great hall with two secondary wings separated from the main hall by rows of pillars. This colonnade occupied the whole southern area of the Temple Mount and its roofs were supported by one hundred and sixty-two monumental pillars. The great hall was used for banking and moneychanging activities as well as for certain judicial functions and by its nature it was also used by non-Jews. Strict measures ensured that no entry into the plateau area was possible. In order to get into the actual plateau the visitor had to leave by the Robinson's Arch staircase, go around to the Huldah Gates or Coponius' Gate, and enter from them.

At the end of Wilson's Arch stood a building known as *The Bet Ha-Midrash* ("The House of Study"), to which the Sanhedrin, the Supreme Court, repaired during the Pilgrim Festival periods from its permanent seat, the *Lishkat Ha-Gazit* ("The Office of Hewn Stone") on the east side of the plateau. The Mishnah records ten changes of location (or "exiles," as it calls them) of the Sanhedrin both before and after the destruction of the Temple. The first removals were in Jerusalem: "From the *Lishkat Ha-Gazit* to the *Hanut*; from the *Hanut* to the *Lishkat Ha-Gazit* and from there to Jabneh." The permanent seat of the Sanhedrin was the *Lishkat Ha-Gazit* on the eastern side of the Temple Mount, and when the royal colonnade on the south side of the Mount and the access staircase were completed, the Sanhedrin moved there temporarily while its permanent quarters were being repaired or renovated. When that work was completed, the Sanhedrin moved back into its original quarters until it finally left Jerusalem for Jabneh. The royal colonnade, the basilica, is known in the Mishnah as the *Hanut,* which means "Shop."

In summation: there were two structures leading into the Temple Mount through the Western Wall, both a staircase and a causeway, and at the point of entry of both of them stood buildings which housed two of the most important secular institutions of the nation – the Sanhedrin (during the busiest periods of the year) and the capital's banking system.

Robinson's Arch.

The Temple Mount; an etching by David Roberts.

The "Place of Sounding" Tower and the Elevation of the Wall

At the southern end of the Western Wall stood a high tower from which, according to Josephus, one of the Temple priests used to sound a trumpet to indicate the beginning and the end of the Sabbath. This spot was indeed most suitable for this purpose since at the foot of the Western Wall and to the south of it was located the "lower market" of Jerusalem consisting of hundreds of shops on both sides of the main road which ran along the length of the Tyropoeon Valley reaching the Siloam Pool. On the top of the tower was an inscription, a fragment of which was discovered in the excavations at the foot of the Temple Mount. The fragment found reads: "For the place of sounding for. . ." and it should be completed: "the announcement of the Sabbath." The inscription almost certainly contained the name of the person who donated the funds for the tower's construction. (For further details see Chapter XI: Four Stones from the Wall.) It can be assumed that during the building of the Temple

The original paved road at the foot of the Western Wall.

and afterwards donations were made for specific sections and that the donor's name was perpetuated in gratitude for his generosity. A good example of this is "Nicanor of Alexandria who made the gates." It is unlikely that he actually manufactured the gates; he most probably donated the funds.

An addition was made to the western Wall in the time of Agrippa II (28-92 C.E.) as a result of his desire to view the Temple from his residence. When Agrippa visited Jerusalem he lived in the old Hasmonean palace. Herod's royal palace and its adjacent citadel were already long occupied by the Roman procurator and his staff and the Herodian prince had to make do with the old palace which was located in the heart of the upper city. Agrippa was accustomed to view the Temple and the activity on the Temple Mount from the roof of this palace and the priests, in order to stop him, elevated that section of the Western Wall which was opposite his palace. Unfortunately, it is not known why Agrippa did not go into the Temple area if he wanted to know what was happening or why the priests decided to obstruct his view. The elevated section was between Robinson's Arch and Wilson's Arch, on that section which today serves as the prayer area. It is possible that the Wall was elevated in preparation for the expected revolt against Rome and that the Agrippa story was an excuse to fool the Romans.

At the Foot of the Wall in Second Temple Times.

In Second Temple times, the Western Wall of the Temple Mount was entirely within the city and in the heart of a very densely built-up area. As described above, at its foot a paved road ran along its whole length. The width of the road was ten metres and it was edged on both sides with raised kerbstones. There were two drainage systems under the road surface; parts of them were hewn out of the bedrock and others were built. The systems were arranged on two levels; the upper level collected all the rain water from the city streets from west to east. When the drainage channels reached the road at the Wall, the water dropped through shafts into the lower system which ran from north to south in the direction of the Siloam Pool.

Shops, attached to each other like row-houses, were located on both sides of the road. The area, known as the "lower market," constituted Jerusalem's most important commercial center in the Second Temple period. The "upper market" was in the upper city and served the residential quarters there. The area of the lower market belonged to the priests who rented out the shops. The income went towards the upkeep of the Temple Mount and its administration. The huge throngs of pilgrims who visited Jerusalem on the Pilgrim Festivals naturally gravitated to this area because of its proximity to the Temple Mount and made most of their purchases and business transactions there. The shops on the east side of the road were built against the Wall and concealed the first three layers of its stones. This state of affairs was not haphazard but originally planned. The use of monumental stones was, therefore, decided upon for constructional reasons; the aesthetic beauty of the Wall was a secondary consideration.

From the main road which ran on a north-south axis along the course of the ancient valley which had once been there, roads branched westward to the upper city. These were narrow alleys about three metres wide with dwelling houses on both sides. The elevation of the upper city was some thirty metres above the level of the road at the foot of the Wall and so each of the alleys contained sections of steps at intervals. The main road itself was not flat. From its southern tip it rose in a slight incline for about half its course northwards until just beyond the fourth gate; from there it climbed and contained blocks of steps as it followed the contours of the bedrock.

In the road's northern section near the Antonia Citadel, the rock rose higher than the road level and so formed the back wall of the shops. In the Second Temple period, the road was called the Tyropoeon Road which name is understood by some authorities literally: "The Valley of the Cheese Makers." According to this theory, the name originated in the large number of dairies situated there. It must, however, be pointed out that in those times milk was not transported to special cheese-manufacturing areas. The cheeses were made in the farms, dried and brought to the cities and markets only for the purpose of selling them. To the name "Tyropoeon" other, more complicated interpretations have been given, some of a folkloristic character and others of an ingenious nature. However, the name can be understood quite simply and in accordance with the manner in which places – then as now – get their names. Frequently, a place is named after its owner – thus the Valley of Ben-Hinom was named after the family that owned it. Similarly, it is likely that the Tyropoeon Valley was named after its owner whose name was Trypon or something like it which was perverted in the course of time. Another possibility is that one of the owners of the valley in the past had been a cheese manufacturer and had taken his profession as his name which, in turn, became attached to his property. This last is a very common process and accounts for very many family names.

In addition to being a highly developed commercial center, the area at the foot of the Western Wall contained some of Jerusalem's most important public buildings in the Second Temple period. Among these, the seat of the City Council and the National Archive building have been identified. The latter was the repository of loan and business documents and records. The building was burnt down by the zealot faction at the start of the Great Revolt; the zealots believed that by destroying these records, they would gain the support of the poor and oppressed who would not have to repay their debts. Needless to say, the small savers and investors were also severely hurt. Josephus mentions a building which stood opposite Wilson's Arch by the name of "Xystus." This Greek term usually refers to the large, paved, open square attached to a gymnasium building and has led some scholars to believe that Herod built a gymnasium in Jerusalem. There is, however, no evidence for this in any other source and, indeed, it would have been contrary to Herod's policy regarding Jerusalem. Josephus' reference should, therefore, be understood to mean that there was a public building there which had a gymnasium-type square attached and that because of the square the building came to be known as the Xystus, whatever its function may have been.

Far-reaching excavations at this section of the Wall have not yet been undertaken but the little that has been done has yielded some very impressive results. Warren's archaeological expedition in the nineteenth century discovered a magnificent hall, the walls of which were embellished with beautiful pillars. He called it the "Mason's Hall" in honor of a conference of Freemasons that was taking place at that time in Jerusalem. After the 1967 war, a large-scale cleaning operation at the site was started by the Ministry of Religions under the archaeological supervision of this writer, and the hall was revealed in its entirety. The hall is today popularly known as the "Hall of Hasmoneans" out of a desire to see it as predating the Herodian period, but there is no evidence for such an identification. Apparently, these are the remains of a hall which was part of a larger public building from the days of Herod or his successors.

The Destruction of the Western Wall: How and When?

When the Romans conquered Jerusalem in 70 C.E., the Temple was destroyed except for its western wall. The support-walls of the Temple Mount must also have suffered some damage during and after the siege and the assault on the Temple, but it was not very great. The parts

A section of the Moslem colonade which runs around the walls of the plateau.

of the walls that rose above the level of the Temple Mount plateau and sections of the colonnade which surrounded it were demolished after the wooden roofs of the colonnade were destroyed by fire and the stonework was damaged. The great building, which had been one of the wonders of the ancient world, now lay in ruins. Jews were driven out of the city and the soldiers of the Tenth Legion who remained were quartered in the royal palace and its adjacent citadel near today's Jaffa Gate.

Hadrian, emperor of Rome, was the first to have any designs on the ruins of the Temple Mount, in 132 C.E. For a variety of reasons he decided to build a temple to Jupiter there and, on the ninth day of the month of Av according to the Jewish tradition, the Romans harnessed oxen and ploughed over the area designated for the pagan temple. This act of ploughing is the equivalent of a modern foundation-stone laying. For Bar-Kochba and the Jewish sages this was the final insult and the spark that ignited the second revolt – one of the bloodiest rebellions the Roman empire had ever known. There were those who saw in Hadrian's act the fulfillment of Jeremiah's and Micah's awful prophecy, "Because of you, Zion will be ploughed as a field!" It took three years to put down the rebellion and, when it was over, the Romans energetically turned once again to building a temple to Jupiter. The ruins of that temple and its statues were described by an anonymous traveller from Bordeaux at the beginning of the fourth century. Needless to say, in order to build their temple, the Romans had first to rehabilitate the Temple Mount which was a comparatively easy task since its walls had not been seriously damaged. Together with the other walls, the Western Wall rose to a considerable height. Of its four gates, two – the ones at Robinson's Arch and Wilson's Arch – were out of commission and were not repaired. Coponius' Gate, today's Barclay's Gate, had been undamaged and apparently served as the main entrance to Hadrian's temple. The northernmost gate, Warren's Gate, was repaired, and an arch was substituted for its original huge stone lintel.

From the beginning of the fourth century until the Arab conquest in the first half of the seventh century, Jerusalem was ruled by the Christian Byzantine emperors. All traces of the pagan Jupiter were removed from the Temple Mount but no other building activity – religious or secular – was undertaken there. The Christian authorities believed it to be of supreme importance to leave the site as a silent witness to the destruction of Judaism and the victory of Christianity. What was left, therefore, was a firmly constructed area, the main buildings of which lay in ruins and the tops of whose outer walls had been damaged. The Western Wall suffered the same fate as the other walls; it stood firm but its top section had been demolished. It was, of course, entirely bereft of its former glory. The main road (the Cardo) which was laid in Byzantine Jerusalem ran from the Damascus Gate to the Siloam Pool and replaced the Tyropoeon road of Second Temple times. It veered some eighty metres west of the old road and the Western Wall, apparently because of the uncleared ruins in that area and in accordance with the new plan.

In 614, the Persians once again invaded the Byzantine empire and, in their battles in Eretz Israel and Jerusalem, were helped a great deal by the Jews. In recognition, the Jews were granted national and religious freedom, rule over Jerusalem and the right to build a temple. Nothing came of this generosity because the Persians reneged on their promises a few years later in order to placate their defeated foe, the Byzantines. It does seem, however, that in those three years of cooperation the Jews started to clean the Temple Mount and rehabilitate it. When the Persians had besieged Jerusalem, the Byzantines had used the whole area of the Temple Mount in their defense of the city. The walls of the Temple Mount were strong and, at that time, quite high, and so the area had served the Byzantines as a redoubt.

In 628 the Persians suffered a decisive defeat at the hands of the Byzantines and Jerusalem returned to Christian rule. The new rulers now proceeded to settle accounts with the Jews and with their last spark of hope – the Temple Mount and the ruins of the Temple. It was decided to destroy the Mount entirely – including the walls and what remained of the gates. Indeed, those original sections of the walls which exist today from before the later Moslem efforts at reconstruction are the only parts that escaped the wrath of the Byzantines. It is also possible that at that time they started to build a church on the Temple Mount. The original plan of the Dome of the Rock which was later built there, is identical with the design of a Christian victory-church. The octagonal design of that mosque is quite foreign to Moslem architecture but it is common in Christian buildings erected to celebrate a victory. An example of this is the octagon-shaped church the Byzantines built on Mount Gerizim after they suppressed the Samaritan rebellion. It would appear that they started to work on such a building on the Temple Mount but did not have the time to finish it because of the challenge of Islam thundering at the gates of the Byzantine empire. When the Moslems took Jerusalem, they built the Dome of the Rock on the foundations they found already prepared.

In the archaeological excavations at the Western Wall, sections of the pilaster-decorated, upper parts of the Wall were discovered in the stratum of the seventh century. This indicates that until that century the Western Wall, together with the others, rose above the level of the Temple Mount plateau to a considerable height.

The Restoration of the Western Wall: Who and Why?

Led by the Caliph Omar, the Moslems conquered Jerusalem in 638, and they used to visit the desolate Temple site and even conduct prayers there. After a time, when the Omayyad dynasty took control of the entire Moslem empire, a golden age dawned for Jerusalem. The tradition of Mohammed's wondrous ascent to heaven became attached to the Temple Mount in Omayyad times. This tradition tells of the prophet travelling from Mecca to the "furthermost mosque" on his fabled animal, Al-Buraq. When the identification of the place in the tradition with the Temple Mount became accepted, the Moslems set about building the buildings in the tradition: at the southern end of the Temple Mount they build the "furthermost mosque," Al Akza, and near the center they built the Dome of the Rock as the place from which Mohammed ascended and the "Gates of Mercy" building which was where the prophet entered the plateau and tethered Al-Buraq.

In order to embark on this grandiose project, the builders had to first rehabilitate the Temple Mount area – and so they did. The ruined walls were built higher; not as high as they had been in Second Temple times because, at this stage, the Moslems did not need a plateau as large as it had been then. The stones used for the reconstruction of the walls were not as large as the original stones and were cemented together with large amounts of plaster. Here and there one can see stones slightly larger than the usual Moslem size, but they are a far cry from the monumental stones of the Second Temple period. Around the walls on the inside, roofed colonnades were built, much in the style of the present colonnades in the Temple Mount. The Western Wall needed less reconstruction than the others. It had been less damaged at the end of the Byzantine rule because at its foot was located a residential quarter which would have had to be cleared of its occupants in order to destroy the Wall completely. This was not the case at the southern wall. Although there had been a Christian residential quarter there, it had been occupied by Jews when the Persians took over. The Jews were driven out when the Byzantines came back and so the quarter was desertd. This fact enabled widespread demolition work to be carried out at the southern wall. This was also the situation

Wilson's Arch as it was in Second Temple times, a sketch.

. . . in the Moslem period.

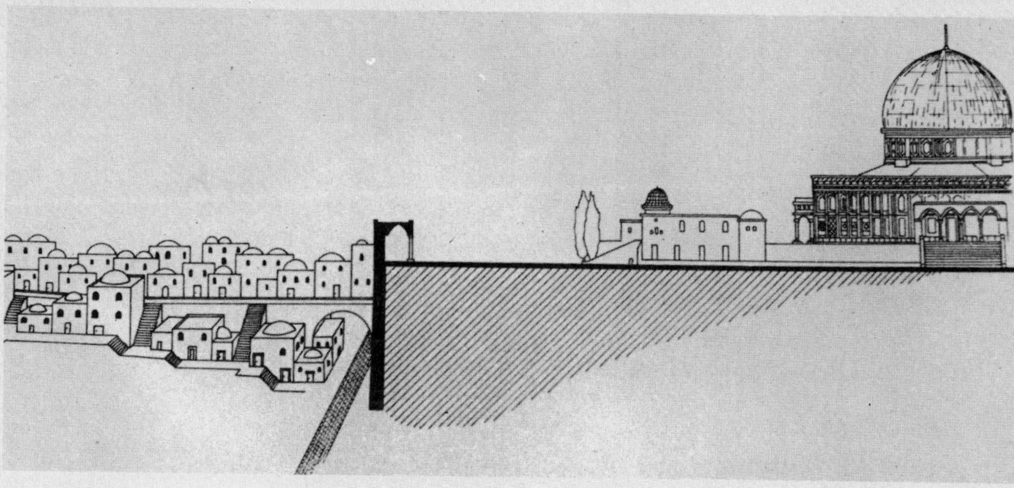

. . . and today.

at the northern end of the Temple Mount. The eastern wall had been the least problematic since it also served as the city wall.

Now, with the Moslems, all the residential sections around the Temple Mount were cleared and a new design prepared for the whole area. The main aim of the new design was to provide extensive public buildings for the needs of the Caliphate. The Temple Mount was rehabilitated and rebuilt as one of the most important sacred sites in Islam and around the Mount an extensive system of secular public buildings was established of which the outstanding feature was a large palace.

Several huge buildings were erected near the Western Wall as part of this extensive system. The southernmost of them was a royal bathhouse built in the Moslem style which itself was heir to the Roman-Byzantine design. The area of the hot-room in this building was one thousand square metres and ovens made of fired brick were located under the floor. Apparently, this was the largest bathhouse ever built in the country. To the north of this building stood a complex building which has not yet been sufficiently investigated. From excavations conducted by the Ministry of Religions it seems that it was a public building connected in some way to the army, a sort of military barracks; when the Caliph visited Jerusalem, units of his bodyguard were quartered there. It is also possible that it served as the living quarters for Jerusalem's garrison. Roads were laid between these buildings of the Moslem period, running north-to-south and east-to-west. The fact that they were narrower than the roads of the Second Temple period would indicate that there was less traffic than then, notwithstanding the area's holiness and public character.

The Western Wall, which had reached its peak in the times of the Second Temple, had been downgraded and damaged in Roman and Byzantine times, particularly towards the end of the latter. Now, under Moslem rule, it resumed its place as a major focal point in the new design but it did not regain its former glory. The area near the Wall, with its markets and its public buildings, had been full of life in Temple times but had been converted into an ordinary residential zone under the Byzantines. It now became a public area once again but in the service of the Caliphate and for its benefit – not for the wider public.

The Vaults of Wilson's Arch adjacent to the Western Wall.

This system of vaults is made up of a large number of vaulted rooms and is underneath the Old City's buildings to the north and south of the Street of the Chain, near the Temple Mount. The largest and most impressive vault in the complex is a complete arch which was discovered by the British archaeologist, Sir Charles Wilson, more than a hundred years ago and which his colleagues called in his honor, Wilson's Arch. It is built on the Western Wall and on a firm pier located thirteen metres west of it. Both the Wall and the lower parts of the pier date from Second Temple times. The original arch was destroyed and stones from it were discovered on the surface of the Second Temple road which lies eight metres beneath the present day surface. It was the Moslems who rebuilt it when they started their extensive building activities in the Temple Mount area and it served a double purpose: it was an overpass or bridge leading to a gate built as an extension of the Street of the Chain, at the site of today's Gate of the Chain, and it created a covered-in usable space within the adjacent system of vaults. To the west, on the ruins of Second Temple public buildings, two multi-vaulted buildings were built with a long vaulted corridor some eighty metres long in them. The entrance to the rooms was located north of the corridor and the lower storeys of the buildings, which have survived practically intact, served as storage rooms and stables for the rooms above. Some of the building stones have the remains of Latin inscriptions on them which indicate that the buildings are later than the Roman period. The several fragments of Latin inscriptions which have been found in buildings in Jerusalem are all connected with the post-Byzantine period because Byzantian Jerusalem itself was merely a continuation of Roman Jerusalem and the first substantial changes were made only after the Arab conquest. The system of vaults was damaged – it seems while it was being built – in an earthquake which shook Jerusalem in 747. It was reconstructed several centuries later and in the tenth and the eleventh centuries it was once again in use, apparently as garrison quarters for the troops of Eretz Israel's Egyptian rulers, the Fatimids. It was this unit's duty to guard the Temple Mount and to prevent demonstrations there against the Fatimid-Shiite rulers of Egypt by the local populace, who subscribed to the Sunnite faction of Islam.

The reconstruction of this area did not always follow the original design. Some of the more heavily damaged vaulted halls were closed completely and others were repaired with supporting arches; thus new vaults were formed. The ceiling of the long corridor was rebuilt but at a lower level than that of its western section which has survived.

A significant change was wrought in the region of the Western Wall at the time of the Crusader conquest and after it. In the wake of the extensive ruin and destruction of those times, building activity was undertaken at a floor level much higher than previously. No effort was made to clear the rubble and descend to the original level. A little to the north of Wilson's Arch, close by the Wall, the Crusaders planned a large structure in the shape of a cross. It is possible that their intention was to erect a large church on the entrance to the Temple Mount and on the Western Wall. They sunk very solid foundations between which a large free area was left. This area was used for a huge water cistern. The foundation walls were plastered with water-resistant plaster and the cistern which was created was also in the shape of a cross. Above the cistern, at today's street level, the church, or whatever the building was meant to be, was to be built. However, it was never built.

A number of buildings were built close to – or at times, on top of – the Western Wall under the Mameluke rule in Jerusalem. Among these were religious schools (*medrasot*), burial vaults for important dignitaries, and dwelling houses for dervishes and other religious functionaries. One of these buildings is known today as the *Mahkameh*, the courthouse, because from the end of the nineteenth century it served as a court for the Moslem community. Originally, it was built for a religious school, a *medraseh*, by Tangiz, the governor of Jerusalem, and it was known by the name Tangizieh. The building rested on deep foundation walls and vaults which are, today, to the north of the Western Wall prayer area. The vaults served as storage rooms for the buildings above them and, in some cases, water cisterns were dug to provide for the buildings near the Wall.

Starting from the Crusader period and through the Mameluke and Ottoman periods, the entire length of the Wall was covered with private and public buildings, at the level of the Old City, whose floors were located on top of the rubble of the earlier period. These buildings effectively concealed most of the Western Wall of Second Temple times as well as the sections reconstructed in the early Arab period.

At the beginning of the British mandate, piped water came into widespread use in the Old City of Jerusalem and the need for a sewage system was felt. Since no such system existed, the system of vaults under the houses was used for that purpose. Slowly, sewage spread throughout the whole system and the Western Wall region to the north of the present prayer area became the central sewage point of the city.

It was only after the 1967 war that a sewage system was built for those streets adjacent to the Wall so that it became possible to clean and reveal the impressive remains of the vaults under the Old City. When the vaults were cleaned of sewage, whole sections of the Western Wall were revealed in all their glory from Second Temple times. Ironically enough, the burial in sewage for generations actually preserved many of the Wall's stones and so, in those areas, it is possible to see origial Second Temple stonemasonry and learn a great deal about stone setting and dressing.

The Gates to the Temple Mount in the Western Wall Today

Today there are seven gates in the wall on the west side of the Temple Mount for entrance onto it and exit from it. Most of them were built in the Mameluke period which was exceedingly prolific in building in Jerusalem, and one of them dates from Crusader times. All the gates were in use during the Ottoman period and in the decades since then. The gates are located at the end of alleys and streets which cross the width of Jerusalem from the upper city towards the Temple Mount.

The northernmost of the gates is called "The Sons of G'anam Gate." The alley leading to it starts north of the Temple Mount but the gate itself is located in the western wall of the mosque compound near the northeastern corner.

The second gate is called "The Prison Gate." At the beginning of the alley leading to it are located a number of Mameluke buildings which served as a prison in Ottoman times and thus the name. This gate also has two other names: "The Council House Gate" and "The Supervisor's Gate," both of which are connected to buildings near it. Not far away is a building which, in Mameluke times, served as the seat of the Moslem Council and the office of the supervisor of the Temple Mount.

One of the most beautiful gates in the western wall of the plateau – and indeed of the whole area – is the "Cotton Gate," so called because it leads out into the cotton merchants' market. This gate is one of the finest architectural creations of the Mameluke period in Jerusalem.

Two gates are situated, close to each other, opposite the northern entrance steps to the Temple Mount. These are "The Iron Gate" and "The Gate of Purity." The latter is so called because from it the Moslems would go to purify themselves in the nearby bathhouses before entering to pray. Both of these gates also date from the Mameluke period.

The only gate from Crusader times is a double gate at the end of the Street of the Chain, above Wilson's Arch. The Street of the Chain, and its continuation, David's Street, is the main thoroughfare crossing the Old City from the Jaffa Gate to the Temple Mount. The face of the gate is decorated with beautiful mouldings and capitals of animal and human figures as well as floral and geometrical designs.

"The Gate of the Chain" is also known as "The Gate of the Divine Presence" and "The Gate of Peace" for each of its respective wings. The names are based on a misidentification of a gate mentioned in the New Testament. The gate there is the main entrance to the plateau at which Peter and John met the lame man and it is the eastern of the two Huldah Gates, which are located in the southern wall.

The name, "Gate of the Divine Presence," evokes echoes of the Jewish tradition that the Divine Presence rests on the Western Wall. The origin of the name may be in the Middle Ages when they identified the western wall of the Temple Mount with the western wall of the Temple.

The last and southernmost entrance to the plateau from the west is "The Magreb Gate." It is located above Coponius' Gate, which is now known as Barclay's Gate. The Magreb Gate was built at the end of the Mameluke period or the beginning of the Ottoman and it has borne its name since then. Refugees from Moslem Morocco and Spain (the Magreb) were settled there by the last Mameluke rulers of Jerusalem and, more intensely, by the Ottomans. The loyalty of the local Moslems to the foreign rulers was suspect and it was thought that the foreign Moslems, who received shelter from the rulers, would be more loyal. A mosque was built at the southern end of the Western Wall for these refugees.

The Magreb Gate is the only entrance into the Temple Mount plateau which is under the control of the Israel Defence Forces and it is guarded by Israeli soldiers and representatives

The passageway under the Al Akza mosque leading to the Huldah Gates.

of the Moslem Religious Council, the Waqf. This state of affairs is the result of an arrangement made after the 1967 war when the Jewish prayer area at the Western Wall was fixed towards the south.

For the last several centuries, Jews have been accustomed to conduct prayers at the entrances to the Temple Mount, from where they could see the plateau and its buildings but into which they could not enter. At first, it was Islam which forbade the Jews to enter and later Jewish law gave its seal of approval to the prohibition. In addition to the Jewish Quarter, Jews also lived in the Moslem quarters and in areas close to the various western entrances to the Temple Mount and so it was convenient for them to pray at them. This tradition became more firmly rooted as the Western Wall was identified as that from which the Divine Presence will never depart.

The Western Wall – a Place of Prayer.

For seven hundred years the Western Wall has been a place of prayer for the Jews. It became so after Jews built their residential quarters near it and after the more accepted Jewish holy places were taken over by the Moslem religion, important Islamic monuments built on them, and Jews denied access. This was the case with regard to "The Gates of Mercy" on the eastern side of the Temple Mount and the Huldah Gates on the southern side. The Western Wall was recognized as a Jewish holy place and the Jews given full exclusive rights to it by the Ottoman sultan, Suleiman the Magnificent, in the second half of the sixteenth century. The section he gave the Jews lay between the Street of the Chain and the Magreb Quarter to its south. An uncovered section of the wall was found there and by excavating downward, it was given added height. Legend has it that gold coins were thrown there and people dug to find them. Such legends appear over and over again in the history of Jerusalem and even today many residents of the Arab quarters believe that the archaeological excavations being conducted at the foot of the Temple Mount are really searches for buried treasure! Access to the Wall was provided by an alley from its north for the residents of the Jewish Quarter and for those Jews who lived in the Moslem quarters of the city, close to the cotton merchants' market. The area of the Wall adjacent to the Magreb Quarter was also safer for the Jews because of the connections between these Moslem Spanish and Moroccan refugees and the Jewish Spanish refugees and also because of the former's loyalty to the regime.

The prayer area was established along a twenty-two metre section of the Wall with a width of three metres which was closed off by a wall running parallel to the Western Wall. The area was paved. Thus a small enclosure was created and it was this space that became the sacred prayer site of the Jewish people. Slowly but inexorably, customs developed about the Wall; one of them was for the visitor to write his name in ink or paint on the stones. When the aspirations of the Zionist movement collided with those of the Arab Nationalist movement, many and bitter were the struggles waged over this tiny enclosure which symbolized the struggle over the country and the status of Jerusalem (See chapter VI: The Struggle for the Wall).

Until 1948, the enclosure at the Wall retained the dimensions and the form which had been established four hundred years earlier. For nineteen years, from Israel's War of Independence when Jordanian forces conquered the Jewish Quarter of the Old City and East Jerusalem, until the Six-Day War in 1967 in which Israel liberated the Wall and the Jewish Quarter, the prayer area at the Wall stood desolate. It was maintained as it had been and no use whatsoever was made of it.

Immediately at the end of the war, the Magreb Quarter was cleared of its inhabitants who were relocated elsewhere and the half-ruined hovels were cleared away and the prayer area enlarged. Later, the floor level was lowered by two metres, that is, two further courses of stone were uncovered. Elementary steps were taken to prepare the enlarged area for visitors; it was paved and separated into separate portions for men and women. Part of the vaulted area and Wilson's Arch were later rehabilitated to be used for prayer in inclement weather conditions. Similarly, arrangements were made for the area's maintenance and a drainage system was installed.

The open air prayer area at the Western Wall today occupies sixty of the 485-metre length of the Wall. At its southern end, it is bounded by the hill of rubble on which the access path to the Magreb Gate ascends and on the north by the Mameluke *Mahkameh* building. Approximately one-third of the area to the south is reserved for women while the remaining two-thirds to the north are for men. Standing facing the Wall, it is possible to see seven courses of massive, monumental stones which are the remains of the wall Herod built. Beneath the surface there are another eight courses of such stones which reach down to the paved road which ran along the foot of the Wall. Underneath the paved road from Second Temple times there are another nine layers which constituted the foundations of the Wall and which have never been uncovered. One can gain some impression of them from the shaft under Wilson's Arch which was sunk by the British Expedition in the nineteenth century and which was left open because it was in the vault system which was not open to the public.

Above the seven visible layers from Second Temple times, one can see four, or occasionally five, rows of large stones. They are easily distinguishable from the Herodian stones; these are approximately one metre square without chiselled borders. These stones are the remains of the Moslem reconstruction in Omayyad times. Above these are rows of smaller stones which reach to the top of the Wall. It is impossible to date this addition with any exactitude. Starting from the early Moslem period, the relatively low courses were built with larger stones and

The entrance to Barclay's Gate. To the left: the lintel of Coponius' Gate which is under it.

the higher ones with smaller stones. Similarly, no attention was was paid to aesthetic considerations; the original intention may have been to plaster the stones over. Later on the Wall was damaged by nature and by human hands and was once again repaired but it is impossible to distinguish between the Fatimid, the Crusader, the Mameluke, and the Ottoman contributions. It must be remembered that the size of the stones cannot serve as an indication, because this whole section of the Wall is built of small stones and is constructed in a manner which was practiced in the country for many centuries.

Two legends have been woven about the small stones in the upper section of the Wall and about two persons as far apart as is imaginable. One story claims that the upper layers were built by Sir Moses Montefiore in his attempt to repair the Wall. The other story claims that it was the Mufti of Jerusalem, Haj Amin al-Husseini, who added a couple of layers to the Wall in order to establish Arab ownership of it. There is no evidence *in situ* for either of these stories and, indeed, no authentic literary sources corroborate either of them. It is possible that Montefiore intended to do something for the Wall, but there is no evidence that he actually did anything. As far as the Mufti is concerned, his rabid hatred of the Jews is well known as are his attempts to drive them away from the Wall; but there is no evidence that he built any addition.

The top three layers of white stones were added by the Moslem Religious Council as part of the general repairs made throughout the whole area. In this case, the repairs were made to the western colonnade which stands, in this section, above the Western Wall.

The Wall continues in both directions from the prayer area but it is hidden by rooms and vaults. To the south, at the end of the women's prayer area, it is possible to distinguish a very large stone under which there is a section built of small stones. This large stone was the lintel of Coponius' Gate, the only complete Temple Mount gate from Second Temple times which survived. The small stones were used to fill in the gate. Above the gate is a vaulted room which the women use in inclement weather. This small room is the remnant of a cellar of a Mameluke building.

To the north of the prayer area is the entrance to the system of vaults which are adjacent to the Wall. In its southern section, this system supports the *Mahkameh* building. These supporting arches continue to Wilson's Arch, above which the Gate of the Chain is located. On the southern side of that area is the entrance to the Tangiz school with its special door and inscription praising its builder, Tangiz the Mameluke governor. All the vault area serves as a prayer area for men but at specific times women may visit it.

The section of the Western Wall which serves for Jewish prayer is called "Al-Buraq" by the Moslems, and is, according to them, the place where the horse was tethered when his master, the prophet Mohammed, ascended to heaven. This tradition was transferred to the Western Wall from the eastern wall and the southern wall about one hundred and twenty years ago when the Jewish nationalist movement chose the Western Wall as the symbol of the renewal of the Jewish settlement in Eretz Israel.

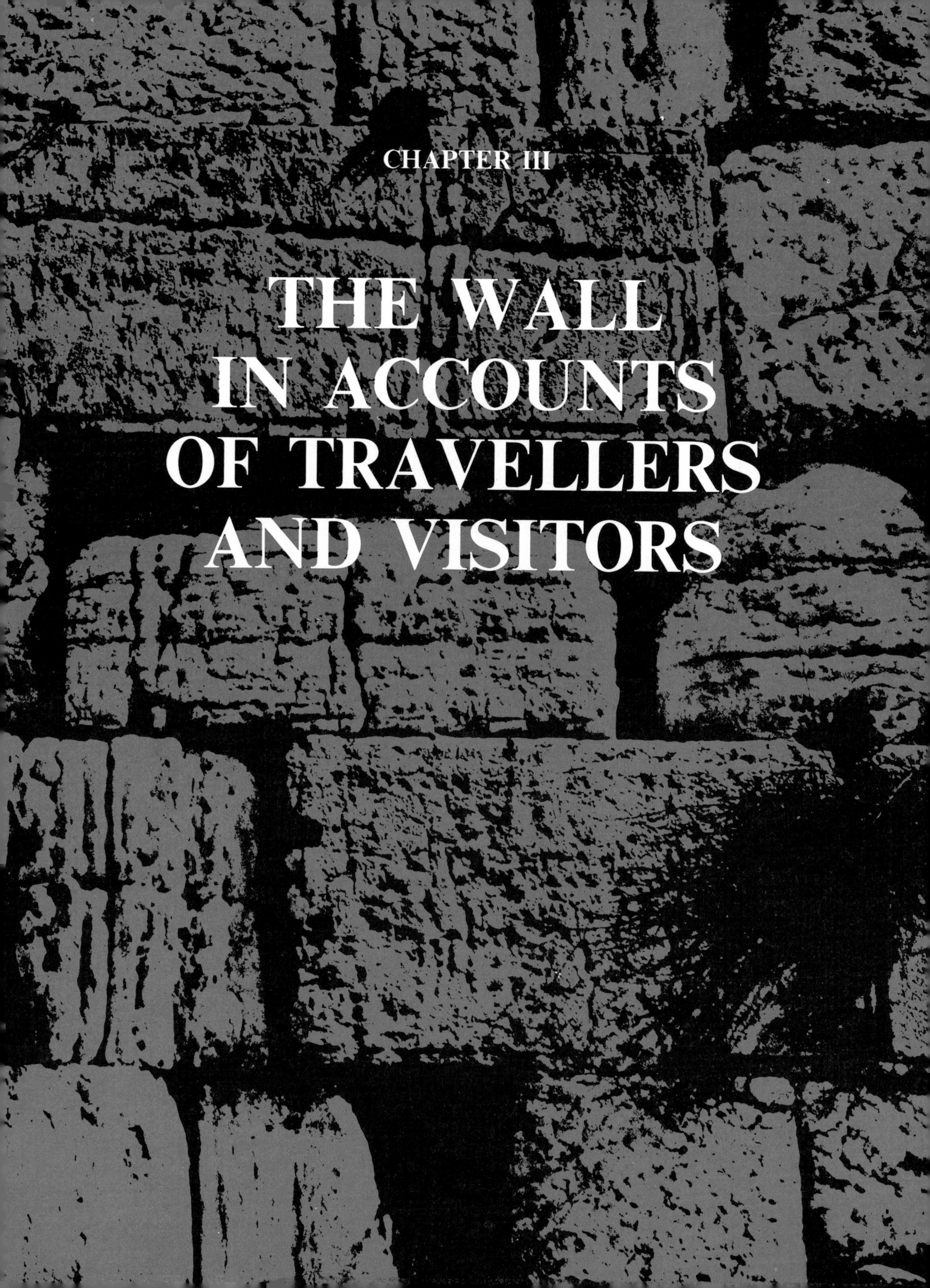

CHAPTER III

THE WALL IN ACCOUNTS OF TRAVELLERS AND VISITORS

The Second Temple was destroyed in 70 C.E. and it is generally believed that the Western Wall, which was a buttress wall supporting the western side of the Temple Mount, is its sole remaining vestige.

The sanctity which is attached to the Western Wall in Jewish tradition today evolved over the generations. The fourth-century rabbi, Rav Aha, is reported in *Shemot Rabbah* as having said, "The *Shekhinah* (Divine Presence) never leaves the Western Wall." The version of his statement in the *Yalkut Shimoni* adds "of the Temple" at the end, and indeed some scholars believe that Rav Aha was referring to the western wall of the Temple itself and that when that wall was destroyed, its sanctity was, so to speak, transferred to the western buttress wall which still survived. In *Shir Ha-Shirim Rabbah* the verse, "Behold, he stands behind our wall" (Songs 2:9) is interpreted: "Behold, He (God) stands behind our wall, behind the western wall of the Temple which the Holy One, blessed be He, swore would never be destroyed. The Priest's Gate and Huldah's Gate will also never be destroyed until the Almighty renews them." The same interpretation is also cited in *Bemidbar Rabbah* with a slight difference: "Behold, He is standing behind our wall – this is the western wall of the Temple which was never destroyed because the *Shekhinah* is in the west."

A.M. Lunz, in his monograph *The Western Wall* (1912), pointed out that although these last two sources have the word "of the Temple," the reference cannot be to the actual Temple wall because Hadrian demolished the Temple completely and built a temple to Jupiter in its place long before these sources were written, and it would have been absurd to say about something that had been destroyed that it would never be destroyed. This reasoning holds good for Rav Aha as well. The *midrashim*, therefore, must be referrring to the western buttress wall which survived the destruction. Lunz finds support for this contention in that the other two sites mentioned in *Shir Ha-Shirim Rabbah*, the Priest's Gate and Huldah's Gate were certainly in the wall around the Temple Mount and not in the Temple Wall itself.

The literary reports of travellers and pilgrims, particularly in the last few centuries, are full of descriptions of the Western Wall. It should, however, be pointed out that for hundreds of years, during nearly the whole of the Middle Ages, there are hardly any references to the Wall. This is most probably due to the fact that Jews were not allowed to approach it or pray at it. Furthermore, it is believed that for a long period the Western Wall was covered in rubble and garbage, which fact is a good indication of the attitude of the authorities – Arab, Christian and Mameluke – to this holy Jewish site.

The Riddled Stone

Early evidence of Jewish prayer at the Western Wall can be found in the *Bordeaux Pilgrim*, (or *Itinerarium Burdigalense*), written by an anonymous French pilgrim who visited the Holy Land in 333.

"The Jews come there (the ruins of the Temple) once a year, weeping and wailing near a stone which survived the destruction of the Temple. . . There are two monuments of Hadrian there and not far away is a stone riddled through with holes to which the Jews come once a year. They anoint it (the stone) and wail and keen and rend their garments and so they return from there."

Presumably, the "stone riddled through with holes" means the Western Wall.

The "stone," i.e., the Western Wall, appears again and again in descriptions written by Christian travellers in the following centuries.

In the eleventh century, for example, an anonymous traveller recorded: "Not far from this place is the stone to which the Jews come every year. They anoint it and weep and wail."

It is in the Middle Ages that the term Western Wall begins to appear in Jewish sources. In *Sefer Ha-Yuhasin*, (*Megilat Ahimaatz*, an 11th-century chronicle) we learn of one, Samuel, the son of Paltiel (980-1015), who "gave 20,000 *drimonim* (drachma) for the poor and destitute, for the rabbis and the preachers who study Torah, for the teachers of the children, for the cantors, and oil for the sanctuary at the Western Wall for the inner altar. . ." The latter section refers to a synagogue close by the Temple site, at the Western Wall.

Other sources tell of Jewish activities near the Temple site, around the gates in the wall and at the Western Wall. During and after the Crusader period such sources increase. A good example is the famous Jewish traveller, Benjamin of Tudela, who visited Jerusalem in the twelfth century (apparently in 1170) and wrote:

"Jerusalem has four gates: Abraham's Gate, David's Gate, the Zion Gate and the Gospat Gate, which is Jehoshaphat's Gate, in front of the Temple of ancient times. The Templum Domini now stands on the Temple site. On that spot Omar ibn al-Khattab built a large and exceedingly beautiful cupola. The gentiles do not take any image or picture into it but go there only to pray. In front of that place is the Western Wall, one of the walls which were in the Temple at the Holy of Holies which is called the Gate of Mercy and the Jews go there to pray in front of the wall in the courtyard."

Benjamin adds that "all the Jews, each and every one of them, write their names on the Wall."

Here we find the term "courtyard" being used for the Western Wall, and it is surely evocative of the courtyards of the Temple, thronged with pilgrims. The term is also used by other Jewish pilgrims. One of them, Samuel ben Shimshon, came to Jerusalem in 1210:

"We came to Jerusalem from the west and when we saw it we tore our garments as is proper and we were filled with pity and we wept a great weeping, I and the high priest from Lunel (Rabbi Jonathan of Lunel, an outstanding rabbi and scholar). We entered by the gate near the Tower of David and we came to prostrate ourselves before the courtyard, and we bowed down before the gate, opposite which, from the direction of Ein Etam which was the priests' place of ablution, is a gate in the Western Wall."

Five years later, Menahem ben Peretz of Hebron visited Jerusalem and wrote: "I was on

An etching of Taylor from the 19th century (below) and the photograph on which it was based (above).

Mount Zion and I saw the site of the Temple and the Temple Mount. The Western Wall still exists."

Exactly one thousand years after the Bordeaux Pilgrim, a kabbalist, Isaac ben Joseph ibn Chelo, wrote an interesting description of the Western Wall in his book *Shevilei Yerushalayim* ("The Pathways of Jerusalem," 1333):

"Because of our sins, on the site of the Temple now stands a mosque which was built by the king of the Ishmaelites (the Arabs) who conquered Eretz Israel and Jerusalem from the uncircumcised (the Christians). And this is what happened: the king who had sworn an oath to rebuild the ruins of the Temple when God would give the Holy City into his hands, asked the Jews to show him those ruins, because the Christians, in their hatred of God's people, had so covered the ruins with garbage that no one knew any more their exact location. There was an old man who said to the king: 'If the king will swear an oath that he will leave the Western Wall, I will show him the ruins of the Temple.' The king immediately placed his hand on the thigh of the old man and swore a solemn oath. The old man then showed him where the ruins were under the mountains of garbage and the king had them all cleared away. The king himself participated in the work until the site was thoroughly cleansed. Afterwards, he rebuilt everything except the Western Wall. He built a very beautiful temple which he dedicated to his God; that is the Western Wall opposite Omar ibn al-Khattab's temple which is called the Gate of Mercy."

It should be pointed out that the terms "The Gate of Mercy" and "The Western Wall" appear more than once as names of the place where the Jews gathered and prayed. This was the case in the account of Benjamin of Tudela as well as in that of Isaac ibn Chelo. According to some opinions, an aura of holiness attached itself to "The Gate of Mercy" in the eastern wall because that was the nearest part of the Temple Mount to the Mount of Olives from which the Jews used to view the ruined Temple Mount. Another opinion has it that the reference is not to today's "Gate of Mercy" in the east but to the Western Wall and the space in front of it.

"Its Stones are Great and Thick"

The first authority to conduct scientific research into Eretz Israel, Estori Ha-Parhi (1280-1355), does not mention the Western Wall in his work *Kaftor va-Ferah.* It is assumed that in his time the Jews were denied access to the Wall, and it is possible that the Wall was completely buried.

From the fifteenth century onwards descriptions of the Western Wall and its environs and the prayers there increase. Rabbi Obadiah of Bertinoro, who emigrated to Eretz Israel in 1488, wrote: "As to the Western Wall which is still in existence – or at least part of it – its stones are great and thick. I have never seen such massive stones in any ancient building, not in Rome or elsewhere."

About a generation later, in 1522 when the Ottoman Turks already ruled the country, an anonymous traveller wrote the following clearer and more recognizable description: "The Western Wall which survives is not the whole of the western side but only a portion of it, between forty and fifty cubits long. For one half of its height it is from Solomon's time as the large ancient stones (show). Below and above (that section) is new building."

Another anonymous source, a short time later in 1537, wrote: "To the west is the Western Wall, an ancient structure from which the Divine Presence has never departed."

The seventeenth century yields mainly Karaite reports about the Wall. Samuel ben David visited Jerusalem in 1644 and wrote: "On the first day we arose and went to seee the courtyard and the Western Wall which remains from Solomon's Temple. The Wall is very high and its stones are enormous."

Fourteen years later, another Karaite, Moses Yerushalmi, gave the following account:

"Now, everybody knows that one wall and one wall only is left from the Temple, and that we must weep and keen for the destruction of the Temple; this wall is called the Western Wall. The (Hebrew) word (*kotel*) is to be divided into two words: *ko* which has the same numerical value as God's name and *tel* which means 'the hill' towards which all turn and direct their prayers; and that is where we prostrate ourselves. Near the Western Wall the Arabs built a house of prayer and surrounded it with a wall, and the Western Wall is also within the wall so that nobody (presumably Christians) may enter. But the Jews are allowed to go there, and they pay a tax of 10 *para* (a small Turkish coin). The Jews of Jerusalem pay the tax for the whole year and may go there as often as they wish. But you must approach from the outside and not from the inside for great sanctity rests on the Western Wall, the original sanctity which attached to it then and forever more."

Yet another Karaite, Benjamin Yerushalmi, tells us of the Wall in 1685.

"Afterwards we went to the Western Wall to pray there. It is within Jerusalem near the houses of non-Jews and it dates from the time of King Solomon, may he rest in peace. It is built of massive stones approximately fourteen spans (a unit of length) long and eight spans wide. We prayed there. On another occasion, when I went there with Zerah Yerushalmi, the Turk, a lad called us into his house in order to show us the inside of the Temple site, through a window in the (house's) courtyard and also the grave of a prophet who is buried in its courtyard under the stones of the Western Wall at the corner of the wall of Solomon's Temple, and we went and we viewed them. There are stones as long as the height of two men in the Western Wall in that courtyard. If a man wants to go to the Wall every day, the Ishmaelites allow him to go and pray; therefore, we went there to pray often and it is also close to our synagogue and communal buildings. But the Ishmaelites will not allow any gentile (Christian) to draw near to the streets near the Wall to see it."

As the years passed, more and more details about the Wall were reported and the accounts by visitors to it became longer. The following is a part of Gedaliah of Semyatitch's description of the Wall in 1699 from his book *Sha'alu Shlom Yerushalayim* ("Seek the Peace of Jerusalem"):

"The Western Wall which remains from the Temple is very long and high. For most of its height it is very ancient and the stones are very large. Some stones are five or six cubits wide and the same is true for their height. But I do not know how thick (deep) they are; if I could see them at the end of the Wall, I could tell but a courtyard (group of buildings) has been built actually against one end of the Wall and at the other end stands the house of an Ishmaelite judge, whom the Arabs call *dayyan*, which is the translation of judge in the Aramaic they speak. The Ishmaelites call him *kadi* in their language. Since these buildings cover both ends of the Wall, it is impossible to see how thick the Wall is. The Ishmaelites have added to the height of this ancient Wall with new building until it has become very high; in these new walls there are also gates to go in and out through them. Only Ishmaelites are permitted to enter the site of the Temple but not Jews or other peoples unless, God forbid, they convert to Islam. Because they (the Moslems) say that no other religion is worthy enough to enter this holy site. Although God had originally chosen the Jews, because they sinned, He deserted them and chose the Ishmaelites. Thus they talk continuously. When we go to the Wall to pray, we are actually standing 'behind our wall' (Song of Songs 2:9), close by it. On the eve of the New Moon and on the 9th of Av and other fasts, (the Jews) go there to pray and, although the women weep bitterly, nobody objects. Even though the Ishmaelite judge lives close by and hears the weeping, he does not object or rebuke them at all. Occasionally, a young Arab comes to annoy the Jews but they give him a small coin (*mahat*) and he goes off. If a dignified Ishmaelite or Arab witnesses such impudence, he severely reprimands the child. The Temple site is far from the streets the Jews live in, and we have to go through markets and other streets to get to the Western Wall. Prayer is generally more desirable by the Wall. When the Ishmaelites enter the Temple site, they take off their shoes outside and leave them there and go in barefoot. They treat the place with great sanctity. I heard a story that in ancient times, when there was a great drought, the Jews proclaimed a public fast and took a Sefer Torah with them to the Wall to pray. God answered their prayers to such an extent that they had to wrap up the Torah Scroll in their clothes when they took it back to protect it against the rain."

"The Most Famous Thing Throughout the Whole Diaspora"

It is impossible to quote all the descriptions of the Western Wall that have appeared in books, brochures, letters and other publications. There is so much material from the nineteenth and early twentieth centuries that considerations of space allow us to cite only a limited number of examples, which actualize the place of the Wall in the Jerusalem experience in particular and among the Jewish people, both in Eretz Israel and outside it, in general.

In 1839, Dr. Eliezer Levy, Sir Moses Montefiore's secretary, wrote: "On the third day I visited the thing most famous throughout the whole Diaspora, the Western Wall, a memorial to ancient times. . . Jews gather in this holy place on Friday evenings to pray before God for the welfare of their brethren who live in foreign lands. They mention their benefactors by name and pray for each one separately."

In the same year, on Sir Moses' second visit to the Holy Land, that Anglo-Jewish dignitary's wife committed his impressions of the holy site to writing:

"We yesterday went to inspect the western wall of the temple of Solomon. How wonderful that it should have so long defied the ravages of time! The huge stones seem to cling together; to be cemented by a power mightier than decay, that they may be a memorial of Israel's past glory: and oh! may they not be regarded as a sign of future greatness, when Israel shall be redeemed, and the whole world shall, with one accord, sing praises to Israel's God!"

In contrast to this optimistic description, Ludwig A. Frankl took a more somber view of what was happening at the Wall. The following citation is from his book, *Nach Jerusalem*! (1859):

"When it became cooler, I set my steps towards the ruins of the Temple, to the one wall that has survived, the wailing place of the Jews who gather there every Friday evening to pray the evening service and to bewail the Temple that was destroyed.

"They have an everlasting *firman* from the authorities allowing them to visit this place, for which privilege they pay a small tax.

"After we passed through many streets, we came into a narrow winding street and from there to the Wall. It is 158 feet long and 60 high, which height is made up of twenty-three stone courses of which the bottom nine are of hewn stones some of which are between twenty and thirty feet in length and five feet wide. Each of these slabs of stone is rounded and on their faces, which have been smoothed as though with an instrument, there is a shining border of about a finger's depth. Lying there, row on row, thin lines can be seen between them, and

A visit by the Zionist leader, Nahum Sokolow, at the Wall.

so the whole Wall looks like a wall of avenues of which the upper courses are of a later origin. From the shape of some of the hewn stones that jut out of the Wall, modern research has concluded that they are the remains of arches leading from the Temple to Mount Zion.

"There can be no doubt that this wall with its courses of foundation stones under the ground, is a memorial for the Jews from Solomon's time which, as Jossipon put it, will never collapse. Anyone who has seen it can testify that it will not collapse until the very foundations of the earth will be shaken.

"From a distance we could already hear the sound of the wailing, a cry of pain which pierced the very heart. In chorus, the appeal rang in our ears, 'How long, Oh Lord!.'

"Jews were gathered there in their hundreds, some in the dress of the Ishmaelites and others in the style of Poland, and, facing the Wall, they bowed and prostrated themselves. At a great distance from the men, stood the women all totally enveloped in white gowns – white doves, tired from their flying, resting on the ruins. When the cantor reached those parts of the prayers to be said by the congregation, their voices rose among the choir of male voices, and spreading their arms on high, they looked in their wide white gowns for all the world like wings spread upwards to the open gates of heaven. Afterwards, they smote their foreheads against the hewn stones of the Temple's wall. Then, when the cantor, exhausted and wasted from his efforts, quietly and slowly weeping, turned his head to the wall, then suddenly, in a moment, a deathly silence covered all."

"The Wall is Ours!"

Thirty years after Frankl's book appeared, a Jewish tourist from Russia came to Jerusalem. This was Mordecai ben Hillel Ha-Kohen who was later to become an important figure in the Zionist movement and the Jewish community in Eretz Israel. His description, which follows,

An *Ashkenazi* and a *Sephardi* at the Wall.

is typical of the reaction of Jews from abroad who saw for the first time the outstanding vestige of Jewish sovereignty, glory and holiness in Jerusalem – the Western Wall.

"I started to organize my stay in the city (Jerusalem), but I soon realized that I did not have the strength to withstand the desire – nay! the urgent need – to hurry to the Western Wall. I remember nothing of the way I went; my legs bore me, and I went blindly like an animal following its herder. My eyes were lifted aloft all the time straining to catch the first glimpse of the Wall. 'This is the Western Wall,' murmured my guide in a holy whisper; but I would have known anyway... I do not remember how my shoes left my feet, how I fell full length on the ground, how I started kissing the flagstones under me or how I began weeping such copious tears that became torrents. My heart was in turmoil. I did not attempt to control myself or stop the flow of tears which I wept like a small infant without sense or words. The attendant did not approve and interrupted me, handing me a Psalter and showing me the verses which were to be recited at the Wall. Idiot! Did he not realize that at that moment I had no need of any verses, of any prayerbook or of any liturgy!?

"I departed the Wall grievously heartbroken. In such a spirit had I left the cemetery in Homel, my home of the previous summer, when I buried my only beloved daughter. I left the Wall and the cemetery and I knew that I was leaving a great part of my life, a whole piece of my heart. Oh! that there should be no such moments in the life of any man! For such moments can bring a man down suddenly or, at least, lead him into madness. I remember and I am distraught! Dread is all around me!

"It was not what my eyes saw or the desolation at the Wall that so struck me but rather my inner soul-feeling. For in its appearance there is nothing in this Wall to so disturb the strings of a man's heart and to incite such a storm inside a Jew. There is not even 'destruction' there. The stones have been burned with fire, the Wall is not destroyed, the rows of its stones do not cast the shadow of death and, generally, surely the terrible destruction deserves a more fitting memorial than that given by this Wall?! After having said all this, I still must say that what this Wall does is truly awesome; for so great is the holy trepidation that falls on the Jew in this place that for the sake of the Wall and for its sake alone every Jew should make the pilgrimage to Jerusalem. The cities of Judah and the streets of Jerusalem are filled with memorials, by their thousands, dear to every Jew and with each step he will hear the echoes of pleasant memories and see memorials which silently will tell him what was ours in days long past. But, even if they all did not exist, even if they were all rolled together and stored out of sight, and only the Wall still remained; even then it would be worthwhile for the Jew to take all the trouble in the world to come and see it with his own eyes. There are scholars who cast doubt on the verity of the traditions about this Wall. They have no heart and they lack understanding! They cannot believe that the tradition speaks the truth, that a wall can stand for two thousand years, and that truly there still exists in the world a survivor from that 'universal house of prayer.' A survivor of all the trials and tribulations which have not ceased to visit this wonderful country from the day that Judah was exiled from it and strangers swallowed it. Let the scholars wonder at it as they will – for us it is no wonder! We know that we are a people of legends. Who knows! Perhaps the whole Jewish people is a legend! But in that legend, there bursts forth a spring of life of exalted strength, and that legend can laugh at the facts of real life! Why do I need to know which of the Wall's stones are from the walls of the Temple Mount and which were added to it later? I know that there is no nation and no people in the world which comes to prostrate itself and pour out itsheart in front of this Wall; but our brethren come from all the lands of their exile to tell their sins before these holy stones. Only Israel – in all its families – cries there! That is the proof that there we stand behind our Wall. The Wall is ours and let no man dare to try to touch it!"

"Hebrew Architecture"

It was not only Jewish pilgrims who wrote emotional and nostalgic descriptions of the Western Wall. Non-Jewish scholars, travellers and tourists also devoted much space in their memoirs and travelogues to the wondrous Wall in Jerusalem.

In 1786 a Belgian tourist Jean Zoualret wrote about the Wall: "Jews come to this place from all over the world out of the special respect they have for Solomon's Temple and the Holy of Holies, in which stood the Chair of Glory, the Cherubs, and the Ark of the Covenant, as well as the Manna and Aaron's Rod."

In subsequent centuries, non-Jews continued to describe the Western Wall. Edward Robinson, the father of modern geographical research into Eretz Israel, wrote of his visit to the Wall in 1838:

"In the afternoon of the same day, I went with Mr. Lanneau to the place where the Jews are permitted to purchase the right of approaching the site of their temple, and of praying and wailing over its ruins and the downfall of their nation. The spot is on the western exterior of the area of the great mosque, considerably south of the middle; and is approached only by a narrow crooked lane, which there terminates at the wall in a very small open place. The lower part of the wall is here composed of the same kind of ancient stones, which we had before seen on the eastern side. Two old men, Jews, sat there upon the ground, reading together in a book of Hebrew prayers. On Fridays they assemble here in greater numbers. It is the nearest point in which they can venture to approach their ancient temple; and fortunately for them, it is sheltered from observation by the narrowness of the lane and the dead walls around. Here, bowed in the dust, they may at least weep undisturbed over the fallen glory of their race; and bedew with their tears the soil, which so many thousands of their forefathers once moistened with their blood."

The Englishman, George Fisk, visited Eretz Israel in 1842 and in his account he, like many others, combines a description of the sorry contemporary state with pious hopes for a better future:

"On reaching the spot, we found a row of aged Jews sitting in the dust in front of the wall, all of them engaged in reading or reciting certain portions of the Hebrew scriptures. There was no such outward manifestation of emotion as I had been led to expect; but yet every one appeared to be intently occupied, and but little disturbed by the approach of European strangers. Among them were several Jewesses, enveloped from head to foot in ample white veils. They stepped forward to various parts of the ancient wall, kissed them with great fervency of manner, and uttered their petitions in a low whisper, at the points where the stones came in contact. I thought of Israel, when by the waters of Babylon they sat down and wept; and could but lift up my heart for the hastening of the time when their King shall be again in the midst of them – no longer in humiliation, but in glory, and when all 'shall know him, from the least to the greatest.'

The French scholar Louis Felicien de Saulay, who became famous on account of his excavations of the Tombs of the Kings in Jerusalem, stressed the "Hebrew Architecture" of the Western Wall in his *Memoirs* (1851):

"I have known for a long time that in Jerusalem at the place of the mosque which stands on the site of Solomon's Temple, stands part of a wall which the Jews have always considered to be a remnant of the original building. I also knew that the base of this wall, access to which has not been denied to the Jews, is, in their eyes, a sacred place, to which they come every Friday evening to pray and at which they can be frequently seen keening, weeping and

"Jews praying at the Wailing Wall;" a photograph from a German travelogue. A picture of the Wall appeared in nearly every book on Eretz Israel or Jerusalem.

thrusting their heads into the spaces in the holy wall so as to wet it with their tears when they contemplate the fall of Jerusalem, and the destruction of the Temple. Since I believed at that time that this was the only remnant of Solomon's Temple, the reader will easily be able to understand that my first visit to the Haram (the mosque compound) was to the Western Wall. When I arrived at this sacred remnant, I was amazed at its beauty. The original structure has completely survived for a height of more than twelve yards, uniform rows of beautiful, extraordinarily square stones (except that their edges are smoothed and serve as a sort of frame) rise up, one on top of the other, till about two or three yards from the top of the wall. A glance for a second is enough to establish, without any doubt, that the Jewish tradition is correct: a wall like this was never built by Greeks or Romans. This is an example of Hebrew architecture."

In 1864, Norman McCleod, a well-known Scottish clergyman, visited Jerusalem and, needless to say, he too saw fit to visit the Western Wall, "one of the most remarkable spots in the world," as he put it. He also wrote:

"On my way out one day I visited the Jews' 'wailing place,' certainly one of the most remarkable spots in the world. It extends 120 feet along the cyclopean wall, which belongs to the area of the Jewish Temple, and which surrounded the sacred enclosure. It begins about 300 feet from the southwest corner. No familiarity with the scenes enacted at this place made

it hackneyed to me. To see representatives of that people met here for prayer – to see them kissing those old stones – to know that this sort of devotion has probably been going on since the Temple was destroyed, and down through those teeming centuries which saw the decline and fall of the Roman Empire, and all the events of the history of Modern Europe – to watch this continuous stream of sorrow, still sobbing against the old wall, filled me with many thoughts. What light amidst darkness, what darkness amidst light; what undying hopes in the future, what passionate attachment to the past; what touching superstition, what belief and unbelief! I found some slips of paper, bearing prayers written in neat Jewish characters, inserted between the stones of the old wall."

A report on the state of the Jews in Jerusalem in general and in the area of the Wall in particular, in the second half of the nineteenth century, was provided by the famous British journalist Edward Dacey, who was the editor of *The Daily News* and *The Observer* of London. He visited the Wall in 1870 and tells of an incident he witnessed in which a prayer book was snatched and how it was returned to its owner. The following, in paraphrase, is his account:

"The Turkish soldiers, doing nothing, wandered about on the parapet above the Wall. In previous years they used to throw stones at the praying Jews below or curse them. Nowadays, the Moslem officials are too afraid of the West (the European powers) to dare show their distaste for the infidels. But the rabble, which do not fear the pasha, still demonstrate their ancient hatred of any religion but their own. On the day I visited the Western Wall a group of hefty Arab women, black-eyed and hard-faced, sat with their children at the corner of the path where the Jews were praying. An old, bent-over Jewish woman put her large leather-bound prayerbook down for a moment on one of the stones while she sank her head into one of the crevices in the Wall. A young Arab girl immediately ran over and took the prayerbook.

The Wall; an etching on copper, 1900.

When the old lady realized that she had lost it, she begged and pleaded of them to return it. She was told that she must pay 5 piastres – about a shilling – to the girl who had stolen it. An interminable argument started with much weeping and wailing, but the Arab girl insisted and the Jewish women were afraid to touch her. In the end, penny by penny, they collected the money between them and gave it to the brazen, arrogant girl. She put it in her pocket and announced that she did not have to return the book since she now realized it was very valuable to the old witch, and so she now wanted twice as much money. One of the Jewish women noticed that our group contained foreigners, and she asked me in German to help them get the book back. I volunteered, through our interpreter, to pay the 2 shillings to ransom the book, but the Arab girl then raised the price. Fortunately, my threat to take the old lady to the British consul had its effect. Sadly, even empty threats, such as mine, often succeed where persuasion fails. The girl, heaping curses on me, the Bible and the Jewish people, lifted the prayerbook on high and threw it as hard as she could straight at the group of Jewish women and ran away shrieking with laughter. Fortunately, the book did not hit anybody. May the blessings the Jewish ladies heaped on me come true! I was reminded of a story I was told in my childhood of the well-mannered boy who picked up an old lady's prayerbook in church and returned it to her. Years later she left him a fortune although he never saw her again. I wonder whether I will ever receive a letter from a lawyer in Jerusalem informing me that I am the sole heir of an elderly Jewish matron who has just been buried in the Valley of Jehosaphat? If I do, I am afraid the inheritance will not consist of more than the prayerbook I saved from the claws of that little Moslem devil. . ."

"How Can a Jewish Heart Not Become Excited?"

"The place to which every Jew who visits Jerusalem turns first" is how A. S. Hirschberg, the author of *Eretz Hemdah*, defined the Western Wall, which he first visited in 1901, the first year of the twentieth century. These words end this small anthology which has indicated the interest – both Jewish and non-Jewish – the Western Wall has aroused for many centuries, from the early days after the destruction of the Temple. This is what Hirschberg wrote:

"On the day after I arrived, I went with one of my young friends to the Western Wall, the place to which every Jew who visits Jerusalem turns first. It was a warm clear day, like one of the days at the beginning of summer in our home country; and here it was the month of Kislev – winter! We came to the vegetable market and from there we passed through narrow, crooked streets, some climbing and some descending, and through alleys, some of which were open and most of which had stone walls on both sides (for the Arabs build their houses inside the courtyards) until we came to a small narrow alley. One side of this was the Western Wall and the other side was a solid wall of one of the hovels of the Magreb Quarter.

"When I arrived, there were only two men standing in front of the wall praying and few Sephardi beggars asking for alms. Some of the beggars were standing and some were sitting on the ground or on boxes that they had brought with them. The Sephardi beadle came over to me and made a tear in the side of my coat and gave me a little prayerbook from which to recite the special prayer for one's first visit to the Wall. I began to mumble the prayer and suddenly I started to weep as I never had until that day, and I was not able to control myself.

"I was in shock. The walk through the squalid streets and filthy alleys, the appearance of the Arabs with their dirty children dressed in rags and barefoot, had depressed me so much that nothing I saw could impress me. When I came to the Wall, I did feel that I was standing in a holy place, but my senses were dulled and my heart laid waste. Then came this prayer

touching on all ills man is heir to, replaying all the aches in the inner heart and the dam broke! All my private troubles mingled with our nation's misfortune to form a torrent. Here I was, standing before the Wall, this silent witness to Israel's glory of ancient times and against it I saw all those places and all those times of suffering and torture throughout the whole world and all history! The inquisitions and the pogroms that have been visited on our pitiful nation passed before my eyes – and these stones do not move... Tears blind me and the letters in the prayerbook dance before my eyes. My nerves jangle and my innermost emotions are totally shaken and sweep over me so that I almost faint ... I turned to escape like a fugitive from this Wall without finishing the prayer I had started, but the beadle held me and gave me a wick to kindle in the small, inferior oil lamp that stood at the end of the Wall. For me it was as though he had given me a memorial candle to kindle for the soul of our people dying there in exile.

"For the six months of my stay in Jerusalem it was the Wall that attracted me most because it is the one and only memorial to our ancient greatness that is authenticated both by our tradition and by scholarly research. The Jews of Jerusalem flock there regularly for prayers, particularly for the afternoon and evening services on the eve of the Sabbath and festivals and for the additional services on those days themselves. Other favoured times are the eve of the Passover festival to read the account of the preparation of the Paschal Lamb and the night of the fast of the ninth of Av to mourn the destruction of the Temple. They stand before the Wall in groups, and the recitation of the holy prayers never ceases. All kinds of Jews are there. Thin, scrawny, sharp-nosed Yemenites dressed in poor, worn Arab robes recite the prayers in their unique pronunciation. A quorum of rich, fat, elegantly clad *Sephardim*, in their black coats with tarbooshes on their well-groomed heads, say the prayers solemnly and with great dignity. At their side is a group of *Perushim*, dressed in a weird mixture of east and west with medieval Polish fur hats on their heads; honoured old men and earnest, pale young men screw up their faces to achieve the concentration fitting for prayer to God. And there are groups of Hasidim, in their kaftans of red, gold or sky-blue silk and velvet, who shake themselves violently until their sidelocks flail, as they respond, 'Holy, holy, holy is the Lord of Hosts' in great ecstasy. And the women! The *Ashkenazi* women stand a way off and jump little jumps as they respond to every *Kedushah* prayer they hear. The *Sephardi* ladies love the Wall with a special love and most of them come to it enveloped in white sheets. Those who cannot read the texts of the prayers make modest prayerful signs to the Wall. All, when they leave, kiss each stone individually and back away as though they were leaving the royal presence, stretching out their fingers towards it with eyes raised on high.

"The square stones of the Wall, arranged one on top of the other, joined together with no sign of cement; these stones which, scratched and cracked though they be, are not consumed in the teeth of time, are a symbol to the people that stands before them in prayer... How can they fail to excite and exalt the heart of every Jew who comes for the first time to the Wall?!"

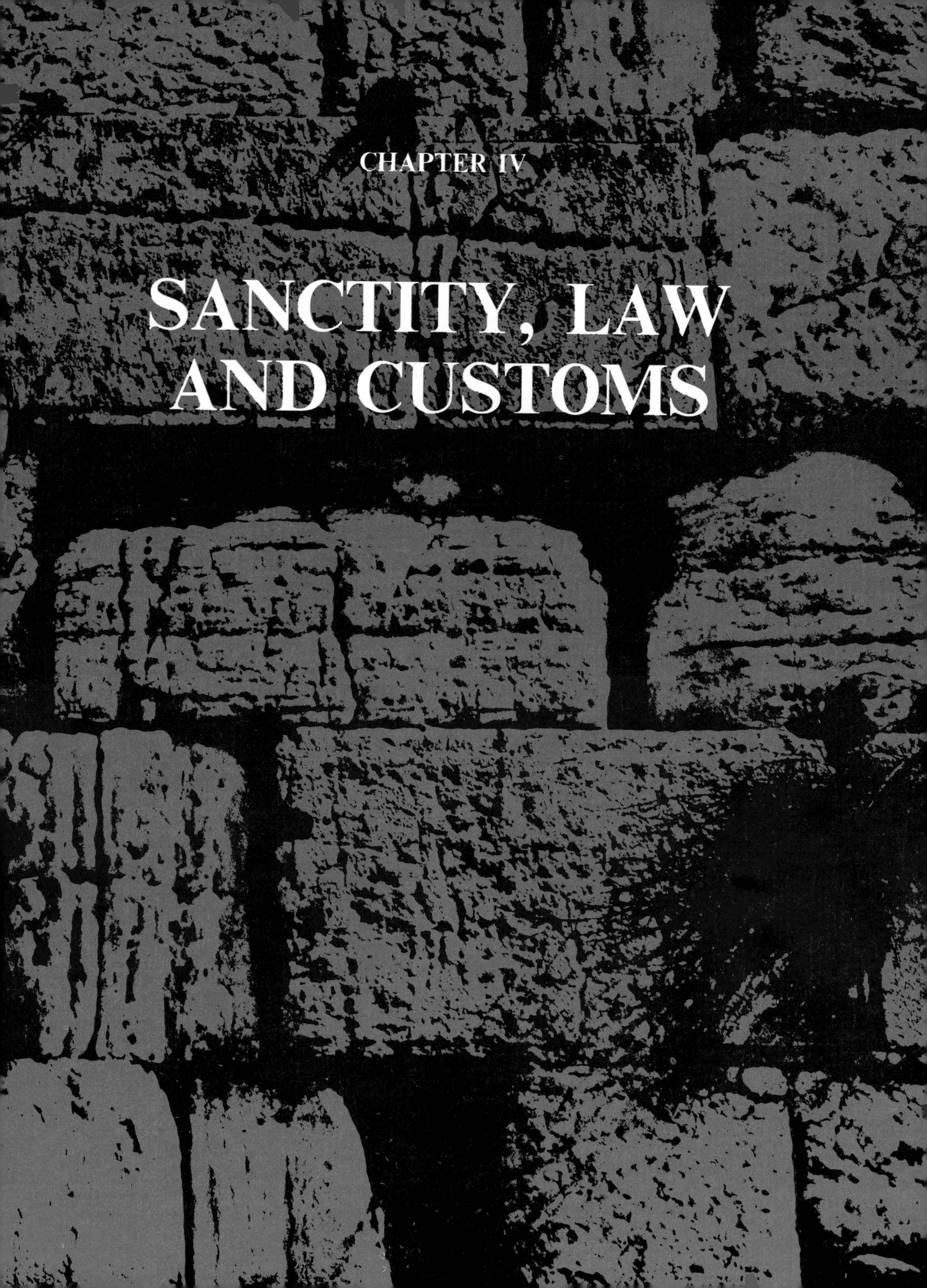

CHAPTER IV

SANCTITY, LAW AND CUSTOMS

Everlasting Sanctity

For the Jews, all the Land of Israel is holy – every piece of soil, every grain of sand and every stone in it. Jerusalem, the capital, is endowed with a special holiness because God chose it for His presence to reside there forever.

In this sacred land and sacred city, there are sites which are exceedingly holy, such as the Machpelah Cave in Hebron in which the patriarchs and matriarchs of the nation are buried, the grave of Rachel in Bethlehem and many more graves of renowned pious men from earliest times until recent generations.

There is one place in Jerusalem which is the most sacred site there is for the whole Jewish people and the holiness of which is equal to all the other sacred sites together – and that is the Western Wall.

The Wall is so sacred for six reasons:

1. Because it is the only remnant of the Temple that has survived. That Temple was the center of the nation; it was the inner heart of the Jewish people through which all the souls of Jews merged and became as one.

2. Because our sages prophesied for centuries after the Temple's destruction that this Wall will never be destroyed because the Divine Presence will never leave it.

3. Because all of Israel's prayers have always been directed to this place as Judah Halevy so poignantly put it, "I am in the west, but my heart is in the end of the east." Similarly a Talmudic source instructs us: "If a man is outside Eretz Israel, he should direct his heart when he prays in the direction of Eretz Israel, as it is said, 'And they will pray to You through the land which You gave to their fathers, the city which You chose and the house which I have built to Your name' (I Kings 8:48). If he was in Eretz Israel, he should direct his heart towards Jerusalem, as it is written, 'And they will pray to God through the city which You have chosen' (I Kings 8:44). Those in Jerusalem should direct their hearts to the Temple, as it is written, 'And they shall pray towards this house' (I Kings 8:30). It thus follows that those in the north face south (when they pray), those in the south face north, those in the east face west, and those in the west face east, with the result that all Israel pray

towards one place. And this is what the prophet Isaiah was referring to when he said, 'And I will bring them to My holy mountain and I will make them joyful in My house of prayer. Their burnt offerings and their sacrifices will be accepted on My altar. For My house will be called a house of prayer for peoples' (Isaiah 56:7)."

4. Because, when the First and Second Temples were destroyed and in the Bar Kokhba revolt, Israel's heroes sacrificed their lives for every stone of the Temple and fought like lions for every inch of it. They have served as the example of bravery for Israel ever since. Like them, our soldiers fought in holy trepidation to liberate the Western Wall and the Temple Mount.

5. Because for more than one thousand five hundred years, Jews in all generations have watered the courses of the Wall with their tears and melted its stones with their kisses.

6. Because the Wall is endowed with everlasting sanctity. The sages of the Mishnah, some of whom lived in Temple times and others of whom witnessed its destruction, explained the verse, "And I will make your sanctuaries desolate" (Leviticus 26:31) as meaning that they still have the sanctity of sanctuaries even when they are desolate (Megillah 3:3).

In the sources, the Temple Mount is also called Mount Moriah and the rabbis explained that name by a play on the word *Moriah*: "That is the place from which instruction (*hora'ah*) goes forth, from which fear of heaven (*yir'ah*) goes forth; from which light (*orah*) goes forth."

The sanctity of the Wall is frequently discussed in midrashic literature. A good example is:

"Rabbi Eleazar said: The Divine Presence never departed from the Temple, as it is written, 'For now I have chosen and sanctified this house so that My name shall be there for ever and My eyes and My heart will be there all the days' (II Chronicles 7:16)... Even when it (the Temple) is destroyed, it remains in its sanctity... Even when it is destroyed, God does not leave it. Rav Aha said: The Divine Presence will never leave the Western Wall, as it is written, 'Behold, He (God) stands behind our wall' (Song of Songs 2:9)."

Maimonides, an outstanding rabbi, philosopher and physician, explained the sanctity of the place thus:

"By a universal tradition we know that the Temple which David and Solomon built stood on the site of Araunah's threshing-floor and that is the place where Abraham had built an altar to sacrifice his son Isaac, and that is where Noah built an altar when he emerged from his ark, and that Cain and Abel offered sacrifices on an altar there, and that Adam offered a sacrifice there when he was created and that, indeed, it was from that spot that he was created."

Maimonides continues,

"And why do I say that the original sanctity of the Temple and Jerusalem applies for ever? Because it stems from the Divine Presence – and the Divine Presence is never abrogated. This is what the verse means: 'And I will make your sanctuaries desolate' (Leviticus 26:31) – even when they are desolate they are still your sanctuaries, i.e., they remain sanctified."

Following Maimonides, one of the great rabbinical authorities of the nineteenth century, Rabbi Jacob Ettlinger, wrote:

"There is a holy light on the Temple and it does not cease even when the Temple lies in ruins; it will never cease! This holy light has a greater influence there than in any other place, for the site of the Temple is opposite the gate of heaven which will never close, and there the holy light always shines with greater strength and greater brilliance. Therefore, well did Maimonides write that the Divine Presence is never abrogated because the holy light which sanctified the Temple has never stopped and never will stop. On this it was said: 'The Divine Presence never leaves the Western Wall,' that is the concealed holy light.

"Since the gate of heaven is near the Western Wall, it is understandable that all Israel's

prayers ascend on high through there, as one of the great ancient Kabbalists, Rabbi Joseph Gikatilla, put it: 'When the Jews are outside Eretz Israel, many hostile and disturbing influences affect communal prayer and, how much more so, individual prayer. Israel, outside its land, is in the hands of the nations' angels and there is no way for their prayers to ascend to heaven because the gates of heaven are only in Eretz Israel... except when the Jews send their prayers from the diaspora in the direction of Jerusalem; from there they ascend by way of the Western Wall.'

"Therefore, Rabbi Abraham Yitzhaki wrote: 'Jews are holy, they believe and they put their trust in the sanctity of Eretz Israel. For although the land is desolate, its king is still there, He resides 'behind our wall' for the Divine Presence has never left the Western Wall and therefore the Jews have never stopped loving it and they go to extreme trouble to go up and appear before God, the Lord, and they pray there: 'As we have seen the Temple in its destruction, so may we merit to see it rebuilt, speedily in our day!' "

"A Great Notice," announcing the public recitation of psalms at the Wall.

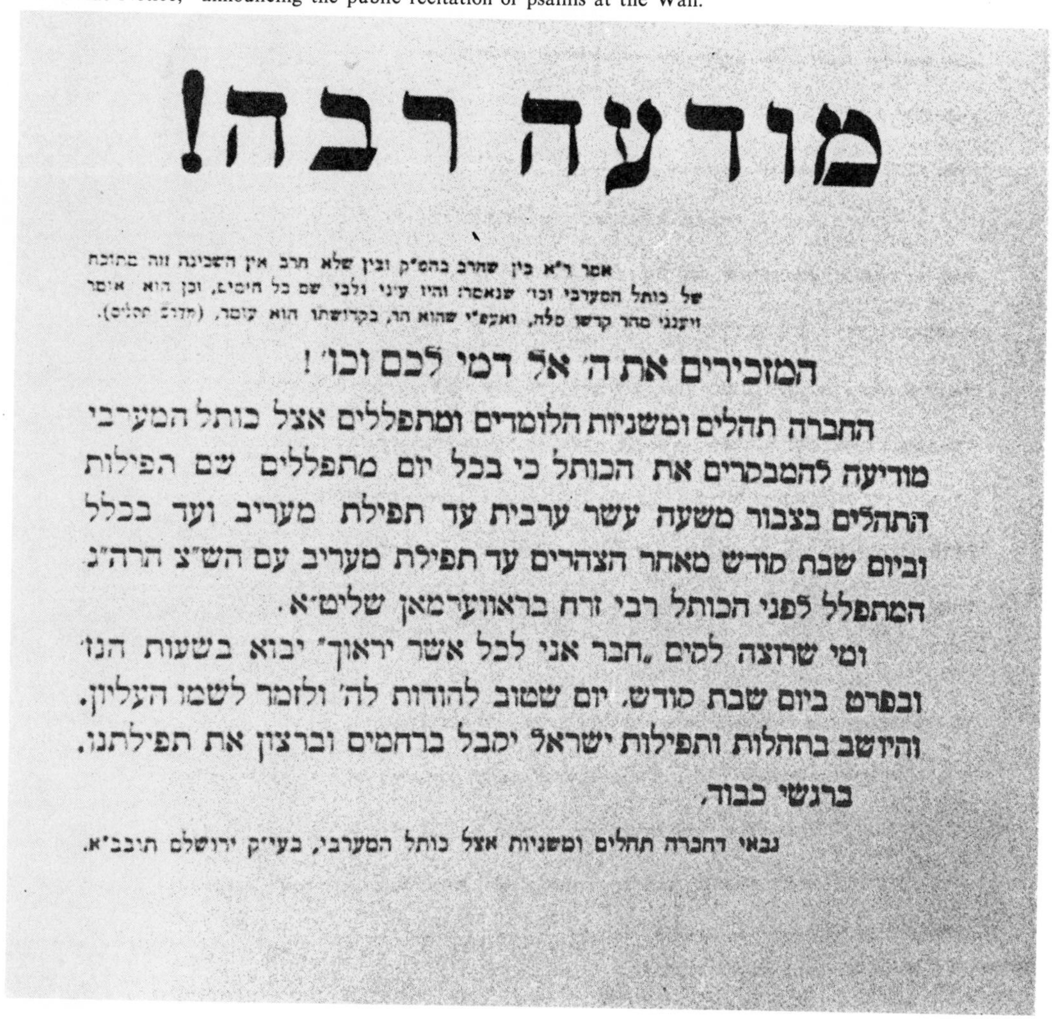

מודעה רבה!

אמר ר"א בין שחרב בהמ"ק ובין שלא חרב אין השכינה זזה מתוכה
של כותל המערבי וכו' שנאמר: והיו עיני ולבי שם כל הימים, וכן הוא אומר
ויענני מהר קדשו סלה, ואעפ"י שהוא חרב, בקדושתו הוא עומד, (מדרש תהלים).

המזכירים את ה' אל דמי לכם וכו' !

החברה תהלים ומשניות הלומדים ומתפללים אצל כותל המערבי
מודיעה להמבקרים את הכותל כי בכל יום מתפללים שם תפילות
התהלים בצבור משעה עשר ערבית עד תפילת מעריב ועד בכלל
וביום שבת קודש מאחר הצהרים עד תפילת מעריב עם הש"צ הרה"ג
המתפלל לפני הכותל רבי זרח בראווערמאן שליט"א.

ומי שרוצה לקים „חבר אני לכל אשר יראוך" יבוא בשעות הנז'
ובפרט ביום שבת קודש, יום שטוב להודות לה' ולזמר לשמו העליון.
והיושב בתהלות ותפילות ישראל יקבל ברחמים וברצון את תפילתנו.

ברגשי כבוד,

גבאי דחברה תהלים ומשניות אצל כותל המערבי, בעי"ק ירושלם תובב"א.

The Priestly Blessing
at the Wall attended
by thousands of
kohanim from all over Israel.

Rabbi Elijah Ha-Kohen of Izmir, wrote in the same vein in his *Shevet Ha-Musar*: "A meal of vegetables with love is better than a fatted ox with hatred' (Proverbs 15:17) – 'a meal of vegetables with love,' is Eretz Israel which God loves continually, and even in its desolation, the Divine Presence has not left the Western Wall. If so, it is better to live there and eat only vegetables than to eat fatted oxen outside Eretz Israel."

Furthermore, when Jews pray at the Western Wall the Holy One, blessed be He, forgives them all their sins. As indeed Rabbi Moses Hagiz wrote:

"And the divine Rabbi Isaac Luria (known as the Ari, the foremost Kabbalist in history), through whom the spirit of God speaks... and he authenticated the Western Wall... which all can see exhibits all the signs and indications that we have by tradition from our ancestors. 'Behold, He stands behind our wall' means behind the Western Wall. For this wall has never been destroyed because it is built on the foundation that David laid, which no enemy hand ever touched. They (the enemies) used to say, 'Destroy it! Destroy it! Even to its base' (Psalms 137:7) but they only succeeded as far as the base but could not touch the base itself. Why? Because God swore to David that that would never be destroyed. And this our eyes can see, for it stands today as though it had only now been finished by that divine craftsman who sunk those pillars to last for centuries not in a natural way but by a miracle, as their height and thickness testifies, which could not possibly be achieved by human means. If not by divine help... and they (the pillars) stand in their sanctity, as it is written: 'God is in His holy sanctuary' (Psalms 11:4) – whether it is built or destroyed. Therefore, Rabbi Joshua ben Levi taught: God said to Israel, 'You caused My house to be destroyed and My children to be exiled; seek the peace of Jerusalem and I will forgive you!' What is the reason? It is written, 'Seek the peace of Jerusalem' and immediately following 'They shall prosper who love you. May peace be within your walls!' (Psalms 122:6-7)."

This being the case, the prayers of Israel have always been directed to the Western Wall opposite the gate of Heaven. Rabbi Jacob Emden, in the foreword to the prayer-book he edited, wrote: "Know and understand! Although the Divine Presence is everywhere, prayers recited outside Eretz Israel cannot ascend directly to heaven. They must be directed to Eretz Israel and Jerusalem, to the place of the Temple opposite the gate of Heaven."

"The Western Wall," wrote Rabbi Ben Zion Alkalai, "is endowed with a special sanctity. Jerusalem, may it speedily be rebuilt, has ten levels of sanctity starting at its outer walls and moving inwards to Zion, which is the Holy of Holies... Even nowadays, these ten degrees of sanctity have not been abrogated and Jerusalem still stands in its original sanctity as, indeed, Maimonides wrote, 'Therefore it is permissible to offer all the sacrifices although the Temple no longer exists.' Unfortunately, there are certain pre-requisites lacking, and so we cannot bring sacrifices. For example, we are all afflicted with ritual impurity from touching the dead and we do not have the ashes of the Red Heifer which are needed to effect purification; furthermore, the lineage of the priests is by no means certain and we grant them priestly privileges only because we assume they are priests. Thus, for technical reasons, we may not today offer sacrifices but, in principle, from the point of view of the site's sanctity, we could bring offerings... But we do have somewhere for our spiritual elevation. 'Behold, He stands behind our wall,' is the Western Wall which the Divine Presence will never leave. Behind this Wall, children cry to their Father in Heaven and the priestly service never ceases – for it is prayer and Torah continually, all the days."

Another pious and perfect rabbi, Aaron Pereira, wrote:

"At any event, everybody admits that the Divine Presence will never leave the Western Wall of the Temple, may it be rebuilt speedily in our days, Amen. A proof for this is that the Wall is standing for some three thousand years since it was built by King David, peace be on him, and not one stone has fallen from it! Thus, we see a miracle every day in that from a wall as enormous as this no stone ever falls. And this is a wonder – really the work of heaven's hands!"

In addition to occupying an important place in Jewish theology and *Aggadah* (religious folk-lore and legend), the Western Wall has raised a number of questions in *Halakhah*, Jewish religious law. There follow some of the problems concerning the Wall which have been discussed in halakhic sources:

1. The law is that it is forbidden to pray in an open space which is not enclosed by walls, such as fields or valleys. How then is it permitted to conduct daily services in the piazza before the Wall which is a large open area? This question, however, answers itself. The reason for the prohibition against prayer in an open space is that prayer is the "service of the heart" and the worshipper must devote all his attention to God's majesty. This is easier in an enclosed area, a room or a synagogue than it is in an open space where the worshipper's attention is constantly distracted. This reason, however, does not apply at the Western Wall for there is no place on earth in which the Jew is as aware of his Maker as at the Wall, from which the Divine Presence never departs.

2. Is the Western Wall actually a part of the Temple Mount? The *Halakhah* rules that nowadays Jews cannot enter the Temple Mount because all Jews, since shortly after the destruction of the Temple, are considered to be in a state of ritual impurity which arises from contact with the dead. The purification process, which it is necessary to undergo in order to become ritually pure and thus able to enter the sacred area, involves the ashes of the Red Heifer (Numbers 19) which no longer exist. If the Wall is halakhically part of the Temple Mount, then it should be categorically forbidden to insert one's hand or even finger in the spaces and cracks between the stones, because partial entry of the body is considered the same as total entry.

This question was discussed in a journal at the beginning of the twentieth century in the following terms:

"Rabbi Joshua Joseph Kolbo of Warsaw has conducted research into old books and various manuscripts in major archives in Rome and England and has built a small exact model of the Temple according to the results of his studies. This model is in the British Museum. The rabbi has proved that the Western Wall, beneath which Jerusalem's Jews pray, is not a wall of the Temple Mount as has been usually thought, but a remnant of the Temple itself. Therefore he warns Jews against approaching it; they must stay at least twenty cubits (approximately 13.5 metres) away from it."

The learned rabbi's opinion has not been accepted and Jews have been accustomed for generations to come close to the Wall and caress and kiss its stones.

There is a difference of opinion among halakhic authorities as to whether it is permitted to insert one's hand or finger between the stones. Some forbid it on the basis of Maimonides' ruling that "the thickness of the wall is considered as being inside," i.e., the Temple Mount begins from the outer surface of the Wall. Others permit it. At any rate, the pious of Jerusalem have always been very careful not to insert their hands or fingers beyond the Wall's outer surface.

In one of the sources that treat this problem an interesting anecdote is reported. The rabbi of Kalisch, Rabbi Meir Auerbach, once entered the cave which is under the Western Wall and saw that the Wall is built on pillars and arches of exceedingly complicated and beautiful construction, a work of wondrous craftmanship.

3. Among some Jerusalemites, particularly those of *Sephardi* extraction, there was a custom for a person intending to travel abroad to take a chip of stone from the Wall or a little

earth from the Wall's enclosure. This was thought to ensure his safe return to Jerusalem. About seventy years ago the question was raised whether it is permitted, from the point of view of the *Halakhah*, to do so.

A long responsum on the question appeared in the Jerusalem newspaper *Havatzelet* in 1898, and its decision was that even if the custom is permitted from the point of view of *Halakhah*, it should be stopped because it constitutes a desecration of the sacred.

Similarly, some people were accustomed to inscribe their names in the stones or write them in ink or paint on the surface. Some used to drive nails into the cracks between the stones as a talisman. Many people viewed this as an act of vandalism and desecration and objected strongly.

4. According to the Mishnah (Tractate Middot), "The priests used to stand guard in three places in the Temple: in Bet Avtinas, in Bet Ha-Nitzotz and in Bet Ha-Moked. The Levites used to stand guard in twenty-one places: five at the five gates of the Temple Mount, four at its four corners, five at the five gates of the courtyard. . . " These priests and Levites constituted guards of honour and the guard was maintained around the clock in honour of the Temple.

At the end of the nineteenth century, a pious kabbalistic rabbi, Hillel Gelbstein, decided to reestablish the custom of "guards of honour" for the Temple Mount. He argued that according to the *Halakhah*, the Jews were obliged to provide such guards and that, furthermore, the re-institution of this ancient procedure would surely bring the redemption and the Messiah nearer. Rabbi Gelbstein was not satisfied with just discussing the matter. He set about putting it into operation. He rented a house near the Western Wall and hired dignified men to stand guard, in relays, near the Wall and around the Temple Mount. However, the "guards of honour" only lasted for a short time, either because of lack of funds or because of the anger of the Arab neighbours. However, Rabbi Gelbstein never gave up hope and kept trying till the day he died.

5. "It is the custom in Jerusalem, may it speedily be rebuilt, to pray at the Western Wall. . . On the eve of every Sabbath the Jews go there to greet the incoming Sabbath Queen. . . Since very many come and the enclosure cannot accommodate them all at once, the people are accustomed to pray the *Minhah* (Afternoon) service and the *Kabbalat Shabbat* (Inauguration of the Sabbath) and *Arvit* (Evening) services at an early hour. Then they leave and others come to pray in their place. So, the worshippers come in waves, one group enters as another leaves until the night. . . " The question asked was: are those who have already prayed permitted to make the congregational prayer responses in the later prayer services? The rabbi to whom this question was addressed wrote a long responsum and permitted the practice. (Rabbi Shalom Gaguin, Responsa *Yismah Lev*, Jerusalem, 1870).

6. A question, similar to the above, was asked concerning the Priestly Blessing which is part of the daily morning services. Jews visiting the Holy Land from other countries are required to observe two days for each festival (except the Day of Atonement) instead of the one day which residents of Eretz Israel observe. It happened that a group of visitors conducted services at the Wall on the second day which to them was a festival. They, however, had no *kohanim* (Jews of priestly descent) among them to recite the Priestly Blessing. The question was: May a local *kohen*, for whom the day is an ordinary weekday, recite the Priestly Blessing for the visitors? The answer was that he may, because although the Priestly Blessing is recited during the prayer service, it is not part of it but constitutes a separate *mitzvah*, religious duty.

7. A contemporary problem. The law is that when a Jew "sees Jerusalem in its destruction, he must tear his clothes as though for his dead, and say, 'Zion has become a wilderness and Jerusalem is desolate!' He who sees the Temple in its destruction must say, 'Our glorious

holy house in which our fathers praised You is a burnt ruin and all our delights are desolate,' and tear his clothes." The question is: now that we have, with God's help, recovered Jerusalem, the Western Wall and the Temple Mount, is tearing one's clothes as a sign of mourning appropriate? On the contrary! Surely today's situation calls for songs of joy and praise!

Many scholars have discussed this problem and they have all arrived at the following conclusion: one should not tear one's clothes for Jerusalem and the Western Wall but rather one must recite the benediction, "Blessed art Thou, O Lord our God, King of the universe, who has established the border of the widow." With regards to the site of the Temple, the ruling is different. Although it is in Israel's sovereign territory, nevertheless the Temple has not been rebuilt and therefore he who sees it should tear his garments and say, "May it be the will of He who has put His name on this place, that as we have merited to see the redemption of our city and our Wall, so may we deserve to witness the House of our Life standing on the heights of the Temple Mount. Amen."

Customs

1. It is an ancient custom for those visiting the Western Wall to remove their shoes. This practice is mentioned in literary sources from early times until recent generations. Moslems also remove their footwear before entering mosques or holy sites as do adherents of many other religions throughout the world. It is possible that this universal religious practice originates from one of the Jewish Temple laws which states: "A person may not enter the Temple Mount with his stick, in his shoes, or wearing his money-belt; spitting is certainly forbidden" (Berakhot 9:1). Because of the site's sanctity, the Jews adopted one of the Temple rules at its surviving remnant – the Western Wall.

The practice of removing one's shoes is mentioned in a seventeenth century collection of special prayers to be recited at holy places: "When he comes to the Western Wall, the visitor should remove his shoes, bow and say. . . " The same formula is found in a prayer-book called *Shaarei Dim'ah* ("The Gates of Tears"). Rabbi Moses Reicher wrote: "It is a good and praiseworthy custom. . . to go to the mount which was the site of the Temple and to stand 'behind our wall,' that is, the Western Wall. . . in white garments after ablution. When they come there, the pilgrims should kneel and prostrate themselves in submission and say, 'This is nothing other than the House of God and here is the gate of heaven!' When they come within four cubits [approximately 2.7 metres] of the Wall, they should remove their footwear. . . "

As late as 1840, the practice is still mentioned by Menahem Mendel of Kamenitz: "We went to pray at the Western Wall of the Temple Mount, as does everybody in Jerusalem. . . and they believe that prayer there stems from the heart. The cantor stands near a certain stone because they say that a pious man once had a revelation at it. And all who approach the Wall remove their shoes."

About a century ago, the Jerusalem physician, Dr. Bernard Newman, wrote:

"The Western Wall is the place known as the Wailing Wall of the Jews, at which, in front of a row of monuments which have survived from Solomon's time from the enormous building of the Temple, the mourning Jew offers his prayers under the open blue sky. Jews visit the place frequently and it is usually crowded with worshippers. Even more people come for the Inauguration of the Sabbath service and for those on festivals and the Fast of the Ninth of Av. On the three Pilgrim Festivals, all the Jews of Jerusalem go there for the Additional Service. Because of the lack of space at the foot of the Wall, people come in groups directly from their synagogues and they conduct the Additional Service, under the open heavens,

Private meditation.

wrapped in their prayer-shawls and barefoot, because of the place's sanctity. In this manner, the Additional Service is recited many times at the Wall. At a distance stand the women enveloped in white gowns from head to foot. When the men recite, in a melancholy, mournful voice, the sad prayer, 'And because of our sins, we were exiled from our land,' the women kiss the stones and strike their heads against them. They all lift their tearful eyes to heaven and groan, 'Until when? How long? Oh Lord!' "

Many non-Jewish tourists also visit this place and none leave it without being deeply impressed. But far more intense are the Jew's emotions who, in his mind's eye, sees the glorious past of the Jewish nation and in his real eyes, sees its present destitution and who prays for a great future.

A.M. Luntz, that indefatigable student of Eretz Israel, also mentions the custom of removing one's shoes at the Wall, albeit in a flowery manner: "Remove your shoes from upon your feet. Draw near and kiss the Wall's stones, the faithful witnesses to your people's heroism, glory and greatness in ancient times!"

In the course of the years, the custom of standing barefoot in honour of the Wall, disappeared. Israel's Nobel Prize-winning author, S.Y. Agnon, gave its abrogation a heart-warming explanation:

"Some tell about the Wall that people never used to come there wearing shoes on their feet, but they used to take them off and leave them at a distance. Not like today when people

The prayer area under Wilson's Arch.

The Wall and the child.

come wearing shoes. Our ancestors were closer to the Temple's destruction and therefore they behaved like a mourner in the first seven days after his loss when he must go barefoot. But we, who are closer to the redemption, may act like mourners after the first seven days, who may wear shoes."

A non-Jewish tourist, Gottfried Millius, who visited the Wall in 1877, wrote: "There, in a narrow alley, old Jews and Jewesses congregate every Friday. They stand barefoot and keen and weep, caressing and kissing the stones which surrounded their ancestors' Temple. They pray, they recite Psalms, or they read Isaiah's prophecies."

2. It was an ancient practice to recite special prayers at the various holy places, prayers appropriate to each place. This was the case regarding the Western Wall and so it is told about Rabbi Moses Galante, a Jerusalem rabbi in the seventeenth century: "On the eve of the Passover festival he used to read there (at the Wall) the Talmudic tractate *Pesahim* which deals with the laws of Passover; on the eve of Yom Kippur, he used to read the tractate *Yoma*, and in addition to the regular prayers he used to recite Daniel's prayer (Chapter 9 to its end), Ezra's prayer (Chapter 9), and a short prayer of Nehemiah (Chapter 1, from verse 5 to the end of the chapter)... He also read the *Zohar*."

3. As at other holy places, so too at the Wall it was the custom that after a person finished his prayer, he would write his special petition on a scrap of paper and insert it in one of the cracks between the stones. On the scrap of paper would be written the name of the petitioner and the nature of his petition or the name of the person who needed divine aid. For full identification the name always included the mother's name (the *Sephardim* are accustomed to use the father's name). A typical text would be: "So-and-so, the son (or daughter) of so-and-so is very sick and needs a cure." The paper would then be folded and pushed into the Wall in the hope that it would thus be continually before Him, whose presence rests on the Wall.

When the Western Wall area was liberated in 1967, it is related that the Minister of Defense, the Chief of Staff and many generals inserted such slips of paper in the Wall. There was a great deal of curiosity to know what they had written but it is a time-honoured rule not to read any of the slips of paper at the Wall and so the curious had to be content with speculation.

4. An old chronicler reported:

"There are those who are accustomed to write their names and the names of their fathers on the Wall as a talisman. Others drive nails into the cracks in the stones in the belief that anybody who is about to make a journey, on land or by sea, will be assured of a safe return if he drives a nail or a peg into the Wall the day before his departure. It is, perhaps, possible to see the origin of this custom in the verse, '... to give us a nail in His holy place' (Ezra 9:8). Although that is not the meaning of the verse, nevertheless those who do it, do so in honest faith, so leave them alone!"

There are, however, three more Biblical verses on this subject: "I will put him in as a nail in a sure place" (Isaiah 22:23); "Out of him, He has taken a nail" (Zacharias 10:4); "... lengthen your [tent] cords and strengthen your stakes" (Isaiah 54:2). At any rate, many objected to this strange custom.

5. It was customary for the visitor to write or inscribe his name and the name of his father on the Wall. Testimony to this practice can be found in the report of that famous Jewish traveller, Benjamin of Tudela who visited Eretz Israel from 1168 to 1170 and who wrote that "the visitors to Rachel's grave used to write their names on the gravestone."

Let the remark of Joseph Klausner, the historian, suffice us here: "Names of Hebrew [i.e., Jewish] men and women are written on the stones in square Hebrew script and between the

A festive day at the Wall.

Colored post-cards (hand-work)
from the end of the 19th century
and the beginning of the 20th.

Sukkot prayers at the Wall.

The seal of a 19th-century Jerusalem charity association; engraved cast brass, Israel Museum collection.

A micrography by Samuel Shulman, 19th century.

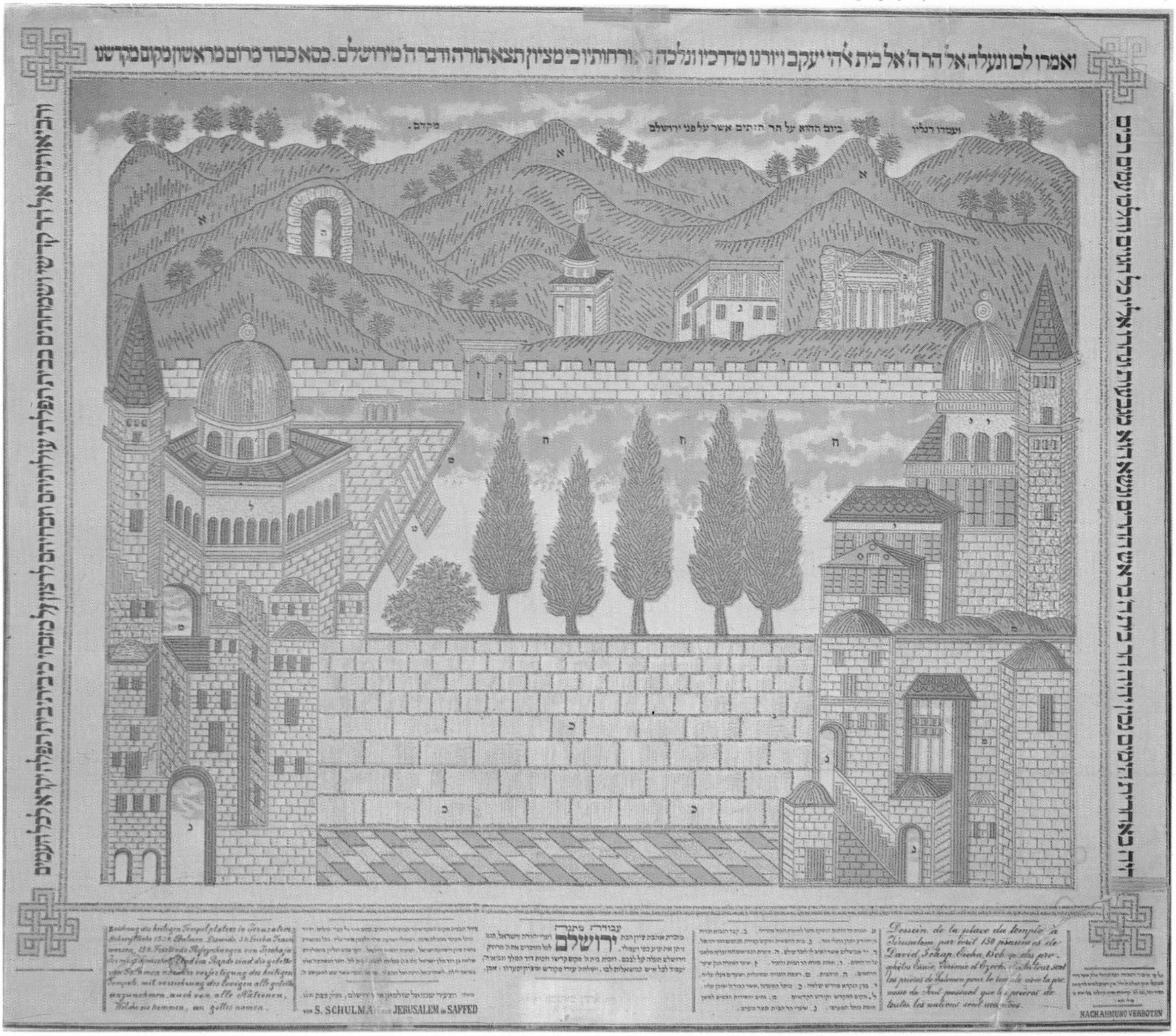

stones nails have been driven in. All this as a talisman. No greater desecration of the holy exists in the whole world!"

6. One of the later rabbis wrote: "A few tourists practice an evil custom which is totally forbidden. They break pieces from the stones and take them as mementoes. This is a custom worthy of the wicked Titus, may his name be blotted out."

7. Pious women, particularly *Sephardi*, in Jerusalem used to cast lots between them for the privilege of sweeping and washing the paving at the Western Wall.

8. Pious *Sephardi* women used to sit at the entrance to the Wall every Sabbath, holding citron fruits or vases of fragrant flowers and spices. They used to offer these to the men who came to pray so that the latter would recite a blessing over the fragrance in order to contribute to the hundred blessings a Jew should recite every day. On the Sabbath, because of the structure of the prayer services, some of this number is lacking and so must be made up other than in prayers. These women would answer "Amen" to each blessing with great joy and enthusiasm.

9. On hot summer days, these women would offer the worshippers cool water to refresh them and in order to answer "Amen" to the blessings recited on the water.

10. In addition to the regular, occasional, and special prayers recited at the Wall in congregation or individually, Jerusalemites had the custom that anybody celebrating a joyous event, such as the circumcision of a child, a *bar-mitzvah*, or a wedding, would come to the Western Wall to offer a prayer of thanksgiving.

However, the actual celebration was never held at the Wall or, for that matter, at any other holy place, so that the celebrants should not be frivolous in a sacred place.

Many pious men were particular to recite the *Kiddush Levanah* prayers, recited as the moon waxes full, especially at the Wall. After it, they would form circles and dance and sing until late into the night.

11. "There was a custom in Jerusalem in the times of its chief rabbi, Rabbi Samuel Salant, to gather all the school children of Jerusalem together at the Wall on the first of the intermediate days of the Sukkot festival, to recite those sections of the Torah which the king used to read in the Temple courtyard at the *Hakhel* ceremony" (*Hakhel Anthology*, Jerusalem 1946).

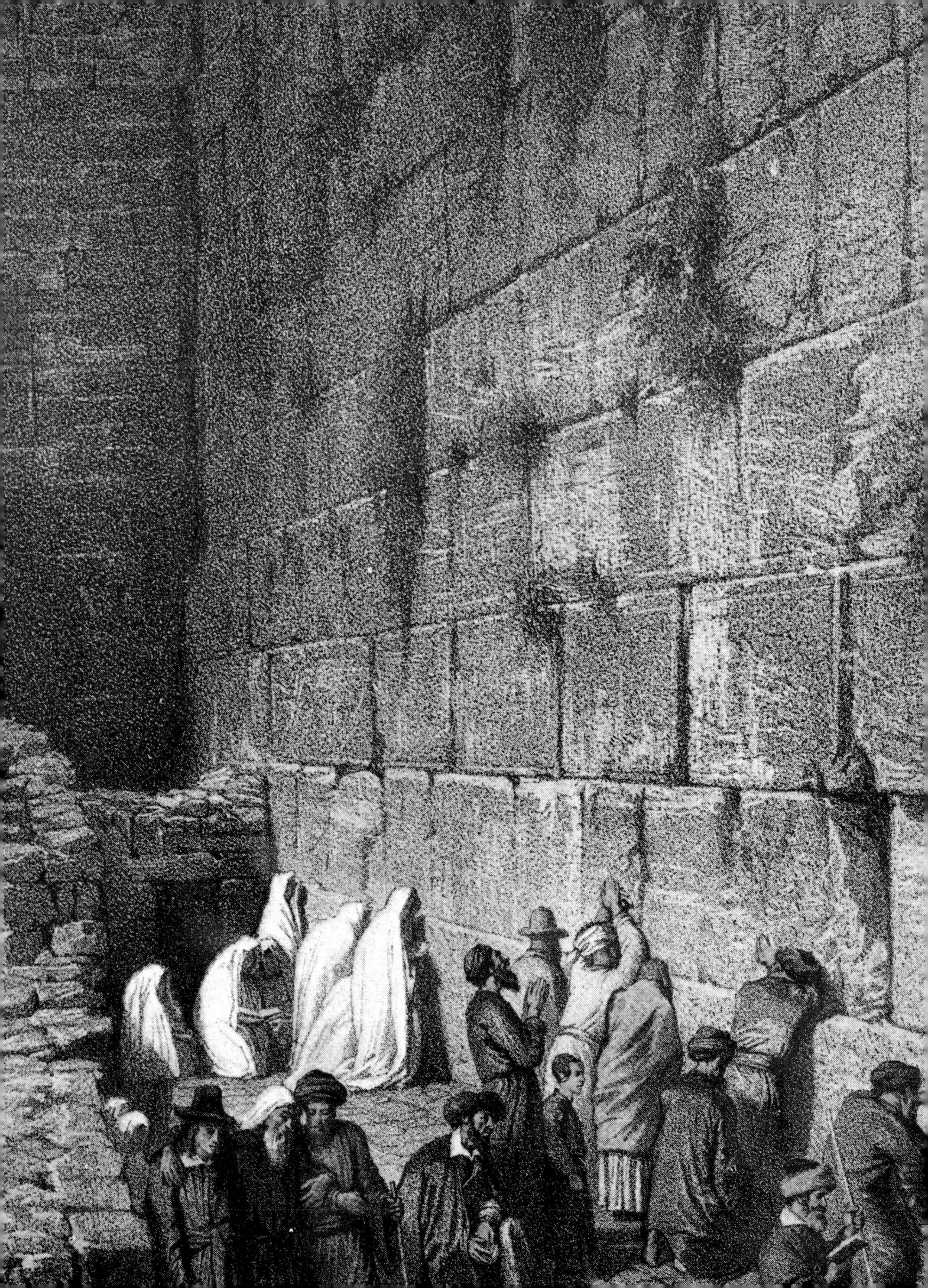

CHAPTER V

FOLK TALES ABOUT THE WESTERN WALL

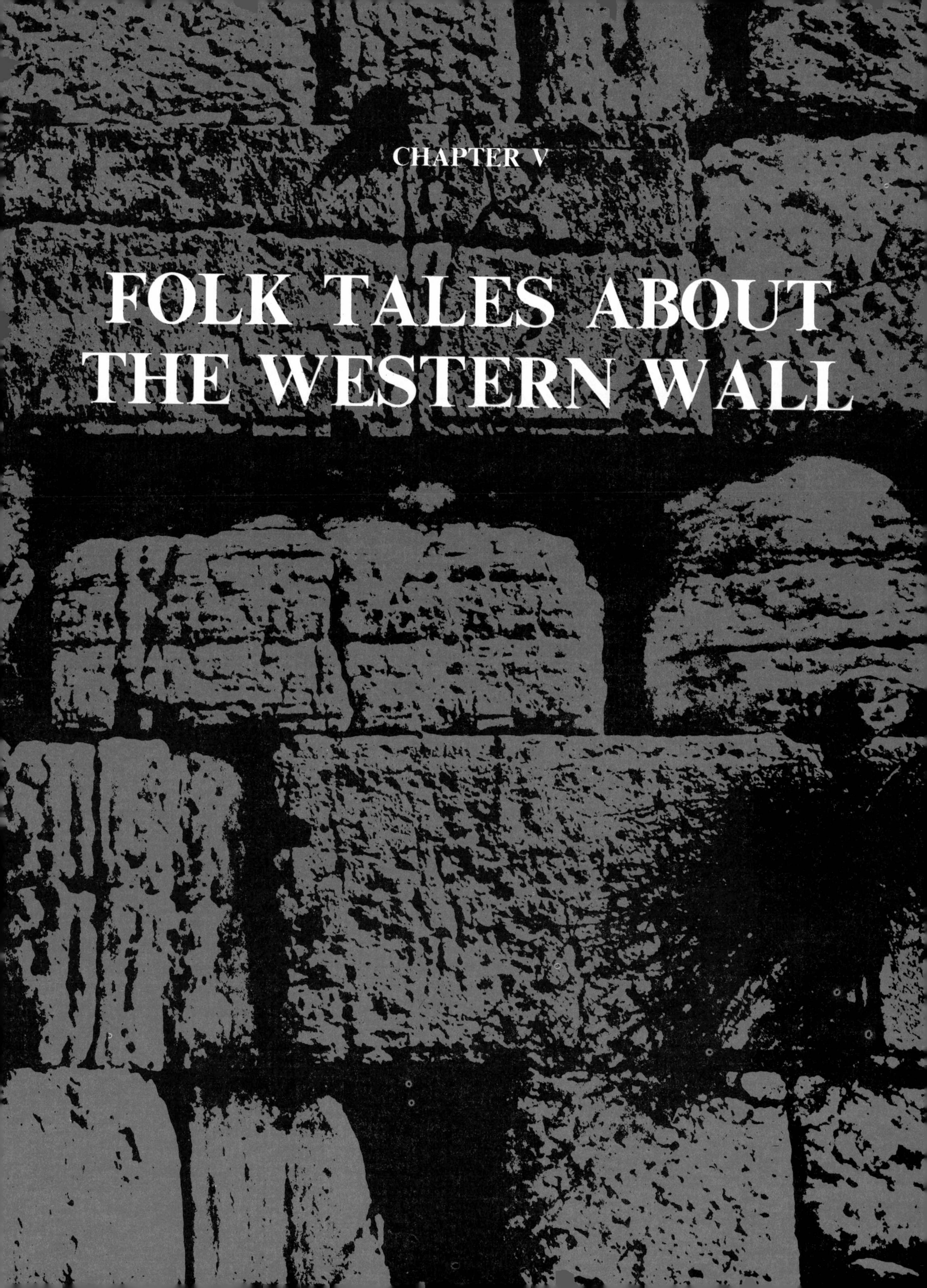

It is the aim of all who experience or feel holiness to escape from the limitations of inner feeling and give an outer, tangible expression to the exalted sensibility that seethes within them. This expression is not necessarily limited to speech or prayer, to acts of faith or customs, which in their tangible form are based on the person himself. The expression frequently takes on an actual material form, which is thus outside the believer himself and manifested in a specific place or article. The more people are naive, the more their religious philosophy is folksy and so popular beliefs which are connected with places and things are more common among the general mass of believers than among the social elite among them. Thus is explained the multiplicity of concrete, outer symbols which express abstract religious ideas, a multiplicity which is typical of folk-creativity, including folk literature.

In folk tales, which are handed down from generation to generation verbally by society, religious artifacts and holy places play a very significant role. The narrator and the preacher, who are trying to evoke visual associations, are interested in having material exhibits because with the aid of concrete symbols, their stories will better perform their aesthetic, educational and entertainment functions. This is the source of the tendency for legends (folk tales on a historical-geographical background) to become woven around material objects which attract, like a lode stone, miracles and supernatural motives. An examination of the special department devoted to religious articles in the *Motif Index of Folk Literature* (6 vols., Copenhagen 1955-58) established by the American scholar Stith Tompson, reveals a whole section on religious buildings including cultic and prayer sites, churches and temples, mosques and holy graves. This section also catalogues stories about religious articles and artifacts which are integral to the buildings such as altars, bells, holy arks, and prayer lecterns. However, a fact that is instructive with regard to Jewish motives should be pointed out: although the index also lists parts of various buildings, the motif of the Western Wall which survived from the Temple building is not mentioned. This motif is exclusive to Jewish folk literature.

The very fact that the holy Western Wall occupies such an important place in Jewish religious philosophy and folk literature notwithstanding the general diminution of external and tangible religious symbolism (in line with the second of the Ten Commandments), indicates the uniqueness of Jewish symbolism and religious philosophy at the base of which is the view that outer, material destruction does not mean that the sanctity is destroyed. True holiness derives from the sources of eternity and the destruction of its symbols is only temporary; it is unable to affect eternal sanctity. This idea is completely foreign to naturalistic realistic systems of thought both of ancient peoples and modern society. For them, the destruction of a holy building testifies to the impotence and ineffectiveness of the holy power which was the source of the building's sanctity, vitality and defence. This is because one of the power's functions is to protect the symbol sanctified to it (in primeval and pagan thinking, the power is identified with its symbol) and the destruction of the symbol is in fact the failure of the power.

It is therefore understandable why there are no holy ruins or holy surviving walls in folk tales. It is interesting to note that in Saul Tchernichowsky's poem, *Shalosh Atonot* ("Three Asses") the "holy ruin" symbolizes Judaism as opposed to the monastery and the mosque which symbolize Christianity and Islam respectively.

"A Holy Ruin"

Of the connection between the "holy ruin" theory and the Western Wall, we can learn from the popular application of a well-known story which is transmitted in the name of Rabbi Jose who lived about a century after the destruction of Jerusalem. The story, which is transmitted in the first person (a memorat narrative), is to be found in the very first discussion in the Talmud (Berakhot 3a):

Once I was walking along the way and I went into a ruin of the ruins of Jerusalem to pray. Elijah the prophet, may he be remembered for good, came and guarded the entrance for me until I finished my prayers. After I had finished my prayers he said to me, "Peace be on you, my master!" I said to him, "Peace be on you, my master and my teacher!" He said to me,

The Western Wall in 1844; an etching by W. Bartlett.

A post-card from the beginning of the 20th century, based on a painting by J.L. Jerome.

A typical etching (by Porter) from the 19th century.

"My son, why did you go into this ruin?" I said to him, "To pray." . . . and he said to me, "My son, what voice did you hear in the ruin?" And I said to him, "I heard a heavenly voice which moaned like a dove and said, 'Alas for sons, because of whose sins I destroyed My house, I burned My sanctuary and I exiled them among the nations!' " Then he said to me, "By your life and the life of your head! Not for one hour only does it so speak, but every day it says it three times. . ."

Folk imagination connected this "ruin of the ruins of Jerusalem" not only with the ruined Temple, which identification is not evident in the text, but even with the Western Wall. From this developed the story told by a Jerusalemite (Vilnai, No. 189)*: "On the eve of every Tish'a Be-Av (Fast of the Ninth of Av commemorating the destruction of the Temple) a dove stands at one of the corners of the Western Wall towards evening. It keens and moans the whole night and the following day until evening."

This is also the source for the stories about the white dove which sighs and participates in the weeping of the Jews mourning the destruction on the night of Tish'a Be-Av at the Western Wall and for the legends about revelations at the Wall (Vilnai, pp. 99). These stories also draw on the motif of the dove of the Congregation of Israel in the *midrashim* to the verse "One is my dove, my perfect one" (Song of Songs 6:9). The legends of revelations at the Wall also draw on the motif of God mourning for the destruction of the Temple which can be found in the *midrashim* on the verse "My soul weeps in hidden places" (Jeremiah 13:17) among others.

However, the Western Wall not only symbolizes the glory of the past and the tragedy of the exile. It is also the symbol of the hope for the rise of the Temple, which although now in ruins will be rebuilt, speedily in our days. For "the redeemer was born on the day the Temple was destroyed", and the two scriptural verses "Lebanon (the Temple) shall fall by a mighty one" (Isaiah 10:34) and "A rod shall come forth out of the stem of Jesse and a branch shall grow out of his roots" (Isaiah 11:1) were treated as though they were adjacent and thus indicating the same thought although they are in different chapters.

In the light of the above assumptions we shall classify and analyze the folk legends that have been woven about the Western Wall over the generations. We will also examine the degree in which these stories reflect the thinking of a people that has been exiled from its land and for which the Wall is not only a substitute and a "small sanctuary" (after all, all synagogues serve that purpose), but also an integral part of the Temple, one of the walls that surrounded the Temple Mount, and as such it will be integrated into the Sanctuary which will arise and which will stand for ever on the self-same spot when the Messiah and the full redemption finally come.

In addition to the Wall stories which have been published* (most of them are also current in the oral folk tradition), we will also use stories recorded from story-tellers of all Jewish ethnic origins, which are preserved in the Israel Folktale Archives (IFA).* *

On What Merit did the Wall Survive?

There can be no doubt that this question troubled the Jewish masses, and was given, like all historical problems in legend, various answers which exhibit two tendencies: 1. Historical-Rational, which tries to explain the cause in historical, social and military terms and connect it to the military campaign and the destruction itself; 2. Moral-Imaginary, which is unconcerned with historical or. pseudo-historical truth which is delineated by the boundaries of limited time. This approach prefers the eternal truth which is beyond the actual happening; the cause for the Wall's survival may have taken place many years before the destruction, for there is no chronological order in eternity, and causes such as "the merit of the fathers" and "a divine decree" have more influence on events whose cause is hidden from man, than what appear to be obvious causes.

The legend which appears in *Ecclesiastes Rabbah* 1:31 (as an explanation to Ecclesiastes 1:4) in Aramaic serves a good example to the first approach described above. The variant readings in round brackets are from *Matnot Kehunah*, a commentary on the *midrash*:

"When he [Vespasian] conquered [Jerusalem] he divided its four walls (sides of the city) between four dukes [commanders] and it was Pengar who got the Western Gate... and from heaven they decreed that it should never be destroyed. Why? Because the Divine Presence is in the west... They [the three other dukes] destroyed the sections that had been assigned to them but he did not destroy his. He [Vespasian] sent for him. He said to him, 'Why did you not destroy your section?' He answered, 'By your life! I did it for the glory of the empire, because had I destroyed it nobody would ever have known what your had destroyed. Now, people will see and say, "Look at Vespasian's power! (a strong city) he destroyed!" He said to

* Many of the folk tales which have the Western Wall as their core, were collected and coordinated (together with legends, articles and works of literature) by: Ze'ev Vilnai, *Aggadot Eretz Israel*, Jerusalem, 1953 (4th edition), Vol. I, pp. 189-196 (henceforth: Vilnai); Jacob Rimon and Joseph Zundel Wasserman, *Yerushalayim Ha-Atikah*, Jerusalem, 1957, pp. 57-94; of importance in this context is Ari Even-Zahav's work, *Be-sod Aniyei Ha-Kotel*, Tel Aviv, 1942, in which there are many stories recorded from the beggars of the Wall (p. 8: "I heard them telling tales among themselves, and they also told me many stories", some about the Wall itself.") Also the two legends which "were collected... from Sephardi elders in Jerusalem" by Asher Ben-Israel and which were published in Booklet No. 1 of *Jerusalem* (published by Hovevei Yerushalayim), Jaffa, 1912, pp. 17-19.

* * As of 1981, there are preserved in IFA 13,000 folk tales recorded from the oral traditions current among the various Jewish ethnic groups. Information about IFA and its inventory structure and ethnic arrangement are to be found in Dov Noy, *Hodesh Hodesh ve-Sippuro*, Jerusalem, The Hebrew University, 1979. Stories cited in this chapter without source are in the IFA.

him, 'By your life! You have spoken well (a correct answer), but because you did not obey my order, you will go up to the summit and throw yourself down [commit suicide]'. He [Pengar] went up and threw himself down and died... and thus the curse of Rabban Johanan ben Zakkai struck him."

This whole legend is on a factual historical plane and underlying it all is the desire of Roman commanders to show the world – by victory parades (including beautiful items of booty) and by leaving some part of the destroyed buildings as a memorial – the extent of their victory and the glory of the victorious legions. For these purposes nothing can be better than physical evidence. Furthermore, leaving some vestige, usually part of a defensive wall or tower, serves another purpose as well. It is a warning and a proof of Rome's power for the local population.

Nevertheless, the second approach is also evident in the legend in the form of a later interpolation (in Hebrew). The phrases concerning the divine decree and the Divine Presence in the west (both originally in Hebrew) transfer the main thrust of this aetiological legend into the realms of morals and eternity. The ending of the legend about the curse of Rabban Johanan ben Zakkai (also in Hebrew!) also derives from supernatural considerations, quite foreign to the body of this Aramaic legend.

The second approach discussed above is very obvious in the independent legend quoted below. It was recorded from the oral tradition more than forty years ago in the Old City of Jerusalem and published by Vilnai (No. 193).

The Wall Exists by Merit of the Poor.

When Solomon decided to build the Temple, an angel of God was revealed to him and said, "Solomon, son of David, King of Israel! Know that the Temple you are about to build will be a temple of the people, belonging to all Israel. Therefore, gather Israel together and let each one participate in the work according to his ability."

The work started. The ministers and barons took their womenfolk's gold jewelry and bought cedar wood to face the eastern wall and hired workers and overseers to urge them on... And the ministers, barons, priests and levites finished their work quickly.

Only the work of the poor dragged on a very long time, for they could not afford to bring the necessary material or hire workers to help them. So they, together with their wives and children, built it with their own hands until, after great and prolonged effort, the Western Wall was finally complete.

And it came to pass that when the sacred work was done and the Temple stood completed in all its glory, that God came down to cause His Divine Presence to live in it, and He chose the western section, for He said, "The labor of the paupers is dear to Me and My blessing will fall on it!" A voice came from heaven and announced: "The Divine Presence will never leave the Western Wall!"

When the enemy destroyed our glorious Temple, may it speedily be rebuilt in our days, Amen, the angels came down from on high and spread their wings over the Western Wall. A voice came from heaven and announced, "The Western Wall, the labor of the poor, will never be destroyed!"

When you visit the Western Wall, you will see destitute Jewish beggars writhing in its dust and begging for alms. They will proudly tell you: "The Western Wall is the labor of the poor and it is only by their merit that it still stands!"

The approach which we described above as "moral-imaginary" derives from the world of fantasy and that is the folk world. People are drawn to supernatural motives and several of the elements in the above legend about the merit of the paupers are part of that world: the revelation of the angel to Solomon, the voices from heaven, and the angels protecting the Wall with their wings. But, in addition to its folk content, the legend contains, between the lines, as it were, a consciousness of social differentiation. It is this that transfers the aetiology of the legend from why the Western Wall survived to why there are begging paupers at the Wall, a sight which often offends visitors to this, the most holy site in Judaism.

The legend, the end of which is directed against those who object to begging at the Wall, was definitely created in recent generations and cannot pre-date the 40s of the nineteenth century, when poor Moroccan Jews took the prerogative of begging at the Wall.

How Was the Western Wall Discovered?

In Talmudic midrashic literature, the Western Wall is hardly given the attention commensurate with its importance as the first of Judaism's sacred sites. It is true that there are some references here and there in early rabbinic sources to the Western Gate, to the Divine Presence in the west, to the heavenly decree that it (the Western Gate) would never be destroyed. To these can be added Rabban Johanan ben Zakkai's request to Vespasian to spare the Western Gate which leads to Lydda, and Rav Aha's interpretation of the verse "Behold, he stands behind our wall" (Song of Songs 2:9) as referring to the Divine Presence which never leaves the Western Wall as well as a few other references. But even if these sources refer to the Western Wall as we know it (which is extremely unlikely; see Chapter I), the paucity of rabbinic material is remarkable when one considers the later importance of the Wall. Furthermore, the later sources which usually reflect the early homilies and interpretations completely ignore the Wall even if the context is such that a connection would seem obvious (cf. Rashi, Ibn Ezra and others to Song of Songs 2:9). Jewish pilgrims to the Holy Land in the Middle

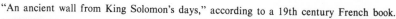

"An ancient wall from King Solomon's days," according to a 19th century French book.

Jews praying at the Wall; an etching by Geikie.

Ages left no stone unturned in their search for holy places at which to prostrate themselves and described them in detail glorifying their sanctity. Yet, the Western Wall is not mentioned. Our earliest pictorial representation of the Wall is from 1743, and in the many etchings of Jerusalem from before that date, it does not appear at all. In them, it is the Dome of the Rock which serves as a symbol of the Temple!

The only possible explanation for this enigma is that for many centuries the Western Wall was not known. And indeed, according to a folk tradition, which certainly has a kernel of historic truth, the Wall was discovered only at the end of the Middle Ages. There are two historical traditions about this matter: the first ascribes the discovery of the Wall to the sultan, Suleiman the Magnificent, the son of Selim who conquered Jerusalem (1517), and the other ascribes it to Sultan Selim himself, who spent a few days in Jerusalem when he conquered it. Both stories have a common motif which indicates a common archetype.

We will begin with the story that antedates the event (Vilnai No. 181). This story was first recorded in approximately 1730, i.e., about two hundred years after the event it claims to describe, by Moses Hagiz, a resident of Jerusalem in the 18th century. The details in brackets are not in the source:

The Discovery of the Wall by Sultan Selim

One day he (Selim) saw from his window, an old gentile woman, more than ninety years of age, bring a sack or box (basket) of garbage and drop it at a spot near his office. He became very angry... and sent one of his slaves to bring the woman and her sack. When she came he asked to which people she belonged and she told him that she was a Roman (Christian). He then asked her where she lived and she answered: "Not far from here, about two days' walk", and explained that that was why she was tired because, according to the custom the Roman leadership imposed, everyone who lived in Jerusalem had to deposit garbage at that spot (the Western Wall) at least once a day; those who lived in the environs of the city had to do it twice a week and those who lived at least three days away from the city had to do it once every thirty days, because that place was the house of Israel's God and when they were not able to destroy it completely, they decreed, by a ban, . . . that the name of Israel should never again be mentioned concerning it.

"Therefore," (said the old woman), "do not be angry that I came with a bag of garbage to your royal court. I meant no offence to you. . ."

The king, may he rest in paradise, listened to everything the woman had to say and then told his slaves to detain her until he had investigated the matter to see if she spoke the truth. . . his slaves brought to him many others who brought (sacks of garbage) and he interrogated them and found that they told the same story as the woman. . .

He (the Sultan) opened his store of silver and gold and took several bags of coins as well as a basket and a hoe which he slung over his back. He issued a proclamation: "All who love the King and want to give him satisfaction, should watch and follow suit!" He then went to the

"The Wailing Place," says the legend in an English book on Jerusalem.

garbage heap and scattered a bagful of coins so that the poor should dig for them, and, out of their love of money, clear the garbage away.

He (the Sultan) stood over them and encouraged them. . . Every day he scattered more coins. . . For some thirty days, more than ten thousand people cleared away garbage until he revealed the Western Wall and the foundations as they can be seen today by everybody.

The hero of the second, parallel story about the discovery of the Wall is the sultan Suleiman the Magnificent, the son of the Selim, referred to above. The author (or source) of this story is Eliezer Nahman Poa (17th century) and he attaches the story to the verse, "He raises up the needy from the earth; He lifts up the poor from the garbage heap" (Psalms 113:7). Poa brings the story from an oral tradition and introduces it with the words, "And this was told to me:"

The Discovery of the Wall by Sultan Suleiman

In the days of the king Sultan Suleiman, nobody knew the location of the Temple, so he ordered a search of Jerusalem to find it.

One day, the man in charge of the search who had already given up hope, saw a woman coming and on her head was a basket full of garbage and filth.

"What is that on your head?" he asked.

"Garbage," she said.

"Where are you taking it?"

"To such-and-such a place."

"Where are you from?"

"From Bethlehem."

A painting by Hunter; 19th century. It was apparently based on a photograph.

The paupers at the Wall.

"And between Bethlehem and this place are there no garbage dumps?"

"We have a tradition that anyone who brings garbage and dumps it here is performing a meritorious deed!"

"This must be it," said the man, and ordered many men to clear out the garbage from that spot, garbage which, because of the great time that had passed, had turned into earth at the bottom. And so he uncovered the holy place. He went and told the king who rejoiced greatly and ordered them to clear and sweep (the place) and wash the Wall with rose-water.

We may assume that the tradition which ascribes the discovery to Suleiman is the more reliable of the two, not only because its source, Eliezer Nahman Poa, lived closer chronologically to the event or because its strands are more true to folk-tradition, but also because Suleiman was famous for his preoccupation with excavation and building. It was he who, in 1538, completed the walls of Jerusalem which are still standing. It would appear that the story line was transferred (by Moses Hagiz?) to the beginning of the Turkish occupation and to the earlier sultan in order to give it more importance. Thus the Selim version was created later. The logic of such a transfer would be: If the new rulers decided to "search Jerusalem" for the unknown Temple site, why would Selim not do it immediately on their arrival?

The stories cited above serve as examples of the general historical legends connected with Wall in the past. Another type of legend is connected with the sanctity of the Wall in the present, a sanctity which is both general and particular. The general sanctity finds expression in the tales about miraculous cures effected by the Wall, in stories about its desecration being punished, and similar motives, which are common in folk literature in connection with other holy places and saints. When they happen at the Wall, however, the miracles that happen are more intense. On the other hand, the particular sanctity is unique to the Wall and derives from ancient dicta about it, such as the Divine Presence there and there alone (thus only the pious and the righteous are granted revelations there) and the fact that the Wall, and only the Wall, sheds tears.

The following two stories from the IFA collection, are examples of the type that has as its motif the general holiness of the Wall. The heroes are Rabbi Shalom Shar'abi, a renowned Yemenite kabbalist and Malkah De Parnas, a daughter of one of Jerusalem's oldest families. In both stories the Wall serves as the site of the action but the action could take place elsewhere. Indeed, similar stories are told about other holy places.

Rabbi Shalom Shar'abi used to go to the Western Wall every night at midnight to recite the special midnight prayers, to mourn the destruction of the Temple and to pray for the redemption.

Once, some local Arabs plotted against him. They formed two lines on the way to the Wall and waited for Rabbi Shalom Shar'abi to beat him while he ran the gauntlet. But when Rabbi Shalom passed between the lines of Arabs, they all turned to stone and were unable to move hand or foot. They remained petrified where they stood.

When dawn broke, the Arab dignitaries came to Rabbi Shalom in the Bet-El Academy, fell at his feet and begged him. "Have mercy on our petrified brethren and return them to life." The rabbi granted their plea and the Arabs were restored to life.

From then on, even the Arabs honoured and venerated the rabbi.

The supernatural motifs, common to international folk literature, of petrification and magical paralysis, are set here in a specifically Jewish setting: the Western Wall, the special midnight prayer, and prayer for the redemption. But the Wall is neither central nor necessary to the story; in IFA there are more than one hundred versions of this Jewish archetype – desecration of the sacred is punished. No specific holy place plays a role in these versions, which is not the case with the pious hero-figure who is always central to them. Stories similar to this legend, in which the miracle working saint is the central figure, can happen anywhere and not necessarily at the Western Wall. In the following story the petrification-as-punishment motif also appears but the miracle-cure element is stressed more strongly. This story also opens with the intense connection between the heroine and the Wall:

A certain woman of Jerusalem, Malkah by name, a daughter of one of the oldest and most pedigreed Sephardi families, volunteered to arrange the water, candles, chairs and benches for those who visit the Wall, and she used to store the various articles in one of the buildings near the Wall. She performed this pious deed for many years and no Arab ever harmed her, because everybody respected this saintly woman. The wives of Arab dignitaries, and even Moslem religious leaders, used to send messengers to her in secret to ask her to pray for them and their families at the Wall.

One night, something happened that put the whole city, Jews and Arabs alike, into a turmoil. A young, wild Arab boy, the only child of aristocratic parents, attacked the pious woman and injured her.

She fainted and, barely alive, she was taken home. The doctor who treated her said that on the same night the Arab boy who had attacked her fell to his bed paralyzed, like a block of wood. His family were panic-stricken.

While the doctor was treating her, the parents of the paralyzed boy burst in weeping and wailing. They kissed her hands and with tear-filled eyes begged: "Have mercy on our son. God is also merciful. Pray for him and us! For without our son, our life is no life!"

The mother of the Turkish governor also came to the pious woman's house and she too pleaded with her to forgive the stricken boy and pray for him. "He is an only child and his parents are fine people and love the Jews."

Malkah struggled to get up out of her bed, even though the doctor forbade it, and said to

"The wailing place of the Jews by Mt. Moriah;" a German etching.

her guests: "Return to your homes and wait for my answer." On the following day she informed the boy's parents: "If you want your son to live, you must bring him in his bed to the Western Wall. Let him confess his sins there, and recite the *Al Het* ("For my sin. . .") prayer before the Holy Congregation (of Jews) and beg forgiveness from the Divine Presence. Only then will his sin be atoned."

The paralyzed lad was brought to the Wall in his bed and, in the presence of a large crowd of Jews and Arabs, confessed and begged for forgiveness and a cure. The saintly woman spread her hands above the boy and prayed: "Please, O Lord, Please cure. . ." and the congregation responded "Amen."

And behold, the stricken boy stirred and began to move his limbs. Cries of gratitude and thanksgiving broke out from the people gathered there. The lad, who lived to a ripe old age, remained a friend of the Jews and respected and esteemed the Wall and those who visit it.

This story is very widespread in various versions. In one Eastern European version in IFA, the narrator claims that in his childhood he actually knew the saintly woman whose name was Malkah De Parnas. In that version all the protagonists are given names: the doctor was Dr. Luzzano, the Frenchman and the Turkish governor, whose mother interceded on the young Arab's behalf, was Arshid Pasha, who governed Jerusalem at the beginning of the renewed Jewish settlement at the start of the eighteenth century. The difference between the versions is in how the cure was effected. In place of "The saintly woman spread her hands above the boy," of our version, the parallels have a man, such as a kabbalist from the Bet-El Academy, doing it.

It should be pointed out that the two stories cited above are not only similar in their main motif (punishment for desecrating the holy) and location (the Western Wall) but also in their endings: "From then on even the Arabs honoured and venerated the rabbi" in reference to Rabbi Shalom Shar'abi as the representative of the Jews and their religion; and "The lad who lived. . . remained a friend of the Jews. . ." These endings are a substitute for the non-Jew's public conversion to Judaism which ends the legends in which the central theme is the confrontation of the pious Jew and a non-Jew who is usually a ruler or a priest.

An outstanding example of this tendency is the following story which is taken from *Yerushalayim Ha-'Atikah* ("Old Jerusalem" by Jacob Rimon and Joseph Zundel Wasserman). In this story the miracle cure is the central and independent element and not just an adjunct to the petrification and its removal as in the previous legend. The historical background is the same – the period of Arshid Pasha who is described in the introduction to the story as "brave and enlightened" and as "the first to be concerned about the cleanliness of the Old City." Similarly, a Jewish woman serves as the intermediary between the governor and the kabbalistic rabbi of the Bet-El Academy and, in light of the abundant praises showered on her, it is possible that in the archetype of the legend, the lady played a more important role. It can be assumed that the female story-tellers, who excelled in the Sephardi community, frequently integrated women as heroines into their stories which were intended for a female audience. The story follows:

The Rabbi of Bet-El - Beloved of Allah

A certain incident brought him (Arshid Pasha) to love the Jews and respect and esteem everything they consider holy. The governor had a daughter, Fatma was her name, who was beautiful and wise. When she was engaged to be married to the son of the mufti, Abdul Kader, she was stricken by typhus and the physicians gave up all hope of saving her. All the

A perpendicular picture of the Wall and the narrow enclosure. Most pictures were vertical.

prayers of the sheikhs, the muezzins and the dervishes did not help. Weeping and wailing filled the governor's house.

In his (Arshīd Pasha's) neighborhood lived a Jewish woman, Senora Malkah De Hazan, of one of the old Damascus families that could trace its descent from King David. She went to the governor and said: "Beg, my lord, the kabbalistic rabbi of Bet-El and then she will be cured!" The governor listened and sent an official to the rabbi with a letter, "In the name of God, Merciful and Graceful," to conduct special prayers to God at the Western Wall for the cure of his only daughter, Fatma who was born by Hasna, the daughter of Ali the son of Salah the son of Mahmud the son of Abdulla...

From midnight till dawn prayers were offered and in the morning the physicians noted a change for the better (in Fatma's condition). On the following day, the governor accompanied by his ministers arrived at the house of the rabbi of Bet-El and bowed before him and said, "Now I know that there is no God in the world except in Israel. My daughter's condition has improved. Please accept my gratitude for your trouble and for your prayers and please take this as a token of my thanks." He wanted to give him one hundred Turkish pounds but the rabbi would not accept the money. The governor departed with profusions of gratitude and blessings at the rabbi's magnanimity and delicacy, at his piety and righteousness, and at his honesty. On Friday at noon, during the Ishmaelites' prayers in the Mosque of Omar on the Temple Mount, the chief sheikh ascended the pulpit and, in the governor's name, announced: "There is no God but Allah and the rabbi of Bet-El is His beloved!"

These and similar legends represent the type about the general sanctity and are also told about other holy places. This is not the case with regards to the following stories. Their dramatic motifs stem from folk beliefs and from traditions particular to the Western Wall and their story-lines would not apply to any other place.

According to an ancient tradition, the Divine Presence has never left the Western Wall of the Temple. In the creative folk imagination this tradition was extended and thus traditions such as: "God stands behind the Wall" (cf. Song of Songs 2:9), looks out from there on the deeds of men, peers out of the cracks in the Wall and the observed does not see the observer. This creativity is also the source for the homily based on the Hebrew for wall, *kotel.* The word is divided into *Ko Tel* , *Ko* being equivalent numerically to God's name. Thus it means: "The hill of God" or "The hill toward which all direct their prayers." This may also be the source for the Arabic name of one of the wings of the Gate of the Chain which stands on the Western Wall - the Gate of the Divine Presence.

In the people's creative imagination all these traditions mean one thing: if anyone merits a revelation of the Divine Presence, it will not be in the Land of Israel, in Jerusalem or even at the Temple site but at the Western Wall! But, of course, not everybody merits such a revelation!

A mystical story preserved in *Tanna de-Vei Eliyahu* (an early midrashic work; Chapter 30; Ish Shalom ed. Chapter 22), exhibits this trend of thought as well as practical attempts to bring about a revelation at the Wall:

"On another occasion, Rabbi Nathan went to the Temple and found it in ruins with only one wall standing. He said: 'What is the nature of this wall?' Another person answered: 'I will show you.' He took (that) ring and stuck it in the wall. And that ring kept coming and going until he saw Almighty God bowing down and straightening up and wailing, bowing down and straightening up and wailing.

Few are the wise and pious men who have merited a revelation of the Divine Presence at the Wall. Stories on this subject are very intense in the collection of "Stories of the Ari" (Isaac Luria, the foremost kabbalist, known by his acronym, Ari, which means "Lion"). Thus it was told about Rabbi Abraham Halevi of Safed, a disciple of the Ari:

Once, the Ari, of blessed memory, said to Abraham Halevi: "Know that your days are up and your time has come to die unless you practice a "correction". I will teach you. If you do this correction, that you go to Jerusalem and go there to pray at the Western Wall and pour out your pleas and you will merit to see the Divine Presence. . ."

Then this pious man Abraham Halevi went home and shut himself away for three days and nights, fasting in sackcloth and ashes. Afterwards he travelled to Jerusalem and came before the Western Wall in prayer and supplication with great weeping. After that, he saw on the Wall the image of a man dressed in black and, straight away, out of his great fear, he fell on his face to the ground. He screamed and wept a great weeping, "Woe is me! Woe that I have seen such a sight! Ah! Woe is my soul!" He carried on crying and screaming and tearing out his hair until he fainted and lost consciousness.

And then, in a dream the Divine Presence came to him dressed in beautiful garments and said: "Be comforted, Abraham, My son! There is hope for your end and the children will return to their borders, for I will bring them back and I have taken mercy on them!"

When he Abraham awoke, he lifted his feet and he returned to Safed and came to the Ari, blessed memory. The Ari immediately said to him: "I can see in you that you have been worthy to see the Divine Presence. You can now be sure that you will live another twenty-two years."

Similar stories, particular to the Western Wall, were created on the basis of other traditions such as: God Himself weeps over the destruction of the Temple in a place no man is permitted to enter (=the Wall weeps); doves participate in Israel's sorrow (=the dove moaning in the corner of the Wall); the privilege of burial in a "faithful place" in which a man drives a peg (=nails in the Wall); the gates of tears which never close through which the prayers and requests of Israel go directly to heaven (=notes and letters placed in the cracks in Wall). For this type of legend, which is particular to the Wall, the following stories are good this type of legend, which is particular to the Wall, the following stories are good examples.

On one of the days of the month of Ellul, 1940, when Jews were at the Wall pouring out the bitterness of their hearts before Him, thin streams of water were suddenly seen running from the cracks in the Wall. Immediately, those present called out, "The Wall is crying!" The news spread quickly and many came to see the tears. Women tried to gather up some of the tears as a special talisman (Vilnai, No. 188).

According to Rabbi Eleazar's statement in the Talmud (Berakhot 32b; Bava Mezia 59a) that the "gates of prayer" were closed on the day the Temple was destroyed, it follows that the gates through which Israel's prayers ascended to heaven were located in the Temple. Since the Western Wall is the remnant of the Temple, it serves as the gate of prayer and there "nothing can come between the Jews and their father in Heaven, not even a partition of iron" (Pesahim 85b).

The use of the Western Wall as the "gate of prayer" for the direct transmission of prayers even by a letter is illustrated in the following legend (Vilnai, No. 192; *Sippurei Yaakov* of Jacob Sofer):

"When Rabbi Hayyim Joseph David Azulai (a renowned bibliographer and rabbi, known by his acronym, Hida) travelled to Jerusalem, Rabbi Hayyim ibn Attar (known as the Or Ha-Hayyim after the title of his major work) gave him a letter to put in the Western Wall. The saintly Hida took the letter, put it among his things and forgot about it. When he came to the Holy Land, he undertook to live from manual labor and he bought a donkey and cut and transported plaster for about two years.

"Suddenly, the donkey died and Hida was left without a livelihood and he remembered his teacher's letter and thought that perhaps he was being punished for not having put it in the Wall. He immediately purified himself with ablution and went to the Wall and put the letter there and prayed for him. When he returned to the study-hall, all who saw him, including the chief rabbi, were struck with a great fear and greeted him in awe. He asked them, 'Why is today different?' and they answered, 'We do not know why today is different. Please tell us!' So he told them about the letter his teacher had given him to put into the Wall and that he had not done it till now and that he had been punished on account of the neglect. The chief rabbi, who truly wanted to see the letter, insisted that Hida show him where he had put it and they went together and read it. And this is what was written in the letter: 'My sister, the bride, I ask you... help my dear pupil when he is in difficulties.'

When they (the local rabbis) saw the letter, they realized that he (Hida) must be a great man and they appointed him as a judge in the Holy City."

The end of this story indicates that its main purpose was to serve as the introductory story in a series about Hida and to glorify his appearance in Jerusalem and his connections with Rabbi Hayyim ibn Attar, who is revered as a saint in the Hasidic tradition. Thus the Eastern European provenance of the story and the many Yiddishisms in it.

The following story (Vilnai, No. 104; *Mas'ot Yerushalayim*, Moses Goldstein), at the center of which stands the Or Ha-Hayyim himself, also derives from Eastern European traditions. An examination of the motifs of the two stories reveals that they are versions, albeit far from each other, of one archetype story. Both testify to the custom of putting slips of paper with prayers and requests on them into the cracks in the Wall and it can be assumed that the stories about God's answering them derives also from the naive piety of the act and not only from the location, i.e., the Western Wall as the Gate of Prayer.

"Once, there was a man who belonged to Rabbi Hayyim ibn Attar's circle and who was close to him, who lived from physical labor and suddenly his luck changed, may it not happen to us! He came complaining to our master, the sainted Or Ha-Hayyim, may his memory protect us!, and poured out to him all his bitterness – that his house was poverty stricken and they were starving, may heaven save us! Pleading, the poor man begged that he do him a favor and ensure that blessings come on him to better his lot.

"The Or Ha-Hayyim was very touched by this tale of woe and he wrote a note with great blessing and he gave it to the poor man and said to him: 'Hold this note and go straight away to the Western Wall and seek out an empty space and there put this note and go home. You will find salvation!' The man went off clutching the note. As he was going, a stormy wind sprung up and blew his outer hat away. He paid no attention and continued on his way in his skull-cap, holding it down with his left hand and still clutching the note in his right hand. The wind blew strongly and took away his skull-cap as well, so he was left bare-headed. When he tried to regain his cap in the strong wind, the note fell from his hand and was blown away. Bitter of heart, he returned to the Or Ha-Hayyim and told him what had happened. The latter said to him, 'What can I do for you? It seems fated to failure.' Later, the missing note, signed Hayyim ibn Attar, was found in the streets of Jerusalem and they brought it to its author. And then they saw that it was addressed to the Divine Presence, so to speak, in the following form: 'My sister, my friend, my dove, my perfect one! I beg you to grant a good living to so-and-so the son of so-and-so.' And he had signed it with the above-mentioned name.

The Stone in the Wall which Prevents the Redemption

The folk beliefs and traditions, which are concerned with supernatural motives generally and holy places in particular, are based on ambivalent elements. Against the sanctity of a holy grave, the believer nevertheless feels discomfort at the impurity of the corpse that is interred there; against the admiration the believer feels for the miracle-worker, he also experiences fear of his wondrous abilities and practical kabbalah.

The Western Wall does not escape this dichotomy. It is the symbol of hope, of the redemption, and of the end of days when the Temple will be rebuilt. Yet, at the same time, it itself prevents the redemption and the rebuilding. It is conceivable that intellectually the Wall is a memorial to defeat and destruction and as such causes a crisis of will. Folk imagination, of course, needs to find a concrete story-line to express this abstract thought.

From this stems the popular belief that among the courses of stones, there exists one stone (of pagan nature) that prevents Israel's redemption. As long as that stone, put there magically by Jeroboam ben Nevat in order to cause Israel to sin, is there, redemption cannot come.

Nobody knows where this stone is and pious men try to locate it and remove it. Thus, for instance, Rabbi Raphael Tarbot, a resident of Jerusalem in the sixteenth century, tells of "a young man" who came as an emissary of "the king of the tribe of Reuben," from far away ("from the ten tribes, his father was of the children of Reuben and his mother from the tribe of Dan") in order "to remove one stone in the Western Wall of the Temple, a stone which Jeroboam ben Nevat built there by magic and as long as it is in the Wall, Israel will not be able to leave the exile." According to Rabbi Raphael Tarbot, this young man boasted that he had taken it out in the presence of the renowned Rabbi Isaac Shulal. . .

It is possible that the storyteller is referring to David He-Reuveni, who visited Jerusalem en 1523 and entered the Temple site.

Similarly, the Sages of Safed, in a letter to the Jewish community of Lunel, France, in 1625, tell of a young man of eighteen years of age, who arrived in Safed on a mission from Hananel, the king of the tribe of Reuben, "to remove a stone which has on it an idolatrous form, from the Western Wall, which was put there by Menashe, the king of Israel." Like Rabbi Tarbot, this letter also testifies that "the said emissary uttered the secret (i.e., the explicit) name of God as King Hananel had ordered him, and the stone with the idolatry inscribed on it fell and was destroyed. . ."

The two versions of this legend are apparently intended to explain why, in a specific period, none of the calculations of the date of the redemption turned out to be true. They are also intended to strengthen the hope for the redemption and to encourage believers. Such legends offer the assurance that now that the impediment has been removed the redemption will soon come.

★ ★ ★

The legends about the Western Wall cited and analyzed above are only a small selection, but they all indicate a general principle: the connection of Jewish legends, in all periods and in all places, to the Land of Israel with its memories of its glorious past and with its hopes for its future redemption. The Western Wall and its folk tales are a concrete expression of this connection and the eternal hope for the perfect redemption to come.

CHAPTER VI

THE STRUGGLE FOR THE WALL

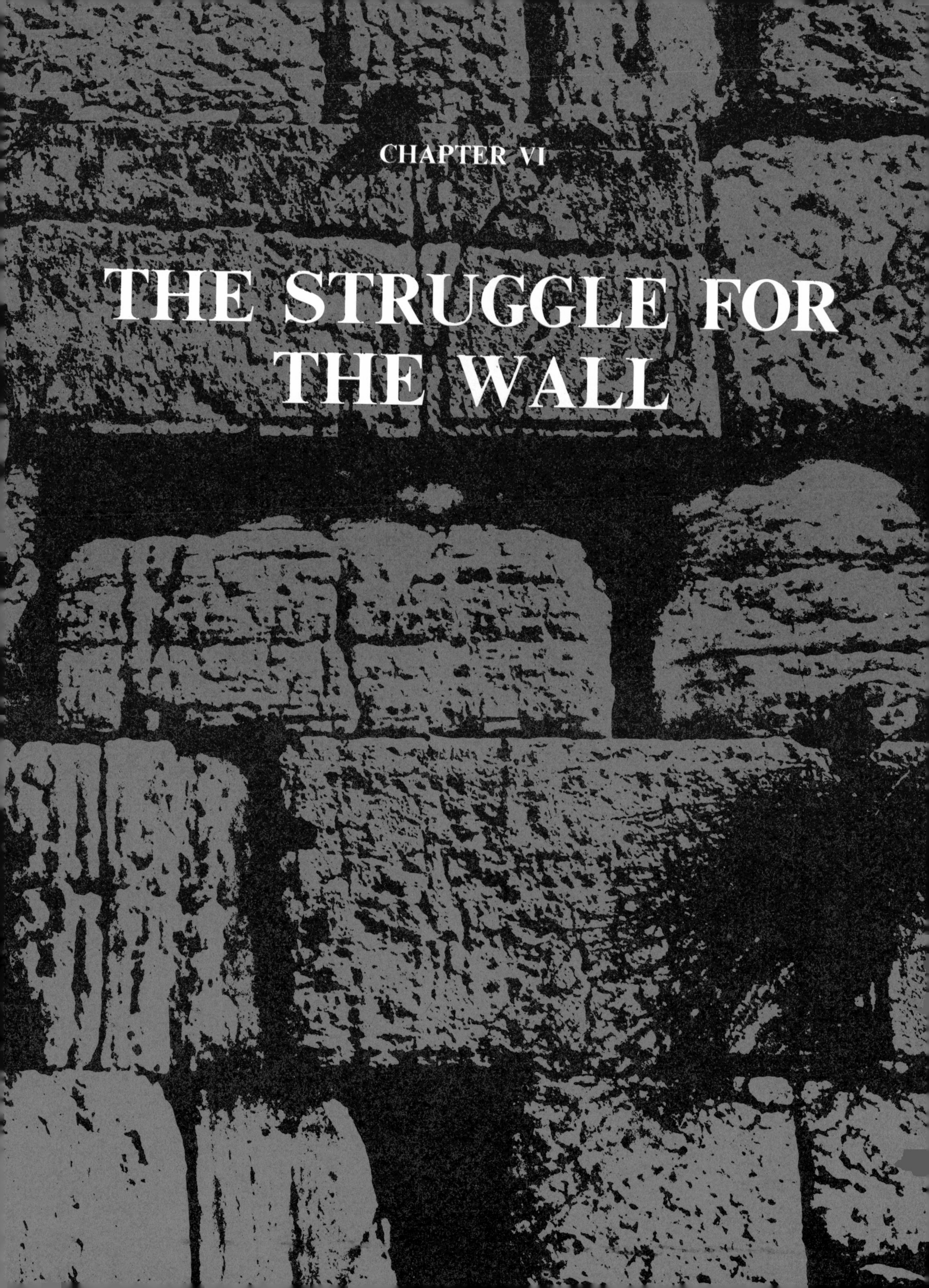

After World War I, the British Mandate in Eretz Israel created a new state of affairs for the Jews in the country after four hundred years of Ottoman rule but also brought about the emergence of new forces in the Arab world. At the beginning of the twenties, the Supreme Moslem Council was established to counter-balance the Zionist Federation. In order to increase its influence in the Moslem world, the Council made the two mosques on the Temple Mount the central focus of its activities, a policy which caused unrest in the country for long periods.

In the twenties, the Jews' claims regarding their rights at the Western Wall intensified. The Arabs believed this to be in preparation for wider claims to the Temple Mount itself and started – both internally and externally – ever growing opposition to the claims. The Arabs' fear of the Jews' position in the Old City of Jerusalem becoming stronger was not entirely without foundation. They remembered the struggle over Christian holy places which had brought about the intervention of the great powers on the side of the Christians. They also remembered that in the nineteenth century, the Jews, with Jewish help from abroad, had tried to buy the area around the Wall. It was true that the Jews' right to pray at the Wall had been recognized from very early times and was firmly established in many traditions, but Jewish rights to the area in front of the Wall were of relatively recent origin. In early times, Jews had gathered there only on special occasions; it was only at the beginning of the nineteenth century, with the growth of Jerusalem's Jewish community and the start of an Ashkenazi community there, that the Jewish presence in the Wall's "courtyard" had become more "established," so to speak. The regular worshippers at the Wall had made arrangements with Arab neighbours to store the various accessories needed for the prayer services and, starting from the 1850s, Jewish organizations in Jerusalem had taken it on themselves to clean the area regularly. However, the Wall had not been transformed into a proper synagogue.

The growth in the Jewish population of the city and in the number of Jewish pilgrims from central and eastern Europe created new conditions at the Wall which led the Jews to install lighting fixtures and even bring chairs and benches there. Concerned about the change in the *status quo* at the Wall, the Moslems complained and, in a decision taken in November 1911, the local Turkish authorities ruled that the Jews had no rights at all at the Wall and forbade

החרות

בטול האסור ע"ד כותל המערבי

ביום הששי בבוקר קבלנו מסופרנו המיוחד בקושטא, מר ב. ר. את הידיעה החשובה הזאת, שפרסמנה בהוספה מיוחדת:

"הודעתיכם כבר כי רבנו הגדול עשה צעדים לפני וזרת המשפטים והדתות ע"ד האסור של „כותל המערבי", שנאסר על היהודים להניח ספסלים ונרות אצל הכתל, עפ"י החלטת מגליש האדארה בירושלם.

"עכשו הנני ממהר לבשר לקוראי „החרות" הירושלמים כי הצעד שעשה רבנו פעל הרבה בחוגים הגבוהים, וביום השלישי י"א שבט (30 ינואר) שלחה הוזרה הנ"ל תלגרמה מיוחדה למותצרף ירושלם בפקודה לבטל את האסור ע"ד של כתל המערבי מיד ומבלי כל אחור."

עתון „איקדאם" הקושטאי מן יום 2 פברואר הביא ידיעה כזו ושם נאמר ג"כ כי הוזרת שלחה למותצרף ירושלם תלגרמה לבטל את האסיר על כתל המערבי.

The beginning of the struggle – a report in Ḣa'herut (a newspaper), 1912.

them to bring to the Wall area any articles, such as lamps, benches, chairs and Torah Scrolls. This decision, which reinforced one taken in 1840, was adopted by the British authorities at the start of the Mandate period out of concern for Arab sensibilities.

Montefiore's and Rothschild's Attempts to Buy the Wall

Towards the end of Ottoman rule in Eretz Israel, several attempts were made to buy the Western Wall from the Arabs. The fact that the Wall and the surrounding area were not privately owned but were the property of the Wakf (the Moslem Religious Trust) made the task more difficult. In 1850, Israel Meir Sofer wrote:

"The Wall stands on the western side of the (Temple) Mount and thus its name, the Western Wall. It runs the whole length of the Mount but, on both sides, the Ishmaelites have built many houses so close to the Wall that it has become the Wall of their houses, in our many sins! Only in the center is a section of thirty cubits open and that is where the Jews stand to pray. There are approximately another ten cubits fenced in with a wall, and Jews are not permitted to go there. The Radbaz (David ibn Avi Zimra, 1479-1573, important rabbi and scholar) was granted a revelation at that spot and, since then, the Jews became accustomed to pray there and weep loudly. So the Ishmaelites fenced it off because it is near to their court where the judges sit, and they claimed that the noise the Jews made disturbed them. The Jews wanted to buy the place to build a study-house (synagogue) there, but the Ishmaelites refused, even for a great sum of money."

James Finn, the British consul in Jerusalem in the middle of the nineteenth century, wrote in his memories, *Stirring Times, 1855-1856*: "Notwithstanding these snatched moments of exalted glory, the Jews are degraded by having to pay 'allowances' to various local Moslem oppressors through the chief rabbi, such as a yearly payment of 300 pounds to an effendi whose house is near the Wailing Wall, which is a portion of the western wall of the Temple courtyard, for permission to pray there."

Yaari Poleskin, in his biography *Baron Edmond Rothschild*, relates that after the Baron finished his prayers at the Western Wall on his first visit to Eretz Israel, he turned to one of the Jewish dignitaries of Jerusalem who accompanied him and said: "The sight of the squalid surroundings in which the Wall stands is heart-rending and insulting. Why should this holiness be situated in the midst of such filth and impurity? While I was praying, I had an idea. I am prepared to donate one million francs to buy all these derelict houses around the Wall, to build for their occupants better and pleasanter houses elsewhere. Let us raze these hovels to the ground and in their place plant boulevards in which we will put benches for the convenience of the worshippers. It will be a beautiful park which will add to Jerusalem." It was a good idea but it was never executed (see below) just as some years earlier, in 1875, Sir Moses Montefiore's initiative had come to nothing.

That had been during Montefiore's seventh visit to Eretz Israel. In his travelogue he wrote: "I made great efforts to make the place at the Western Wall into a place filled with awe, and I had already drawn up an agreement to achieve this, my earnest desire, but an unforeseen obstacle arose which could not be overcome and the whole plan was brought to nought. Recently, one dignitary tried to get permission to put a few benches there for the convenience of the many worshippers who visit there daily; but he did not succeed. He again asked permission to at least put a few blocks of marble in the prayer enclosure to be used as benches and for this he was granted permission. But they were not there for long; they were stolen one by one to the last.

May Jews bring benches to the prayer enclosure? A question which occupied Jews, Arabs and the British in Mandate times. This photograph from the beginning of the century proves that then they did.

In 1913 the Board of Directors of the Anglo-Palestine Bank made another effort to buy the Wall. In his memoirs, the managing-director, Zalman David Levontin, wrote that an effort was made for several years to find a way to buy the Wall. And indeed, it seemed as though success was at hand: "In order that the Wall should be ours, it was necessary to buy the area near it, and, in the course of time, to build a cultural institution – or better still, a large synagogue – there. It is impossible to buy property belonging to the Wakf with money; they will only take other real estate in exchange. It is necessary to build nicer houses on the property offered. We could have done it with an outlay of approximately 150,000 francs. In the meantime, World War I started and negotiations were suspended."

The Wall, as is clear from the above citations, occupied the center of Jewish life in Jerusalem, in Eretz Israel and, indeed, in all places Jews lived. Some Jews prayed at it; all Jews prayed to it, albeit from afar, and saw it as the most sacred object left to them – which was not the case with the other religions, Islam and Christianity.

Guarding the Wall – a British policeman.

The Yom Kippur Incident, 1928

Above, we have described the situation in the second half of the nineteenth century and the beginning of the twentieth. In the twenties, the course of events led to the bloody Arab outbursts of 1929 and to a change in British policy in Eretz Israel. One of the main causes was the success of Haj Amin al-Husseini, the mufti of Jerusalem, in establishing himself, after internal Arab struggles which lasted most of the twenties, as the most important leader of Eretz Israel's Arabs. He well knew how to manipulate Arab sentiments regarding the Temple Mount.

Incitement increased in 1928 and, as a result, the Jewish-Arab situation deteriorated rapidly. *Sefer Toldot Ha-Haganah* ("The History of the Haganah, the Jewish Defense Force") describes it thus:

During Turkish rule, when Islam was the dominant religion in the country, the authorities frequently persecuted Jews who prayed at the Wall and forbade them to bring chairs or set up a partition (to separate men and women) there. But they never questioned the Jews' right to come and pray there. When the British took over, they proclaimed absolute freedom of religion in the country and the authorities were charged with the task of protecting the rights of all religions to their holy places. There was talk of 'a special committee which would examine, define and fix the rights and claims regarding the holy places' (from the committee's mandate). The government undertook to maintain the *status quo* until the committee would be formed; it never was. From the first days of the Mandate the Wall constituted one of the cards in the hands of the mufti and his aides. From time to time the Supreme Moslem Council complained about disturbances of the *status quo* by the Jews. Shortly before the arrival of Herbert Samuel as the first High Commissioner, Ronald Storrs, the Governor of Jerusalem, renewed the Turkish regulation which forbade the bringing of chairs and benches to the Wall. Nevertheless, the Jews did bring chairs and benches there, particularly on Yom Kippur, and periodically the police would remember the prohibition and enforce it. The Jews' status regarding their most holy place – from the point of view of both religion and nationalism – was wretched. Hooligans from the nearby Magreb Quarter used to molest worshippers, throw stones at them and even beat them. The Arab police showed no concern. When Samuel and Plumer (the second High Commissioner) were in charge, they were able to stop this behaviour without causing a fuss. In the days of Lock (the First Secretary, second in the hierarchy of British command after the High Commissioner), however, events took an entirely different turn."

On the eve of the Day of Atonement (September 23rd, 1928) many Jews came to pray at the Wall and the beadle set up a partition to separate the men from the women. The Deputy Governor of the Jerusalem area Kitroach, accompanied by a police officer named Duff, arrived at the Wall in the course of his tour of the neighbourhood and when he saw the partition, "he was stricken with horror," to quote *Sefer Toldot Ha-Haganah.* He immediately asked the sheikhs, who were guards appointed by the Wakf, if they had not seen what the Jews had done. "The cunning old men," Duff wrote later, "put on a show of insulted innocence and began to interpret the Jews' action as an open attempt to turn this Moslem holy place into a Jewish synagogue." Kitroach ordered the police officer to remove the partition. On the following morning, Yom Kippur day, a delegation of the worshippers visited Kitroach and asked him to postpone the removal of the partition until after the Day of Atonement. He immediately sent Duff to remove it by force, if necessary. Duff came to the Wall with a squad of policemen and as soon as the worshippers began the Silent Prayer (during which they are not permitted to move), he decided that the prayers had ended and approached with

A military ceremony at the Wall.

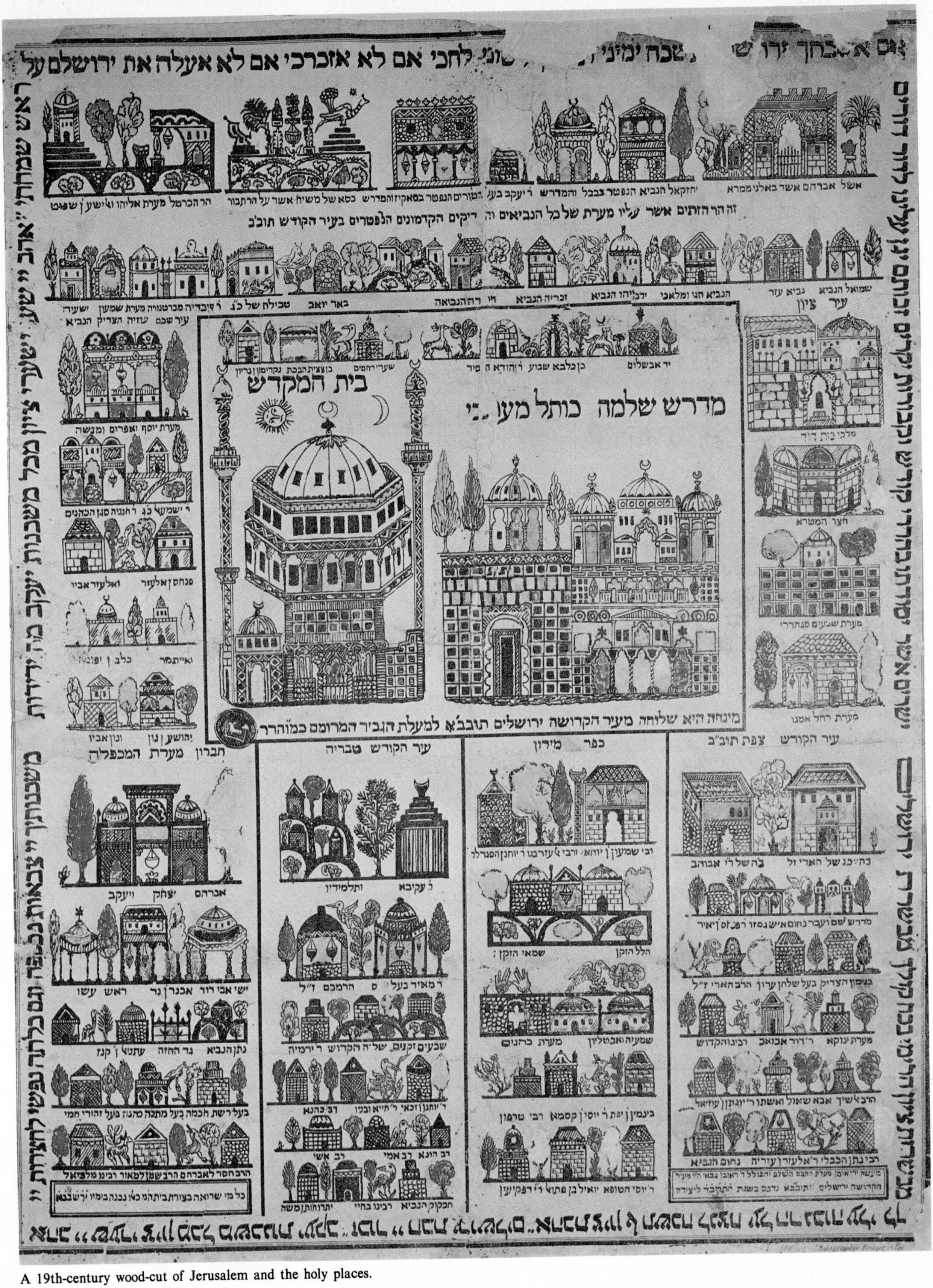

A 19th-century wood-cut of Jerusalem and the holy places.

למען הכתל המערבי בירושלם

קול קורא לעם ישראל בכל מקום שהוא!

A manifesto about the Wall by Joseph Klausner, 1928.

his men to take down the partition. Some of the worshippers tried to stop them, but the police overcame them and carried out their orders. This disgusting behaviour raised a furor in Eretz Israel and its echoes resounded throughout the Jewish world. The Jewish national institutions complained to the heads of the British government and even to the Mandate Commission of the League of Nations. An indication of the anger and shock felt by the Jews can be found in a newspaper article written by Itamar ben Avi, the editor of *Doar Ha-Yom*, at the end of the Yom Kippur day:

منظر اليهود يبكون عند حائط البراق الذي يسمونه «المبكى»

The Arabic legend reads: "Jews weeping at the Buraq wall which they call the Wailing Wall."

"For the fourth time since the British began to rule our country, English officers, accompanied by Arab policemen, have found the courage to attack the sanctity of the Day of Atonement – the greatest of the Hebrew festivals of the oldest living nation. For the fourth time, we say, because we are only referring to scorching insults; ordinary and isolated insults have been our lot for years. . . For the fourth time the commander of our police force has had the audacity to give a signed order to a brutal officer with the deliberate intention on both their parts of giving a resounding and insulting slap on the face to the bearers of that great and holy faith from which their messiah emerged some two thousand years ago. . .

"An abomination has been wrought in Jerusalem by officials of the English administration. Let this be the last time our revered Wall is desecrated! Let yesterday's Yom Kippur be a day of warning to all who would defile our name, wherever they may be. In future, let no man touch, let nobody dare to touch, the last vestige, the one living symbol of our people as a people, of our sovereign state as a sovereign state! . . ."

Jewish Attempts to Calm the Situation

During the course of that year, the end of which saw the disturbances which became known as "The Events of 1929," the Wall was the focus of many incidents, serious and trivial, with the British authorities doing nothing to assuage the situation. The White Paper, published at the end of 1928, stressed the need to maintain the *status quo* with regard to the Wall, which meant that the Jews could bring there "only those prayer accessories which had been permitted in Turkish times." The Chief Rabbinate was requested to prove which accessories had been permitted but, arguing that the Jews had a right to pray at the Wall with no restrictions, it refused to do so.

Until that period, the Western Wall had had no religious significance for the Moslems, and it had even been frequently desecrated by Arab hooligans who threw rocks and garbage into the prayer area. Suddenly it became very sacred and a Moslem tradition was established fixing it as the place where the prophet Mohammed tethered his wondrous horse, Al-Buraq, when he ascended to heaven. At first, this new "tradition" was totally rejected by many Moslems, but, with the passage of time, it became a common belief. Furthermore, the mufti and his men constantly spread the fiction that the Jews were planning to conquer the Temple Mount and its mosques. One of their proofs was that on plaques indicating the direction in which Jews should pray (*Mizrah* plaques), the Temple Mount with the Dome of the Rock appeared with the legend, "The Place of our Temple." The situation became so serious that the National Committee, the highest authority of the Jewish community, saw fit to publish an open letter addressed to the Arabs in the following terms:

"We hereby affirm, in all honesty, that it is inconceivable for any Jew to think of damaging the Moslems' rights to their holy places. But our Arab brethren must also recognize the rights which the Jews of the country have to their places... Any attempt to describe the desire of the Jews to pray in this holy place (at the Wall) in peace, with dignity, and without hindrance, as the establishment of a strategic basis from which to attack Moslem mosques is the figment of a lying imagination or a vicious libel. The purpose of this libel is to sow discord and confusion and to stir up hatred and enmity betwen two brother-peoples. Such action can only bring disaster to both sides."

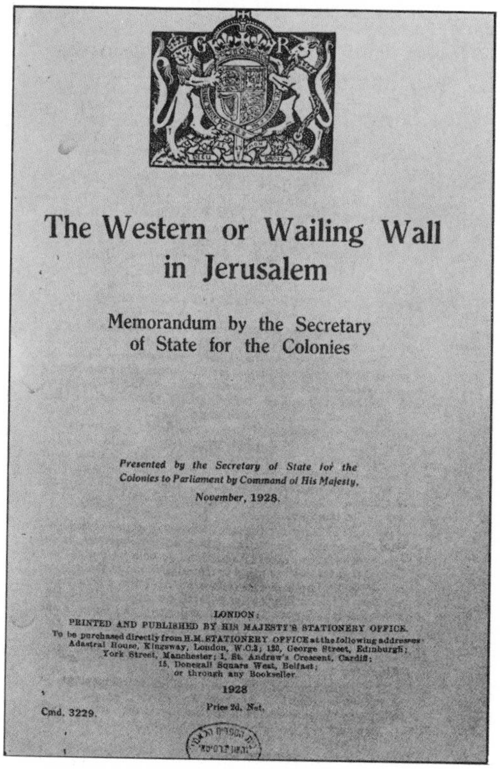

The Western or Wailing Wall in Jerusalem

Memorandum by the Secretary of State for the Colonies

Presented by the Secretary of State for the Colonies to Parliament by Command of His Majesty, November, 1928.

LONDON:
PRINTED AND PUBLISHED BY HIS MAJESTY'S STATIONERY OFFICE.
To be purchased directly from H.M. STATIONERY OFFICE at the following addresses:
Adastral House, Kingsway, London, W.C.2; 120, George Street, Edinburgh;
York Street, Manchester; 1, St. Andrew's Crescent, Cardiff;
15, Donegall Square West, Belfast;
or through any Bookseller.
1928
Price 2d. Net.
Cmd. 3229.

The Events of 1929

In the summer of 1929 the situation in Jerusalem worsened. The mufti gave the order to repair one of the walls near the Western Wall and created an entrance for passage from the Temple Mount directly into the prayer area at the Wall. Every day donkeys passed through the prayer area and disturbed the Jewish worshippers. Somewhat later, the Moslems started major building projects in the neighbourhood which restricted Jewish access and further oppressed the worshippers. In addition to all this, the adjacent Magreb Quarter started to hold wild, noisy ceremonies in order to trouble and provoke the Jews who prayed at the Wall. Notwithstanding Jewish protests, the British did nothing to stop this deliberate harassment and the mufti, encouraged by this tacit approval, incited Jerusalem's Arabs more and more. As the incitement increased, a demonstration was organized by the Jewish youth movement, Betar, which marched to the Wall where, contrary to an earlier agreement, the demonstrators waved Jewish national flags and heard a short speech. On the following day an Arab demonstration was held and on Friday, August 23rd, 1929, thousands of Arab worshippers gathered on the Temple Mount. The kadis delivered inflammatory sermons and the bloodthirsty mob surged out of the Temple Mount towards the Jewish Quarter of the Old City and the Jewish neighbourhoods of modern Jerusalem. Riots started throughout the whole country. Most of the victims of these "Events" were members of the old Jewish communities in Hebron, Safed and Jerusalem. In all, 133 Jews were murdered by Arab rioters and more than 300 were injured.

After the riots died down, the Western Wall remained a troubled question. The British government sent a parliamentary committee to Eretz Israel to investigate the disturbances at the Wall in all their manifold aspects. Jewish and Arab representatives appeared before the committee and made their claims with regard to the ownership of the prayer area at the Wall and the rights to it. Particularly exhaustive was the evidence of Nissim Bachar, who, aged 81, analyzed the change in the Moslem attitude to the Wall from the middle of the nineteenth century until 1929:

"I can remember from my childhood how, when the month of Ellul arrived, all my family used to go down to the Wall in the early hours of the morning, in order to pray the morning service there. We always used to find the place filthy with hair clippings of the neighbouring Arabs who used to perform their toilets there. The poor Jewish beadle used to clean up the mess before the first worshippers arrived. We once asked him why he did not complain to the Moslems in the nearby courthouse and he told us: 'I have complained and objected many times, but the effendis in the courthouse laugh at me. You know, we are in exile.' All this proves that the place has never been considered holy by the Moslems. On the contrary! In accordance with the accepted practice in the east, the faithful of one religion do not respect the holy places of any other, but despise them. When Baron Edmond de Rothschild visited Eretz Israel (for the first time in 1886), I interested him in the possibility of buying the prayer area at the Wall including the buildings occupied by the poor Moroccan Arabs. The idea was to offer them suitable compensation in the form of a house surrounded by a garden for each family, in one of the light, airy sections outside the city. The Baron wholeheartedly accepted the proposal and the governor of Jerusalem at that time expressed his happy agreement. Even the mufti himself thanked me because thus the area would be cleaned up and cease to be a disgrace to all Islam. All the other dignitaries, including the chief rabbi, not only welcomed the idea joyously but congratulated me for having initiated such a clever proposal. In the meantime, the Baron travelled to Damascus and two days later I joined him there. To my great astonishment, he showed me a letter, signed by the chief rabbi of Jerusa-

רק כך

הודעה

השתא **לא** התפרצו שוטרים בריטיים אל רחבת הכותל־המערבי בזמן תפלת יום הכפורים, שנסתיימה **ללא הפרעות**, בתקיעת שופר ובשירת „התקוה".

מנהג מחפיר, שהונהג על ידי שלטון הדכוי. על מנת להרגילנו לכניעה בפני רצוננו ולחיי עבדות רוחנית, „מנהג" שלא נתקל בעבר בהתנגדות מעשית של הישוב ומוסדותיו — הופר זו הפעם הראשונה אחרי שלש עשרה שנה.

עובדה זו, אשר את ערכה המוסרי־המדיני אין להגזים ואין להפחית, תלמד שוב את כולנו, **כי רק בקומה זקופה ובעמדה ללא רתיעה אפשר להגן על כבוד האומה ולהלחם לחרותה.**

הארגון הצבאי הלאומי
בארץ־ישראל

The Wall in underground literature. An Ezel manifesto of the 40s (on the right) declaring that national honor can be protected "only by standing upright without fear." A manifesto of the Haganah (above, left) called "the Wall." Near the Wall in the War of Independence (above); Jordanian soldiers attacking the Jewish Quarter.

lem, Raphael Meir Fenijal, urging the Baron to withdraw from the proposed exchange and to give up the idea completely lest it arouse Arab feelings. I pointed out to the Baron that the letter was writen in French, a language which the chief rabbi neither understands, reads or writes, but he (the Baron) asked me not to talk to him any more on the subject. I personally was sure that the matter could have been arranged, but some Jews interfered and because of their personal interests the deal did not go through. However, this incident, in addtion to the other proofs, is absolute and irrefutable evidence that the governor of the city, the mufti and the dignitaries of that time, did not attribute any importance to the Western Wall and did not consider it a holy place or a place of Moslem prayer.

"When the present mufti complains that the Jews have put up a partition at the Wall to separate the men from the women, the British authorities should answer him: 'This is a Jewish holy place and you should thank them for keeping it clean as befits a place of prayer. No man has the right to question whether they can put up a partition in their place of prayer, just as they will not interfere if the Moslems build a wall or partition in their mosques to separate women from men and just as no one can stop the Christians from doing so in their churches.' Such an answer would have put an immediate end to the argument and would have completely foiled any evil intentions. As it happens, the mufti was encouraged by the support of the authorities who used force to disturb the Jews while they were fasting and praying to their God on the holy Yom Kippur day. The authorities' interpretation of the *status quo* has contributed to the growth of hatred between the two peoples in that it has allowed bands of rowdies to use this place for free passage between the Dome of the Rock and the Wall, something which was not allowed even by the Turkish government. This cleared the way for those terrible 'Events' and for all the atrocities that came in their wake. . ."

The Struggle Continues

The British parliamentary committee recommended, *inter alia*, to appoint an international inquiry commission on the basis of Article 13 of the Mandate for Palestine, in order to define the rights at the Western Wall. The League of Nations appointed the new commission in January 1930, and its three members arrived in Eretz Israel on July 19. All in all, the commission heard fifty-two witnesses, of whom twenty-one were Jewish, thirty were Moslems and one was British. David Yellin, who appeared before the commission, said:

"Being judged before you today stands a nation that has been dispossessed of everything that is dear and sacred to it from its emergence in its own land – the graves of its patriarchs, the graves of its great kings, the graves of its holy prophets and, above all, the site of its glorious Temple. Everything has been taken from it and of all the witnesses to its sanctity only one vestige remains – one side of a tiny portion of a wall which, on one side, borders the place of its former Temple. In front of this bare stone wall, that nation stands under the open sky, in the heat of summer and in the rains of winter, and pours out its heart to its God in heaven. And even against this pitiful privilege, acquired by the myriads of tears that it has shed on the stones of this wall for thousands of years, there have suddenly arisen protestors. . . For the last two thousand years Eretz Israel has passed like a ball from ruler to ruler: from the Romans to the Persians, to the Byzantines, to the Arabs, to the European Christian Crusaders, and again to the Arabs and the Turks. And during all these rules, and the disturbances they created, the People of Israel never stopped praying at this place. . ."

The commission tried to find a compromise between the Jews and Arabs, but the mufti Haj Amin al-Husseini rejected all proposals and continually claimed: "We own the Wall and the prayer area at it. They are part of the precincts of the mosque and we will not give the Jews an inch. If they are to have access to the Wall, it will be an act of grace on our part and we will decide everything regarding the use of the place" (according to Joseph Nedava). In 1931, the commission's report was given the force of law by a King's Order in Council in England. This legislation ruled that the *status quo* at the Wall would be maintained. This meant that the area belonged to the Arabs but they were constrained from executing any repairs which might disturb the Jewish worshippers. The Jews were permitted to bring prayer accessories to the area, but all articles of furniture were forbidden. The law also forbade sounding the *shofar* at the Wall at the close of the Yom Kippur services, but many young Jews took the risk of trial and imprisonment and every Yom Kippur there were attempts to blow the *shofar* there.

One of those young Jews was Moshe Segal, a member of the Betar youth movement. Although he was arrested, tried and sentenced to six months in prison, from an entry in his diary, written a few days after Yom Kippur, it seems that he thought it was worth it:

"... some time ago I had decided to pray on Yom Kippur at the remnant of our ancient Temple, the Western Wall. This is the Wall that our enemies and those who manipulate them have started to desecrate in recent years, in order to abuse our deepest feelings; abuse which signifies the beginning of an attempt to deprive us of our rights in our land. In the month of Av, 1929, we all swore an oath at this Wall to guard and protect it, and so it is the duty of us all, of every Jewish boy, to visit it whenever possible and to participate in the traditional prayers there, particular on our people's most holy day. I went up to Jerusalem. Because of the difficulties of the journey from the Galilee, I said the evening prayers in the Hebron Yeshivah which I love because of its wonderful atmosphere... The following morning I went to pray at the Western Wall. Notwithstanding the fast, very many people visit the Wall on this day and a great number stay there the whole day to pray, without leaving it at all. This year, the British policemen guarded the place properly; they accompanied the Mugrabis (Arabs) whenever they crossed the area, necessarily or otherwise, with trays laden with steaming cups of coffee and various kinds of sweetmeats, to aggravate the thirst of the fasting Jews. The cantor, a very old man, led all the day's prayers... When he came to the prayer, 'Close the mouths of our adversaries and accusers! Rid us of pestilence, the sword, captivity and destruction! Raise up the glory of Israel, Your people!' he put special meaning into his mighty voice which stirred the worshipers greatly. The sun began to set. The *Ne'ilah* prayer, in which our fate is sealed until next Yom Kippur, is full of warmth and emotion and exalted ethical meaning and stretches out its hand to welcome penitents. You forget all the intrigues and conspiracies around the Wall. There is only one feeling: The eyes of all Jews, wherever they are, are turned towards these stones; all Jewish hearts are praying this sublime prayer together with you, and with you they are confessing 'The Lord is God!' and in honour of His majesty the *shofar* is sounded every year. And then, suddenly you remember: Sounding the *shofar* is forbidden!... Who forbade it? The evil government under whose auspices innocent blood is shed. Do we have to accept the yoke of this government? And with all the emotion in your heart you want to grasp the *shofar* and sound it with all your strength to acknowledge that the Lord of Israel is God and there is none other... the innermost thought of your heart drives you to action...

"A hand, by force of its orders, arrested me... Darkness in the hearts of the surprised worshippers; a darkness which spread in the hearts of all our brethren in their exiles. How long will gentiles defile our holy sanctuary?"

The Wall in captivity – an empty prayer area and a Jordanian policeman.

The Wall – In Jordanian Captivity

In the following years, until the establishment of the State of Israel, the Arab-Jewish tension over the Western Wall abated a little, perhaps because of other tensions that took its place. But the struggle for the Wall was not over. Members of Betar and the Irgun Zeva'i Le'umi (a Jewish underground armed organization) continued to sound the *shofar* at the Wall year after year in spite of the prohibitions and the difficulties, and the question of the Wall was frequently mentioned in underground publications. The Hagana even adopted it as the logo of its regular manifesto, *Ha-Homah* ("The Wall").

In 1948, the Wall, together with the Jewish Quarter of the Old City, was conquered by the Jordanian Arab Legion, and the struggle over it found different forms of expression. According to the cease-fire agreement Israel and Jordan signed in 1949, Jewish worshippers from Israel were to be permitted to visit the Wall, but the Jordanians ignored this paragraph (no. 8) of the agreement, as they ignored other important paragraphs. Only a few Jewish tourists who were not Israeli citizens, had the good fortune to visit the Wall and the prayer area there was totally desolate for more than nineteen years. All Israel's efforts to bring about a change in Jordan's policy were in vain. This situation continued until June 1967.

יוני 1967

CHAPTER VII

THE WALL IN THE SIX-DAY WAR

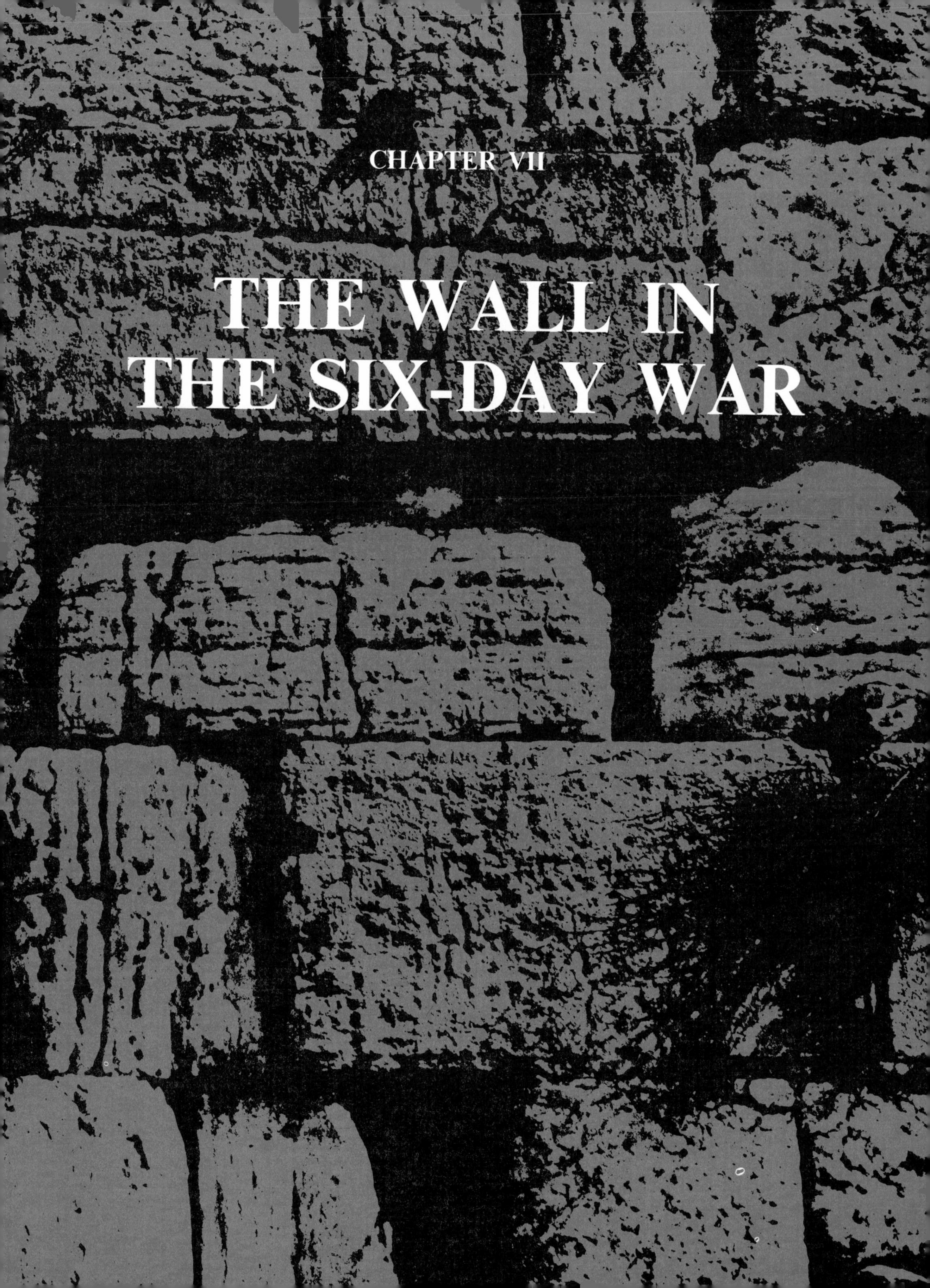

" 'The Wall' was a concept that everybody understood. There, we began to listen to the radio again and to discover what was happening on the other fronts of the war. Only here did we begin to understand that what we had done in Jerusalem was the heart of the matter, the heart of all the things that had been done in those June days."

These words, spoken by Jonathan, the intelligence officer of Battalion 66 of the paratroop brigade commanded by Motta Gur which liberated the Old City of Jerusalem, sum up in a few words the dramatic events of the Six-Day War, which reached its climax on June 7, 1967, in Jerusalem, in the narrow prayer area in front of the Western Wall.

The Six-Day War was a defensive war which was forced on the nineteen-year-old State of Israel. It began in the south, in the wastes of Sinai and it seemed that it would follow the course of the previous war, the Sinai War (or the Kadesh Campaign, as it is sometimes called), which took place eleven years earlier. But, in contrast to 1956, this time Syria and Jordan joined in on Egypt's side and within a few days, they too were defeated. The Jordanian army was driven out of all the territories it had occupied west of the Jordan river and the Syrians suffered the same fate in the Golan Heights.

One of the results of this war was that Jerusalem, long divided by a winding, mine-strewn border, was reunified. The Old City, and in it the Jewish Quarter which had fallen in 1948, and deep in that, the Western Wall, was the dream of many who did not dare to utter the hope that one day these places would once again be in our hands.

In 1962, Hayyim Guri wrote about "The Torn City": "Occasionally you remember that it is torn. Not always. You are far away; you are busy. Then, one day you find yourself standing opposite it as though trying to see it anew. You walk, walk and then stop. Before you are steps. A rusting garbage can, a piece of fifteen-year-old barbed wire. Stop! for your own good. If you carry on, at best you will be thought to be mad; at worst you will be shot. For here they shoot. Everything is as though dozing in the noon's sun. Stones and trees and domes and crosses. But it is a mighty stillness full of lookout posts and snipers."

That is how it was until 1967. And then, suddenly, without any preparation, all the great events happened. The war broke out. First in Sinai and within a few hours in Jerusalem, as well. Hussein, King of Jordan, believed Nasser, Egypt's ruler, that he was winning and so he joined him. Israel warned Hussein not to embark on any adventures but in vain.

The paratroopers at the Wall, an historic photograph, June 7, 1967.

On the Jordanian front, event followed event as though of their own momentum. Israel hesitated to open a second front but Hussein pushed his country and his army towards war. Israel began to reinforce its forces in and around Jerusalem.

The First Day of the War

In his book, *Six Years, Six Days*, Moshe A. Gilboa wrote as follows:

"Already on the first day of the war, when the Legion's artillery started to pound Jerusalem, a few of the cabinet ministers began to wonder whether the time had not come to liberate Jerusalem and reunify it. Levi Eshkol, the Prime Minister, had a conversation on the subject with his colleagues, Menahem Begin and Yigal Alon. In consequence, the government of Israel met in the cellar of the Knesset building to the screams of the shells which were exploding round them.

"The Prime Minister opened the meeting and said: "I understand that you have heard a review of the battle situation and I assume that tonight we will have to discuss the continuation with regards to Jordan, if they continue their attack. It all depends what subjects will occupy us, particularly Sinai."

On the night of June 5, towards the end of the first day's fighting, the picture was becoming clearer. In Sinai – success. The Air Force had almost totally destroyed the Arab Air Forces but in Jerusalem and in other places along the border the Jordanians continued the shelling and sniping. The decision was taken. Motta Gur's paratroop brigade would break into East Jerusalem in order to join up with the Israeli enclave on Mount Scopus which the Jordanians were attacking. At this time, the taking of the Old City was not yet discussed.

At approximately 8:30 p.m., the commanding officer of the Central Command, Uzi Narkiss, arrived at the Evelina de Rothschild girls' school which was serving as the headquarters of the paratroop brigade. The commanding officer, Motta Gur, explained his plan of attack which included far more than opening up a route to Mount Scopus. When he finished, he looked at Narkiss. In his memoirs, Narkiss continues:

"The room was silent; they were all waiting for my decision. I weighed up the plan in my mind. The brigade commander had understood what I had told him earlier, 'Pull to the right and be prepared for entry into the Old City.' In his plan he committed only one battalion to the "official" goal of the brigade, to break through to Mount Scopus, whereas most of the brigade, two battalions and the commando company, he had earmarked for 'the pull to the right', to the walls.

"I said: 'The plan is authorized. Take these objectives and let's see how things develop. And you, Motta, keep thinking about the Old City all the time.' "

The battles in East Jerusalem continued one night and one day. Ammunition Hill, the Police Academy, the Rockefeller Museum, are among the places that witnessed acts of great heroism and also the fall of many fine men. And they were still outside the walls. On Wednesday morning (June 7, 1967) the government authorized the conquest of the Old City after much hesitation on the part of some ministers because of the negative reaction that could be expected from world public opinion at Israel taking places holy to Christianity and Islam.

During the morning the paratroopers stormed into the Old City by way of the Lions' Gate and immediately advanced to the Temple Mount. Over his communications system, Motta Gur made the most emotional and electrifying announcement of the war: "The Temple Mount is in our hands!". And then the Wall.

It seems that until that time, in the battles, the sniping and the death and injury, the paratroopers had not thought of the Wall. That was so – if it was so – until the "Assembly on the Temple Mount", when the paratroopers gathered on the plateau, a few steps away from the Western Wall. Now they all began to rush there.

In *The Lions' Gate* which tells the story of the fighting in Jerusalem, we discovered the following lines:

"Everybody wanted to get to the Wall. The deputy brigade commander was ready to get there first but Motta asked him to wait. He promised company commander Yoram Zamosh that he would be the leader. Some of the soldiers ran from the direction of the eastern steps and Zamosh came after them. They were hugging each other, shouting, confused, patting each other on the back, laughing, shouting and embracing again. Zamosh made sure the flag was in its place, and the group disappeared in the direction of the Wall.

"Motta was leaning against one of the walls feeling as though he had come home, to the goal of all his aspirations. Names out of history jumbled together in his mind. The Temple

Paratroopers raising the Israeli flag above the Wall.

David Ben-Gurion at the Wall, June 1967.

The piazza – empty and full.

The flag of the State of Israel is raised above the Wall for the first time (1967).

Mount, Mount Moriah, Abraham and Isaac, the Temple, the Maccabees, Bar Kokhba, Romans, Greeks. We are on the Temple Mount. The Temple Mount is ours!

"The men below just could not stop looking. They kept staring at every stone of the mosque and kept going around it. The inscriptions, the mosaics, the colored arabesques, the ornamental archways, the stone pulpits, the washing cistern in the middle of the plaza between the two mosques, the crescent roofs and the golden spheres all drew amazed, bewildered eyes.

"The deputy commander's force reached the Western Wall. An Israeli flag is flying above it. Embraces, kisses, Le-Hayyim!

"Paratroopers are pouring down the narrow steps. Their feet take them down but their eyes are lifted on high. Paratroopers are weeping.

"The paratroopers are clinging to the Wall and thinking: 'What am I feeling? Why am I so emotional? Am I emotional?'

"Company commander Zamosh at the head of a group of paratroopers hurries to the Wall. He is carrying an Israeli flag under his arm. 'This is a home-made flag,' he tells everybody, 'which was made in the Jewish Quarter during the War of Independence.' Later, after his story spread and the flag had been photographed and the photographs published in hundreds – if not thousands – of newspapers, magazines and television programs, it was discovered that this flag's past had been far more prosaic. The paratrooper had got it from an old couple, recent immigrants, in the Bet-Ha-Kerem quarter of Jerusalem. They had bought it in honor of their first Independence Day in Israel! But the hands of time cannot be turned back and the myth became the accepted truth."

Forward! To the Wall

Moshe Amirav, a paratrooper, described the first minutes at the Wall:

"It is with a smile that I remember how we looked for the Wall. We ran there, a group of panting soldiers, lost on the plaza of the Temple Mount, searching for a giant stone wall. We did not stop to look at the Mosque of Omar even though this was the first time we had seen it close up. Forward! Forward! Hurriedly, we pushed our way through the Magreb Gate and suddenly we stopped, thunderstruck. There it was before our eyes! Gray and massive, silent and restrained. The Western Wall! I remember that I had such a feeling only once before in my life; it had been when I was a child when my father brought me near to the Holy Ark in the synagogue. I, a little infant, had been afraid that something would come out of the Ark, something big and terrible from another world...

"Slowly, slowly I began to approach the Wall in fear and trembling like a pious cantor going to the lectern to lead the prayers. I approached it as the messenger of my father and my grandfather, of my great-grandfather and of all the generations in all the exiles who had never merited seeing it and so they had sent me to represent them. Somebody recited the festive blessing: 'Blessed are You, O Lord our God, King of the universe who has kept us alive, and maintained us and brought us to this time,' but I could not answer 'Amen.' I put my hand on the stone and the tears that started to flow were not my tears – they were the tears of all Israel, tears of hope and prayer, tears of hasidic tunes, tears of Jewish dances, tears which scorched and burned the heavy gray stone."

Abraham Duvdevani also described the first encounter with the Wall:

"Narrow alleys, filthy passageways, garbage at the entrances of shuttered shops, the stench of dead legionnaires – but we paid no attention. Our eyes were fixed on the golden dome

After the
great battle.

which could be seen from a distance. There, more or less, it had to be! We marched faster to keep up with the beating of our hearts; we were almost running. We met a soldier from one of the forward units and asked him the way and hurried on. We went through a gate and down some steps. I looked to the right and stopped dead. There was the Wall in all its grandeur and glory! I had never seen it before but it was an old friend, impossible to mistake. Then I thought that I should not be there because the Wall belongs in the world of dreams and legends and I am real. Reality and legend, dream and deed, all unite here. I went down and approached the Wall and stretched out my hand towards the huge, hewn stones. But my hand was afraid to touch and of itself returned to me. I closed my eyes, took a small, hesitant step forward, and brought my lips to the Wall. The touch of my lips opened the gates of my emotions and the tears burst forth. A Jewish soldier in the State of Israel is kissing history with his lips.

"Past, present and future all in one kiss. There will be no more destruction and the Wall will never again be deserted. It was taken with young Jewish blood and the worth of that blood is eternity. The body is coupled to the rows of stones, the face is pushed into the spaces between them and the hands try to reach its heart. A soldier near me mumbles in disbelief, 'We are at the Wall, at the Wall...' "

The Commander's Story

The brigade commander, Colonel Motta Gur (later, General and Chief-of-Staff), relived these dramatic events in his book, *The Temple Mount Is In Our Hands:*

"In the streets on the way to the Wall our boys are moving in groups. It is easy to see their deep satisfaction and their enormous tiredness. Now that the first excitement of the conquest and liberation of the Old City has passed, the pain and the sadness emerge, the feeling of man's insignificance faced with war and even success. Opposite us men are coming and going. Some civilians have already managed to get here. They are coming back from the Wall with sparkling eyes, gesturing excitedly as they talk.

"Our soldiers are sitting at the side and watching: it is good for men to be able to be happy. Over them there does not hang the memory of comrades who did not make it.

"Before we went through the Magreb Gate we could already hear the sound of prayer arising from the Wall. We lowered our heads, for the gate is low and you must bend down. A narrow, dark passage. The sound of prayer from the right and below a narrow area crammed with men. To the right and above – the Western Wall. Large, gray, bare, silent stones. Only the small hyssop bushes in the Wall, for all the world like piercing eyes, give it life. We stop for a moment on the winding steps. Khaki dominates the area; the soldiers are praying, swaying back and forth devoutedly. A curtain has been spread on the Wall – for the moment it is a military synagogue. Rabbi Goren is standing there, reciting a prayer out loud, pouring out his soul. He is already hoarse. He has not stopped praying there for two hours. After our emotional encounter on the plateau, he and his aides went straight to the Wall.

"The iron gate leading from the Magreb Gate was still locked, but two paratroopers helped the rabbi and they broke it open. The area is empty of people and clean. Above the Wall an Israeli flag flies, put there by the deputy-commander's unit. The rabbi and his men were the first at the Wall. He sounded the *shofar*, put the Torah Scroll he was carrying in a space between the stones of the Wall, prostrated himself on the ground and kissed it, and recited the 'Who has kept us alive' benediction. The excitement and ecstasy increased. Psalms celebrating the Return to Zion filled the air as dozens of paratroopers came from all directions.

The paratroopers
and the Wall.

When the Deputy Chief-of-Staff and the commander of the central command arrived, Rabbi Goren started to conduct the first prayer service at the liberated Wall...

" 'Ha-Tikvah' – the national anthem, a hymn of strength but mingled with sadness, united everybody. The soldiers sprang to attention, the officers saluted.

"The anthem had barely finished when the Chief Chaplain said the memorial *Kaddish* prayer "in memory of those who have fallen... for the liberation of holy Jerusalem". Emotion takes control; the throat is choked.

"Rabbi Goren, Major-General Narkiss and the Deputy Chief-of-Staff, Major-General Bar--Lev embraced each other publicly. Narkiss just said, 'This is extraordinary, indescribable,' and Rabbi Goren once again recited the *Kaddish* 'in memory of those who fell for the liberation of Jerusalem, the Temple Mount and the Western Wall'... The sounds of weeping joined with the words of the prayer... and, towards its end, overcame them. The unity of the dead and the living hovered over the Wall and the worshippers there."

"This year in Rebuilt Jerusalem!"

"At 12:11 the Afternoon Service began. Rabbi Shtiglitz, a paratrooper, began to recite the *Tahanun*, a prayer of supplication said on non-festive days and Rabbi Goren interrupted him: 'Today *Hallel*, [a joyous prayer of thanksgiving said on festivals], must be recited!' 'I cannot, Rabbi,' answered Shtiglitz, 'I have been recovering the corpses and I cannot say *Hallel*; I will say *Tahanun*.' So the two rabbis prayed, *Hallel* and *Tahanun*. I drew near to the praying soldiers. They noticed me and cleared a path for me. I thanked them and stayed at the back.

"Among this huge crowd I wanted to experience a private moment. I did not listen to the prayers; I was aware of them and that was enough. I stared at the stones and contemplated the praying paratroopers, some wearing helmets and others skull-caps. I surveyed the buildings closing us in on three sides and giving such an air of intimacy to the prayer area.

"I remembered our family visits to the Wall, twenty-five years earlier, walking through the narrow alleys and the markets. I cannot remember details; I was only a child then. But I do remember the impression the worshippers at the Wall made on me, or am I remembering a picture from a later, older date? White-bearded Jews dressed in caftans and wearing *shtreimels*, the round fur hat they brouhgt with them from Eastern Europe]. For me, they and the Wall formed one unit.

"I returned to reality. Rabbi Goren, in battle-dress, is reciting a prayer and behind him the soldiers are praying.

"In the right-hand corner, slightly apart from the crowd, a man is standing. No, not standing! He is as though attached to the stones, a part of the Wall. He is wearing a long, brown caftan and a black hat from under which long hair peeps out. Nothing moves. Not his head or his hair. Not his body or his feet. His arms are bent and the palms of his hands spread flat on the surface of the stones. I 'locked' onto him like radar; I just could not take my eyes off him. I stuck to him from afar just as he was stuck to the Wall. Through his seemingly paralyzed body, I could feel the Jewish heart beating from within the stone. So we stood glued together for a few moments – him, me, and the Wall.

"I turned around and went back to the Temple Mount plaza."

A moment of relaxation after the great battle.

The President Must Come to the Wall

In the wake of the soldiers, hundreds and thousands started streaming to the Wall. The fighting had not yet stopped, but Jerusalem and the whole country was drawn to the ancient stone wall as though to a lodestone. A mighty pilgrimage started. Nothing could stop it; not the sniping that was still going on, not the barbed wire, not the road-blocks. Statesmen and politicians of the present and the past (led by David Ben-Gurion), rabbis, army officers, and other public figures with, perhaps, the right connections...

One of the few that did not get to the Wall in the early hours was Zalman Shazar, the President of the State of Israel. In his book, *Jerusalem is One*, Uzi Narkiss decribes how the President's visit was arranged:

"The telephone rang and on the wire was the President's military aide, Colonel Arie Raz. 'Listen, Uzi, the President wants to visit the Wall!'

'That does not come into the question,' I answered, 'there are still snipers about and the mopping up operation is not yet completed!' He refused to listen and with, 'This is not a discussion for the telephone, I am on my way,' he hung up. Before I could get out of my chair, he was in the doorway. 'The President insists. I cannot convince him. You try...' We travelled to the President's house. He shook my hand, congratulated me on the victory and got straight down to business: 'Everybody has been to the Wall. It's inconceivable that only the President hasn't!'

'But, sir, they are still shooting there! How can we endanger the life of the President of Israel?'

"No matter, I'll wear a helmet."

"But, sir, not all the security arrangements in the world can stop a bullet!"

He drew himself up, his face became stern, his eyebrows arched and looked me straight into the eyes:

'Young man! Pay attention! The President of Israel must go to the Wall! I am not talking about Zalman Shazar. He is already an old man; what he could do in life, he's already done. It is not important whether he lives or dies. But the President of the State of Israel must go to the Wall. It's in your hands! I ask you to consider what security arrangements can be made for the President of Israel and then give me your estimate of the risk involved. If it is very serious, I will not go, "lest the daughters of the Philistines rejoice." But if the risk is not very great, the President will go up to the Wall.'

I was struck dumb.

'Your Excellency, when will you be ready to go?'

'Immediately'. And he did."

The Paratroopers are Happy and Sad.

Major-General Uzi Narkiss first arrived at the Wall in the morning. A few hours later he returned with the Chief-of-Staff, General Yitzhak Rabin and the Minister of Defence, Moshe Dayan. The picture of the three of them entering the Old City through the Lions' Gate has become the "frontispiece" of the Six-Day War in Jerusalem.

The following is an extract from Uzi Narkiss' diary, written that day:

14:00. We arrived at the Western Wall. The crowd now is larger than this morning. Cheering soldiers clear a place for the Minister of Defence and his entourage and we all get to the Wall. Dayan takes a piece of paper from his pocket and pushes it in a space between two

The Chief-of-Staff, General Rabin, the Minister of Defence, Moshe Dayan and the commanding officer of the Central Command, Uzi Narkiss (partly hidden) at the Wall while the Jordanian road-sign was still in place.

stones. Kobby Sharett asks him what was written on it and Dayan replies, "May there be peace on Israel."

He has a statement ready and reads it facing dozens of cameras and batteries of microphones: "We have returned to our most holy place, never again to leave it. To its Arab neighbors the State of Israel extends its hand in peace, and assures all other religions that it will maintain full freedom and honor all their religious rights. We have not come to conquer others' holy places or to curtail their religious rights but to guarantee the unity of the city and live in it with the others in harmony."

The paratroopers are still there, happy and sad, as Gad Meir, one of them, described it: "A mist of tears and a mist of thoughts together overcome you. Some stand opposite the Wall like mutes, as though they are afraid to draw close. Everybody is bewildered by the occasion. The sound of the *shofar* wakes us up for a moment but quickly the mixture takes over again, the mixture of history and reality, joy and sorrow."

Abraham Schechter, Gad's comrade-in-arms, adds:

"When I used to go up to Mount Zion to look at the Old City from afar, there were moments when I used to close my eyes and imagine it as a castle standing on a high hill with a sparkling halo hovering above it. A sort of fantastic background to the city... When I saw the Wall in front of me, after all the stories about it that I had heard, I was in shock. I had thought that the Wall too would have a halo on it which would illuminate the whole city. I was in shock and kept trying to decide whether I was seeing things or dreaming them. The company commander, who was standing next to me, touched me and asked, 'Are you wounded?' I was leaning sideways and just could not move. And then, when I woke up, I saw the Wall. I started to pray, but the words which I have said every day of my life were different. I felt as though I was adding a plea that we should never give this place back. It is so dear to us and it cost so much blood after so many long years of waiting. I also made an addition to the 'Silent Prayer' and begged God that this place should be ours forever... I got the feeling that Somebody was listening, that He was pleased with the prayer and that He had granted my plea. Thoughts were running through my mind with supreme intensity and I felt as though I was floating on air. When I first heard the *shofar* I became dizzy and my body burned. People told me later that I wept like a baby. I found some paper and I wrote home that now I envy no man – for I was in the unit that broke into the Old City and reached the Western Wall."

The Soldiers are Weeping

The Wall did not only draw to it the soldiers, the public figures and the rabbis. It drew everybody! Among those who squeezed and pushed themselves into the packed prayer area, were representatives of the press from Israel and abroad; writers and poets many of whom set down their impressions of those early hours for posterity. Among them was Yehuda Ha-Ezrahi:

"I ran after a group of soldiers to the southwest corner of the compound (The Temple Mount), towards a little green gate, the Magreb Gate. The gate was wide open and soldiers were coming and going through it to the noise of their heavy boots and their heavy tired breathing. From it leads a narrow alley with a sharp right turn to narrow steep steps – to the Western Wall.

"In this suddenness, I at first saw only the stones. It was a suddenness long awaited for interminable hours mingled with fire and explosions but sudden nonetheless. I saw the sacred stones and, wondrously, it was as though I had already been there only the other day. They are so familiar. No, not the other day. But generations ago! They are so old; breathing in the touches and the kisses and the weeping and the dirges and the supplications and the prayers of generation after generation. And maybe, even before then, outside of time, when, motionless, my mother stood by them, her frozen posture like a prayer to God, I first saw them and I had already known them for generations. 'The stones,' my mother said then. Here they are, now, in front of me, in their courses. Suddenly, I remember their smoothness, every crack, every bit of roughness, every sign of the stonemason's hand, every corrosion of the rain and the wind, every indentation where the strange bushes laid down their roots, every flicker of light and shadow. But first, I saw only the stones.

"They towered above me, course on course, and I stand by them. Then my gaze started searching for their secret places, looking for redemption. Slowly it went up, searching from below, from the course my hands were touching, to the course above it; from the deep dimness like a waterless river pressing its dry banks, to the courses above it, higher and higher. So close! The stones of themselves lead my eyes from the depths upwards, until they come to the living roof, to the patch of blue sky.

"Soldiers are standing there. Standing in their sweat-stained, dusty camouflage outfits, dirty with the smoke of shooting and the blood of wounds – maybe their own, maybe their friends' who were hit or killed while fighting at their side. They are wearing steel helmets and

Prayer in a temporary field synagogue.

they are laden with rifles, machine-guns, ammunition, mines, and frozen faces. Look! One of them stretches out his black hand, hesitantly, to the old stones and touches them lightly. Another pushes the palms of his hands against the stones, then his body and his face into the courses. Another looks up, to on high. And I see, astonished, tears flash in their eyes. Perhaps it is the Divine Presence, in the form of a white dove which cries human tears, that hovers above them in the little patch of blue sky. Hardened, frozen-faced soldiers are standing here – and they are weeping.

My mother is standing here. She is wearing a large straw hat with a wide brim, shadowing her forehead. 'Mother,' I called to her.

"Her hand touched and did not touch these stones, known so well, so ancient, that rise up above us."

"I Am Touching the Stones of the Wall"

The liberation of the Old City, and particularly the scene at the Wall, on the third day of the Six-Day War, did not only excite and affect those who had been present and those who had managed to make their way to the Wall. The same evening, the radio announced the news to every house in the country and to every fighting unit. "The Transistor Generation", which had been so censured before the war, used that small, magical instrument to hear the news. There can be no doubt that of all the stirring broadcasts in the war – and there were indeed many – none had the effect of that of Raphael Amir of the Israel Broadcasting Services:

Raphael Amir: "It's 10:20 on June 7th. At this moment we are going through the Lions' Gate in a jeep with the Deputy Chief-of-Staff and the commander of the Central Command. I am now in the shadow cast by the gate. Now we are in the sun again, in the street. We are inside the Old City. The soldiers are up against the walls." (Sounds of shooting. Soldiers shouting, "To the Wall! To the Wall!")

Uzi Narkiss: "Regiment Commander! Come on Motta, say something. What do you feel?" (Voices of soldiers cheering and the sound of the *shofar*.)

Motta Gur: "It's hard to express what we're feeling in words. We saw the Old City to our right when we were on the crest of Augusta Victoria. We enjoyed the view and now we are hoarse from so much shouting and the excitement of coming in at the head of all this convoy. Our half-track broke open the gate and went over a motorbike. It went through the Jordanian camp and we were the first to get up to the Temple Mount, in great excitement. Moishele, who's been my deputy for many years, took some men and ran to raise the flag above the Western Wall. Now, the whole Old City is in our hands and we are very happy." (Sounds of a *shofar*; soldiers singing "Jerusalem of Gold".)

Uzi Narkiss: "Say, where's the Wall? How should we go?"

Raphael Amir: "At this moment, at this very moment, I am going down the steps to the Wall. I'm not religious and never have been, but this is the Wall and I am touching the stones of the Western Wall!"

(Rabbi Goren recites the "Who has kept us alive. . ." benediction and another one, "Who comforts Zion and rebuilds Jerusalem". The national anthem, "Ha-Tikvah", is sung spontaneously.)

"The Heart of the Matter"

What did the listeners, wherever they were, feel? Joseph Hermoni, of Kibbutz Ayyelet Ha-Shahar, describes how he heard the news in *Si'ah Lohamim* ("Fighters' Talk") written after the war:

"Wednesday, 28th of Iyyar, the third of the six days. We were sitting wherever it was, glued to a tiny transistor radio. The generation of the transistor.

"This little instrument, with its batteries breathing their last, succeeded in letting us hear the beat of the wings of history.

"Just so!

"Those were the ten seconds when we accompanied the voice-choked reporter of the Israel Broadcasting Service on his way to the Wall.

"I do not know that broadcaster's name, but he deserves the thanks of all of us because he succeeded in suddenly making clear how stupid is the devious controversy over 'Who is a Jew?'.

"He succeeded because he stood before us naked, vulnerable, after he had lost all his armour of professionalism. He did not talk with the newspaperman's objectivity, he wasn't articulate, he couldn't even control the recording machine he was carrying. That's why we all felt how history was beating its wings. . ."

Others' hearts ached because at such a time they were far away from what was happening. That is how Major-General Ezer Weizman, Chief of Operations in the GHQ, felt. On June 7 he had joined the forces which were meant to take Sharm el-Sheikh and in his memoirs,

The narrow prayer enclosure packed with soldiers. It was soon to be extended beyond recognition.

Yours are the Heavens; Yours is the Earth, he writes: "We started to get organized there. I radioed: 'Tell Motti (Hod) that he should tell Dayan that everything is under control and the straits are in our hands, open to Israeli shipping.' They answered: 'We cannot tell Dayan, he is at the Wall.' I nearly fell over. Somebody was with me and I said to him, 'My lousy luck! For years I've been dreaming of it! And look. At this historic moment when everybody's at the Wall, where am I? Stuck in the most faraway place of the war!' "

In Sinai, in the course of being conquered, the news of the Wall spread like wildfire. After the war, Yehoshua Bar-Dayan published a book of his experiences in the tank corps and among descriptions of battles the following piece is to be found:

". . . my friend Benjamin has gone mad, he is screaming with all his strength: 'The Old City of Jerusalem – Jerusalem of Gold!' It is hard to describe how we look. Dirty four-day old stubble, dirty from the dust, from the soot of the shells, from the torn-up tarmac of the roads. But morale is very high. About seven in the evening we are gathered around our only transistor radio to listen to the news. Our unit is parked together with a number of artillery pieces and half-tracks. The transistor's batteries are weak and reception is poor. Seven pairs of ears are glued to the transistor. A cold evening in the desert. We are receiving a broadcast about the conquest of the Old City. We listen hard. The Chief-of-Staff is speaking and also Rabbi Goren. The broadcaster, Raphael Amir, is describing how he is going down behind the soldiers to the Western Wall. His voice is excited; choked with tears. We, hundreds of kilometres beyond the border, are no less excited. On the radio, we hear the *shofar*. Staff sergeant Harel, a religious fellow who prays every morning at dawn, cannot hold back his tears. After they said the *Kaddish* prayer at the Wall, we heard the 'Ha-Tikvah'. There, at sunset in a yellow waste surrounded by purple ridges, we stood to attention spontaneously and joined the singing coming from the radio. Seven men in seven hoarse, tired voices sang. Before we finished the last stanza, the mobile artillery crew realized what had happened and they joined in and before they finished the half-track's crew also joined in. The desert echoed with the strains of 'Ha-Tikvah' from the truck to the half-track and from the half-track to the tank. . ."

So it was, just as Jonathan said in the opening to this chapter. The scene at the Wall, on Wednesday, Iyyar 28th, 5727, June 7, 1967, the third day of the Six-Day War, was "the heart of the matter". In every place, near or far, for soldiers as for children, for new immigrants as for old-timers, the "heart of the matter" touched every heart.

CHAPTER VIII

PLANNING THE PIAZZA AT THE WESTERN WALL

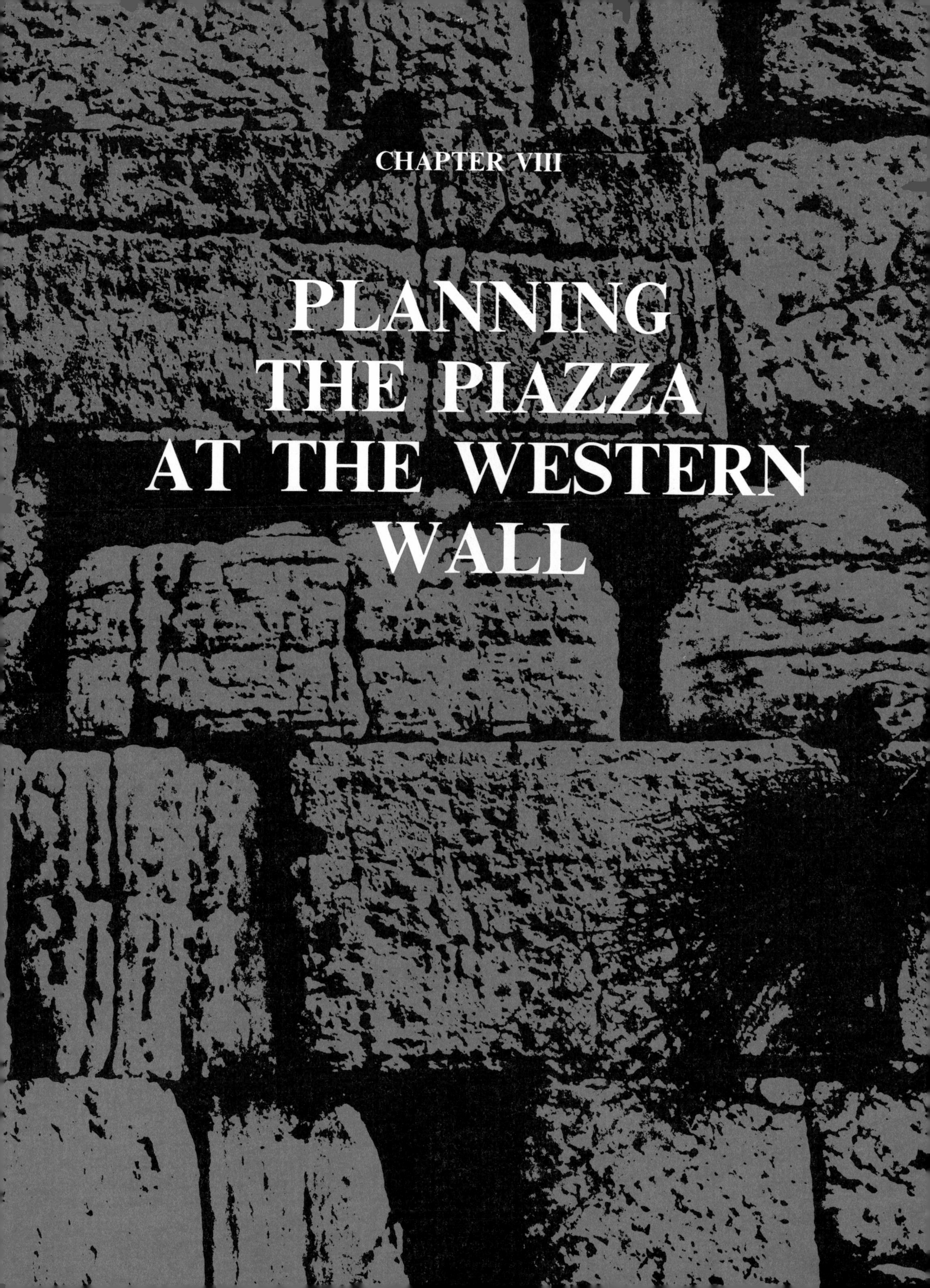

The First Design

The area at the Western Wall was first designed as a prayer area under the influence of Sinaan, the court architect of the Ottoman sultan, Suleiman the Magnificent, in the first half of the sixteenth century. As the king-pin of his Eretz Israel policy, the Sultan had decided to populate the country, and particularly the major cities, with minorities in order to blunt the edge of the local Arabs' opposition to Ottoman rule (For further information, see Chapter I, From the Temple to the Western Wall).

Within the framework of this policy, Jewish immigration in Eretz Israel was greatly encouraged. This was particularly true regarding the Jews who had been exiled from Spain and Portugal in the wake of the inquisition; Turkey was interested in absorbing them in its empire and in resettling a portion of them in Eretz Israel. In order to encourage Jews to immigrate to the country and to Jerusalem, the Sultan granted the Jews that section of the Wall which had become holy to them and at which they had become accustomed to pray from the time of Mameluke rule, and he instructed the court architect, Sinaan, to design the place as a prayer area. An area of twenty two metres along the length of the Wall in the heart of the Magreb Quarter was set for the purpose and it was designed with simplicity and without any ostentation. The area was paved with stone slabs and when completed it was twenty metres long and slightly more than three metres wide. Some scholars believe that in Suleiman's time, the area was several metres wider and that it was reduced to three metres only two hundred years ago. Stone walls were built at the extremities of the area and sealed it off on the south, west and north. The eastern side was, of course, the section of the original Western Wall from the Second Temple period. The walls around the area separated it off from the houses of the Magreb Quarter; the entrance was from the north directly from a narrow alley which crossed the Magreb Quarter. The first sight the visitor had of the Wall was when he entered the narrow closed prayer area. He was then suddenly faced with the massive stones of the Second Temple period, and, on them, the smaller masonry of early Islamic times. In order to magnify the impression on the visitor and increase the sanctity, the pavement level was lowered so that five courses of Herodian stone were visible. Because of the relationship between the size of the Wall and that of the prayer area, the worshipper was forced to raise his eyes and stretch his neck if he wanted to see the upper courses. The Wall dominated the prayer area entirely. It was nine metres high – five of Herodian masonry and four of Arab – whereas the other walls around the area were only three metres high. The size of the massive Herodian stonework heightened the impression when it was compared to the small stones of which the other walls were constructed. The result was that the Wall drew all the worshipper's attention – a state of afairs that had surely been the objective of the designers.

The sight of Jews in their distinctive dress, *Sephardim* and *Ashkenazim*, bowed low over the stones of the Wall, caressing them, kissing them, and pouring out their prayers and supplications before their Maker – all in a small, narrow area with the Wall towering above it – was one of the most impressive and touching scenes in Ottoman Jerusalem. And indeed, accounts of both Jews and non-Jews from those days have preserved the special atmosphere of that small square and that huge Wall.

The piazza at the Wall soon after the Six-Day War and the demolition of the Magreb Quarter.

Changes in the Wake of the Six-Day War

The excitement and emotions which gripped the Israeli soldiers who conquered the Temple Mount and were the first to go down from there to the Wall have already become part of the folk-history that surrounds the Wall. Already before the shooting had stopped and the storm of battle had died down, the national and military leadership was unable to hold itself in check and came to visit the place that had stood desolate for nineteen long years. Those who had known the Wall before 1948 were particularly emotional. The prime minister, Levi Eshkol, gave instructions to quickly prepare an access road from Mt. Zion to the Dung Gate. This road was laid outside the walls of the Old City, to enable the masses of Israelis to flow to the Western Wall. This was before the Old City, with its alleyways and hidden treasures, was opened to visitors. Already at this stage, it was clear that huge numbers of people would visit the Wall and that it would be necessary to create an area capable of accommodating them. It was also clear that in the future the area around the Wall would become a major national and religious shrine and would be a place of constant pilgrimage. The prayer area which had existed for more than four centuries would obviously be unable to cope with the new situation and the order was given to demolish the half-ruined hovels of the Magreb Quarter and to relocate the few occupants who still lived there. It should be remembered that many of the occupants had left the quarter long before the Temple Mount was liberated, as soon as it was known that the Israeli soldiers had cut off the city from the north. These Magreb Quarter occupants realized that the Wall to which Jews had been denied access for so many years, would become a national attraction and they preferred to leave their houses and find other accommodation. The buildings of the Magreb Quarter were among the poorest and the most derelict in the Old City; even the two or three important buildings could not in any way be compared to the beautiful houses in Hagai St. and the alleys leading from it towards the Temple Mount.

Who gave the order to demolish the Magreb Quarter and create the great piazza at the Wall? There is no unequivocal answer to this question. The generally accepted account of what happened is that Teddy Kollek, the mayor of Jerusalem, got in touch with several Jerusalem construction companies and persuaded them to make heavy earth moving equipment available and undertake the task as a donation to the city. He asked them to work around the clock and gave orders that they should not interrupt the work on any account, even if the Prime Minister or the Minister of Defence ordered them to. "Tell the workers," he said, "that they should stop the work only on the direct order of Teddy Kollek and I will make sure that I am unavailable until the job is finished!" And so it was.

Within a week the area at the Wall had been cleared: from the *Mahkameh* building in the north to the ramp leading to the Magreb Gate in the south and from the Wall in the east to the edge of the Jewish Quarter in the west. The result was an enormous square measuring sixty metres from north to south and slightly more from east to west. This large area made the wall itself appear smaller since it could now be seen from afar and the element of surprise which existed previously now no longer existed. In order to minimize this negative effect, it was decided to lower the pavement level and thus increase the height of the Wall, but in order not to prematurely destroy any archaeological remains that might be under the ground, the level was only lowered by the height of two courses of stones. This action did not really solve the problem which remains one of the most important considerations in planning the area. In the first stage, the part of the piazza adjacent to the Wall was paved and prepared as a prayer area for all the sixty metres of the revealed Wall.

Those responsible for this stage of the work, the architect Joseph Scheinberger and the Public Works Department, decided to elevate the section to the west of the prayer area to create some contrast and distinction between it and the general piazza which is visited by many tourists and sightseers who do not come to pray. The *Sephardi* chief rabbi, Rabbi Yitzhak Nissim, insisted that the piazza be all on one level and a compromise was reached according to which the planners reduced the elevation of the outer section by twenty centimeters. In the course of time the upper level was also paved and a drainage system was installed. Arrangements were made for orderly entrance to the square and norms for behavior in it were fixed.

Notwithstanding all that was done, it was clear to everybody concerned that the arrangement was temporary and that a comprehensive design project would have to be undertaken based on research into all the variegated aspects of the problem: the sanctity of the site as a holy place and prayer area; the archaeological considerations and arrangements for visitors who do not come to pray, such as people celebrating some happy event and foreign pilgrims and tourists who visit the Holy City. It must be remembered that the present piazza is the result of hurried demolition of the Magreb Quarter in order to make the minimal arrangements needed for the huge numbers of visitors who come to the Wall. Those arrangements were temporary, and it is only proper that a full and comprehensive design program be undertaken for this most important site.

Planning Involves Emotions – The Wall till the Temple Will Be Rebuilt

The Ottoman design of the prayer area at the Wall which existed until 1948 was a successful design in that it created a small prayer area for a small community. Its success was a direct result of its small size; it confined a section of the Wall with its massive stones within a tiny enclosed area, the result being an atmosphere of isolated intimacy in which the Wall dominated the worshipper without any distractions. With the demolition of the Magreb Quarter, all this disappeared. The *Mahkameh* building with its supporting vaults is revealed to the north and continuing westward stands a complex of buildings which creates a line dividing the piazza off from the Old City. To the east rises a rock outcropping on which living houses, some old and others relatively new, are built. These houses are on the edge of the old Jewish Quarter where it touched the Magreb Quarter, which, when it existed, concealed the rock outcropping. The view to the south is the wall of the Old City and the Dung Gate. Today's visitor to the Western Wall piazza is surrounded by a number of interesting visual elements – the houses on the rock outcropping on the the one hand and the *Mahkameh* building on the other and Suleiman the Magnificent's wall with its turrets to the south. Unless there is human activity at the Western Wall, it is just a high wall which is built of big stones in its lower section. At a little distance from the Wall it is possible to see the golden cupola of the Dome of the Rock and other buildings and trees on the Temple Mount. This view also distracts attention from the Wall.

There are two essential points which must be considered in any proposal for designing the piazza at the Wall and both of them are basically emotional. This is the source of the many planning difficulties because it is not always possible to translate emotion into stone. It is also exceedingly difficult to find a common denominator for the wide range of emotions in a heterogeneous community and express it in architectural design.

Firstly, it must be remembered that the Western Wall, like the other walls of the Temple Mount, is a buttress wall of the Temple Mount from the Second Temple period. Only the fact

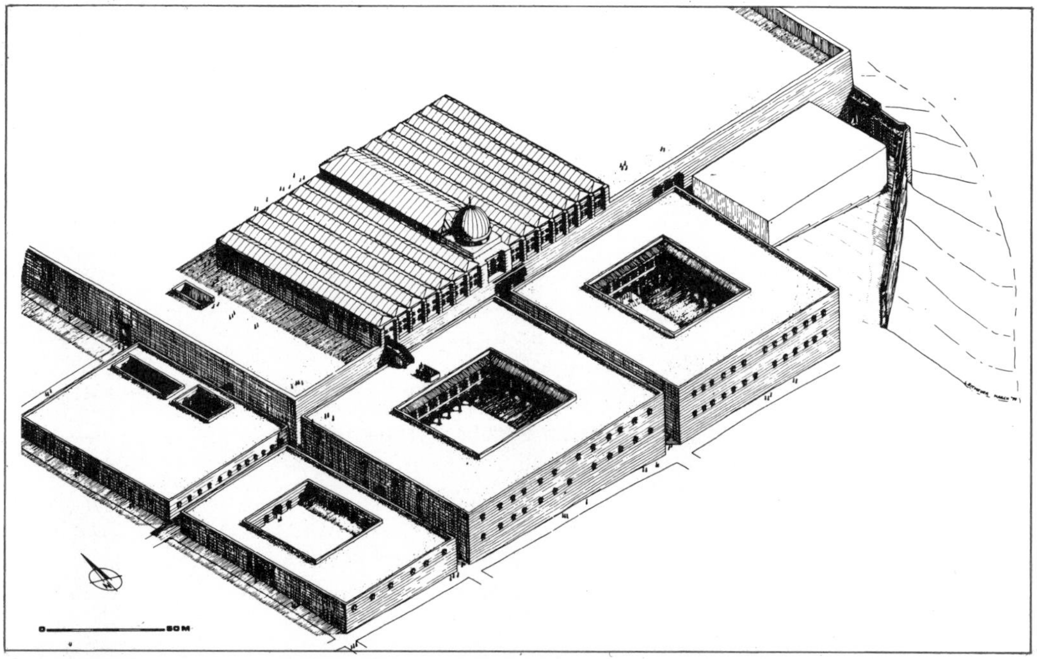

The early Moslem plan for the Temple Mount and its environs. Notwithstanding its holiness in Moslem eyes, the dense building would indicate that huge throngs did not visit it as they did in Second Temple times.

that they were denied access to the Temple Mount itself and cut-off from the site of the Temple, caused the Jews to see a site outside the Temple Mount as a sacred spot. This was after Islam had reconstructed the walls around the Mount and erected its shrines, the Dome of the Rock and Al Akza, on it. In the early years after the destruction of the Temple, it was the southern and the eastern walls which were considered holy and it is only during the last thousand years that the focus shifted to the Western Wall because of political and practical exingencies.

However, when a Jew prays, "May the Temple be rebuilt speedily in our days," he is praying for the rebuilding of the Temple *on* the Temple Mount and, in the Jewish tradition, that event, when it happens, will herald a new world with the coming of the Messiah. These utopian and messianic hopes are focused on the Temple and not on the Western Wall or any other secondary structure in the area. Prayer at the Wall became important as a result of a compromise – because the Temple is not rebuilt – but cannot, in any way, serve to transfer the spotlight from the center to the periphery. No matter how holy its traditions have become, the Wall cannot be a substitute for the Temple and should not contribute to the demise of the Jewish people's messianic aspirations. It is possible that, without intent, that is what the Wall has become for many but such a status is not within Jewish tradition. Any design for the Wall area must, therefore, realize that the Wall does not represent the achievement of Judaism's ultimate hopes; that will be in the rebuilding of the Temple however theoretical that may be and however delayed it may be till the arrival of the Messiah. In effect, the Wall must symbolize destruction and imperfection; it must represent a reality which is not ultimate but only a stage on the way to better times.

Nothing is more difficult than to give these ideas architectural expression. As far as this is concerned, it would have been preferable had the miserable pre-1967 situation continued to exist and the Wall remained confined in the Magreb Quarter slum, symbolic of the Jewish people's status regarding the Temple and the Temple Mount. It is easier to dream of a great past and a glorious future standing near a piteous symbol than it is in a splendid, complete architectural monument which can only divert one's thoughts from the hopes for the future and create the illusion that it has already arrived. However, leaving things as they were is a very un-Jewish solution; if the present can be improved, then it must. But with the proviso that man realizes that improvement is not completion and that perfection can only come with the Messiah and the rebuilding of the Temple. This is the main problem in designing the piazza at the Western Wall – a way must be found to preserve the element of destruction while making the site as splendid as we can.

The opinion of this author is that the solution already exists at the Wall in the form of the road which ran along the foot of the Wall in Second Temple times. The surface of this road, which lies some eight metres below the present surface, is strewn with pieces of masonry from the Wall which were thrown down in the destruction of the year 70 C.E. This road should serve as the prayer area, and the Temple masonry should stay where it is and how it is. This will drive home the whole message of the Wall in the best possible manner.

The second basic problem in planning the piazza at the Wall is its immediate surroundings. This problem is primarily one of design; the emotional content is less than in the first. As has

The buildings on the rock outcropping to the west of the Wall.

been pointed out above, the weakest of the four sides of the piazza is the Wall itself since that is a smooth stone wall and must compete with the variegated visual elements contained in the other three sides. How, then, can the project be designed so that the other sides do not divert the visitor's attention away from the Wall which, after all, should be the main focus? Will not "hanging" houses built on the rock outcropping prove to be a stronger visual attraction than the Wall itself? This problem must be taken into consideration and the design must be such that nothing competes with the main attraction, the Wall. An easy solution would be to insist that all building around the piazza be dull and drab; but that is a proposal that can hardly be made. It is possible, however, to achieve the desired effect by simple, monotonous building. If the buildings to be erected on the rock outcropping are composed of simple lines which repeat themselves, they will not compete with the Wall for the visitor's attention. Buildings with individual, complicated lines will have the opposite effect.

Should the Design be Integrated into the Style of the Old City?

At first glance, it might appear proper to design the area at the Wall so that it fits into the general style of the Old City. However, this view should not be taken as axiomatic and the question should be considered at a basic level. The Temple Mount itself is not an integral part of the Old City and even the David's Tower complex at the Jaffa Gate and other public buildings do not fit the general style of the Old City. The basic question is: Should the piazza which is being built today be an archaeological reconstruction or should it have a character of its own? There is no unequivocal answer to this question. It is quite conceivable to have a piazza, the periphery of which blends into the surrounding city but it is equally conceivable that the piazza stands out as the product of a new generation. While one may regret the disappearance of the Ottoman buildings that were cleared to make way for the piazza, there is surely no point in doing any new building in the Ottoman style using Ottoman techniques. The buildings that were cleared were unimportant to the architectural annals of Jerusalem and technically they were in a sorry state. They represented their generation – and that not very well. Even the remaining houses on the outcropping are unimportant. Although some date from the Middle Ages, extensive reconstruction has been done to them in the twentieth century. One of them has a concrete roof supported by iron railway tracks! The balconies of the buildings are also constructed of railway tracks which proves conclusively that they do not predate our century. The presence of these buildings in the area is purely accidental; a decision to remove them would be just as legitmate as one to leave them there.

Once the order to demolish the Magreb Quarter was given, a new era in Jerusalem's architecture was announced. The designers of the piazza at the Wall can decide as they see fit. They can merge the piazza into the adjacent Jewish Quarter or they can ignore it. The style of the surroundings is not strong enough or authentic enough to dictate the style of the piazza. Retaining the buildings on the edge of the piazza and integrating them into its design can be seen as the creation of a link with the Ottoman past. On the other hand, it is possible to see the Jewish Quarter as just another stage in Jerusalem's architectural history.

For examination of Jerusalem's public buildings reveals that their design always differed from that of the private buildings around them. This is true of the Temple Mount, The Church of the Holy Sepulcher and the fortress at the Jaffa Gate, among others. These buildings stand distinct in their surroundings as though they had expropriated sections of the city. There is no reason why this should not be the case with regards to the piazza at the Western Wall. This is not stated as an absolute but as a legitimate alternative. The architectural history of Jerusalem is multi-hued which is, in fact, one of the distinctive attributes of the city. The Church of the Holy Sepulchre is a monumental building with huge cupolas in the heart of an area densely packed with simple dwelling houses; the same is true of the German Church of the Redeemer, the adjacent Monastery of Alexander which belongs to Pravoslavian Church, the Dormition Church on Mt. Zion,the synagogues of the Jewish Quarter – the Hurvah and Tiferet Israel – which were destroyed in the War of Independence, and, above all, of the Temple Mount and the Dome of the Rock. All these were very different to their settings but contributed to the general architectural atmosphere of their city. Each of the buildings had its own plan and style and each testifies to its own historical period. The piazza at the Wall can, therefore, legitimately express its period, the twentieth century – or, more exactly, the period after the Six-Day War. Without that war the piazza could never have had the dimensions it now has and that fact must also find expression in its design.

The plan proposed by Louis Kahn in 1967 for the reconstruction of the Hurvah synagogue and the piazza at the Wall.

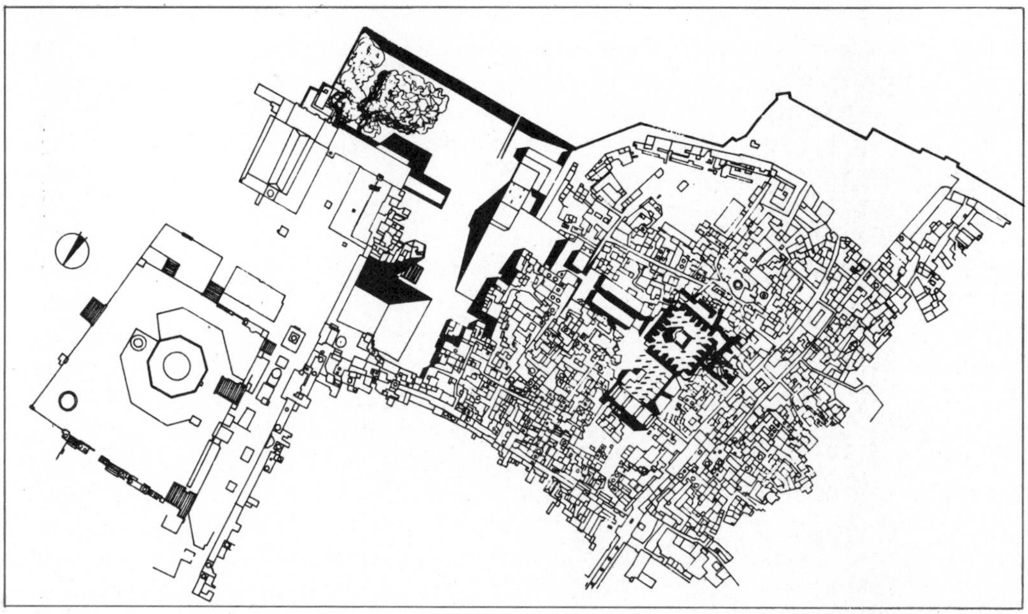

The conceptual plan of Isamu Noguchi. In the center is the black basalt stone symbolizing the Holocaust.

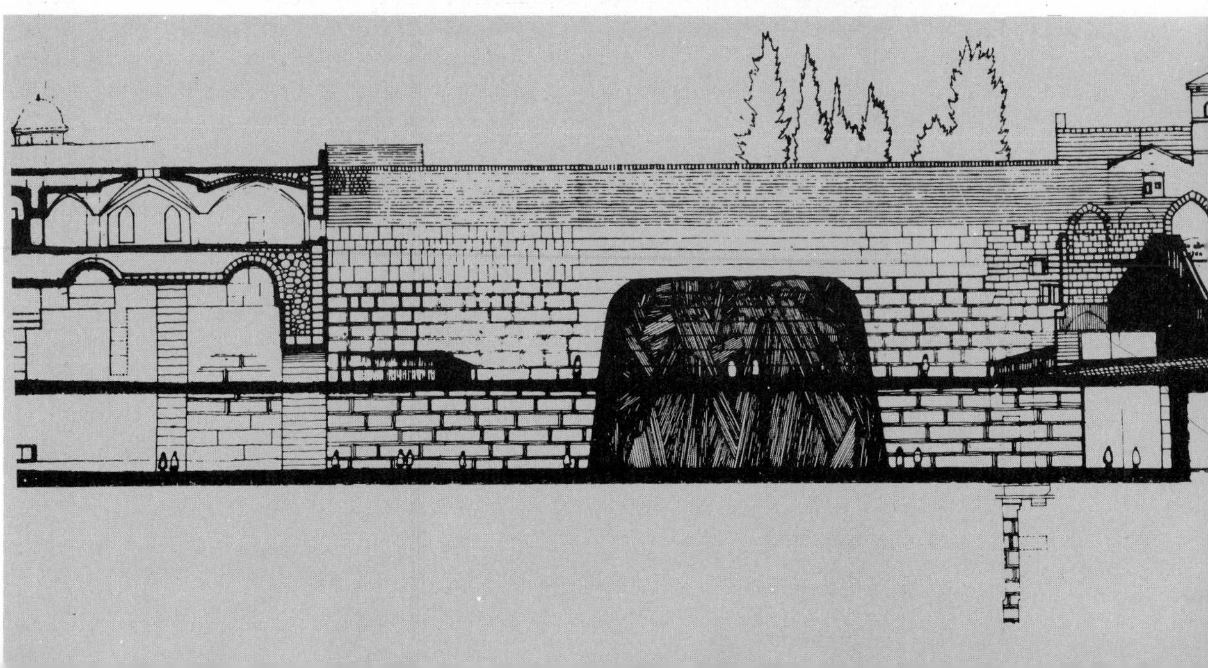

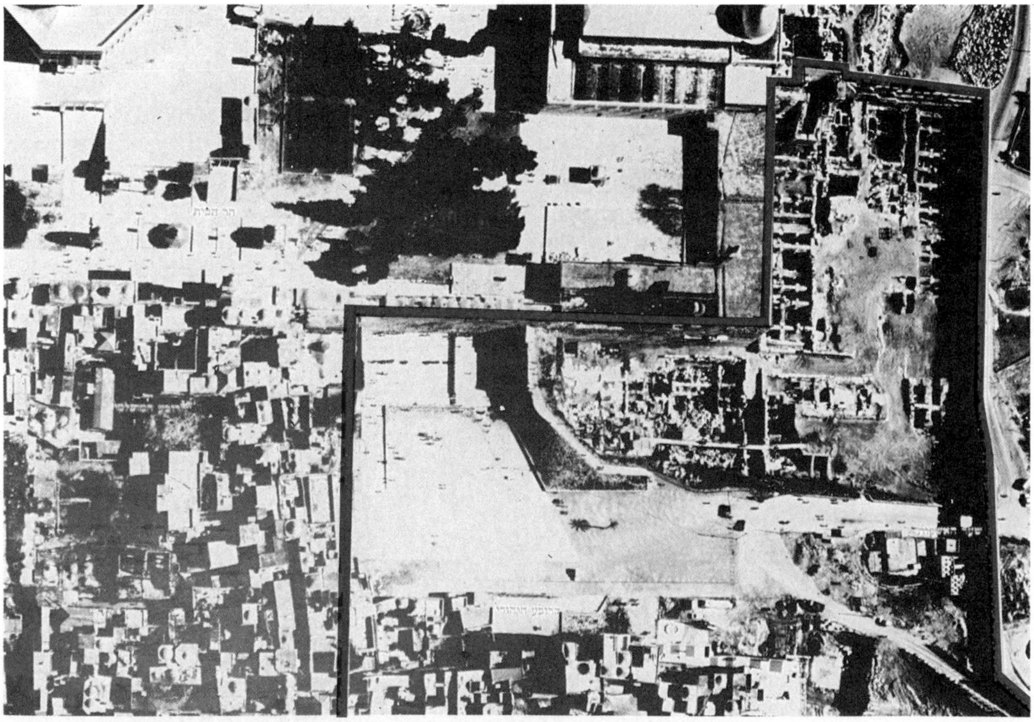

Aerial photographs of the piazza and the archaeological site; the heavy lines indicate the limits of the Safdie proposal.

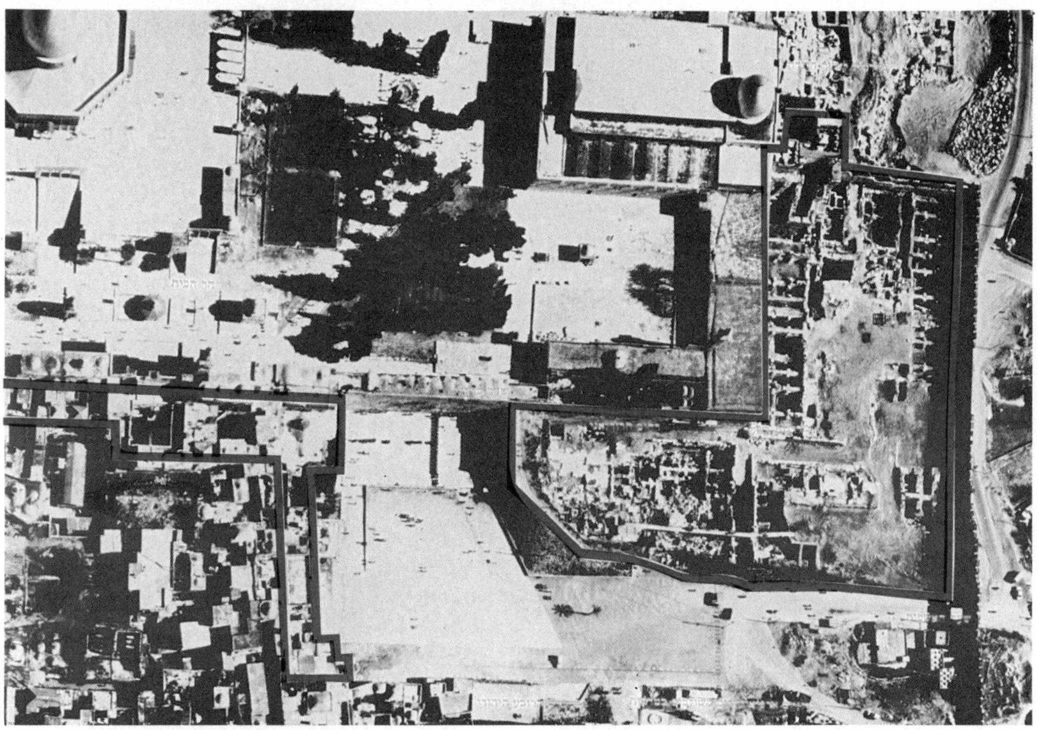

Plans for the Piazza at the Wall

Immediately after the Six-Day War, representatives of the Minisitry of Religions approached the Japanese architect-sculptor, Isamu Noguchi, who had designed the sculpture-garden at the Israel Museum, and asked him to submit a design for the Western Wall area. Noguchi was not acquainted with the history of the Wall; what he knew of Israel's history was mainly in the modern period and he was deeply impressed by Israel's renewal under the shadow of the Holocaust in Europe. He decided, therefore, to design the upper area of the piazza, at its 1948 level, for prayer. In the center would stand a block of basalt which would be suitably inscribed and would symbolize the Holocaust, which, notwithstanding the terror and the pain, contributed to the establishment of the State of Israel. Similarly, his proposal provided for other symbols of specific events in Israel's history connected with the Wall. It also provides for archaeological excavations to be carried out below the level of the prayer area and the preservation of that section as a roofed-over archaeological-garden which would be open to visitors for the study of the Wall's history.

A perspective of the Wall area from above; a sketch of the present state of affairs.

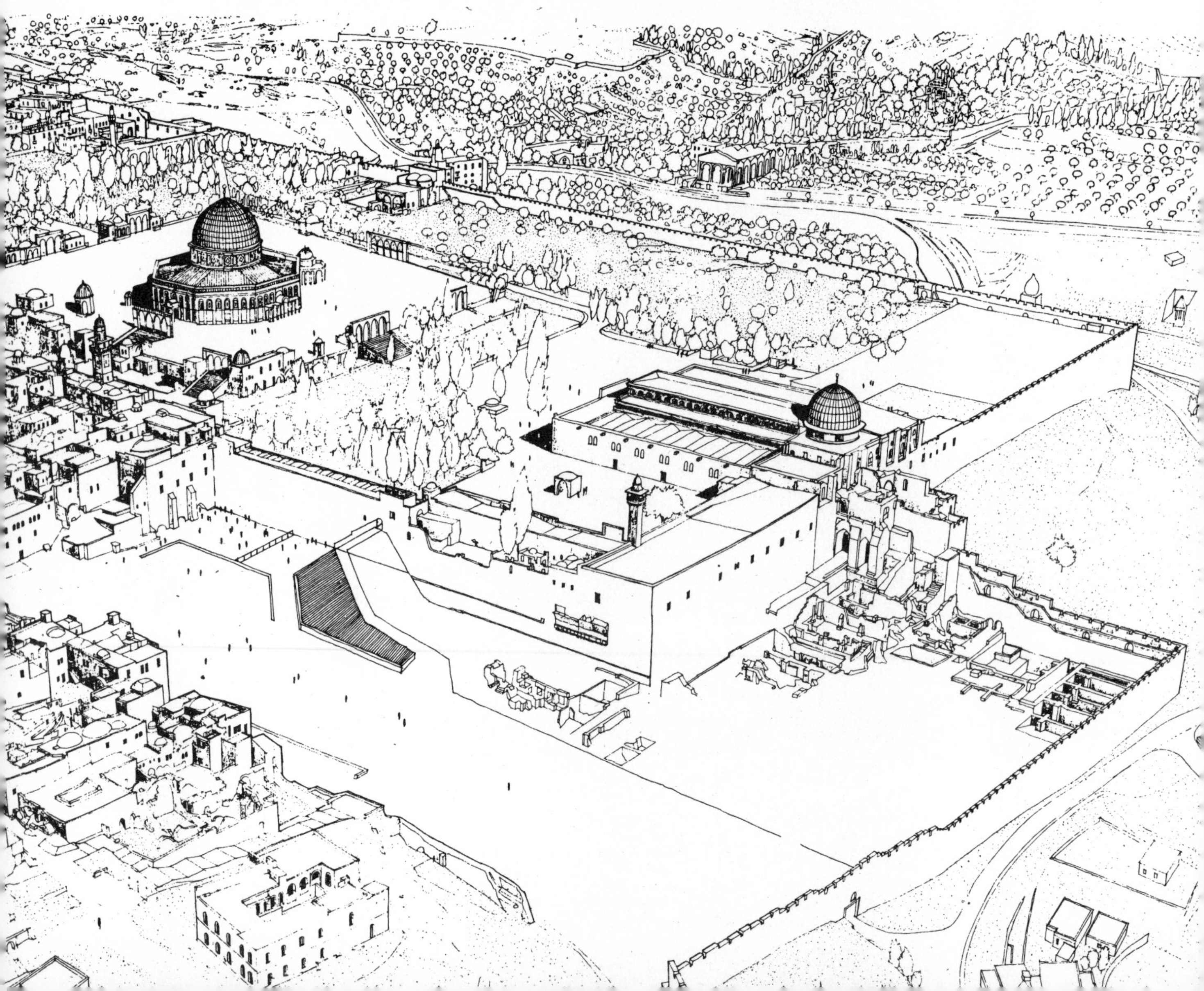

Joseph Sheinberger, an architect who served as the minister of religions' advisor for architectural matters, conducted a special survey which recorded the situation as it was then including the archaeological findings. However, at that time the excavations were in their early stages and thus the information available was, at the best, incomplete. A result of this survey was that a plan was put forward for the piazza as it is today with a few minor changes and improvements. The enormous square was to be left as it was with all its drawbacks, ignoring the fact that the Magreb Quarter had been demolished in 1967 only in order to create an open space which would be later designed. As a justification for leaving the present dimension, the plan cited the example of one of the most famous squares in the world, the San Marco piazza in Venice. There is, however, no real basis for comparison. San Marco is a public business piazza of the type that was built in medieval cities to be the commercial center with the façade of an important church serving as one of its sides. Clearly, there can be no comparison between the façade of a church and the Western Wall, with its status and symbolism, except for the fact that they both close-off sides of large squares. It is important to stress that there is no similarity between the piazza of a medieval city and the square at the Western Wall – with regard to essence, purpose or, certainly, historical period.

In the course of the years many proposals were made for the design of the Western Wall area. They were generally based on one of two principles: preserving the area in its existing form with a few "cosmetic" improvements and with an underground archaeological site in which the archaeological finds would be preserved; or a new design incorporating intensive symbolism and utilizing all, or nearly all, the Jewish symbols. Some suggestions had twelve gates leading into the square, symbolic of the twelve tribes of Israel; others wanted the seven-branch candelabrum of the Temple to occupy center of the stage. Since Judaism and Jewish history have a considerable amount of symbols, there was no shortage of such suggestions.

Exceptional among all the design proposals was that of Moshe Safdie. In the light of the solutions it proposed, it is possible to examine the problems that the area presents. Safdie's proposal had one major advantage over all others – it was commissioned by the official bodies active in the project and it was adopted by the government which appointed a committee of experts to examine it.

Safdie's Proposal – the Birth of a Design

In 1969, Meir Ben-Dov, representing the archaeological expedition, requested Moshe Safdie, an architect, to serve – in an honorary capacity – as the architect of the archaelogical expedition to the Temple Mount, with the aim of arriving at a design to rehabilitate the site of the archaeological excavations and to prepare it for the throngs of people who would no doubt want to visit it. One condition was attached to the request. The site had already been designed – by Herod's architects as well as those of the various Ommayad caliphs and builders throughout the ages. What was required was to find some way to coordinate the work of all those periods and, particularly, to fix visitors' itineraries through the excavation site. Further thought on the subjects and the execution of the first practical steps made it clear that it is impossible to design the excavation site by itself. Furthermore, the site is only a part – albeit a large part – of the general area of the piazza at the Western Wall. And so the archaeological expedition turned to the Company for the Rehabilitation and Development of the Jewish Quarter, and its energetic chairman, Yehudah Tamir and he undertook to deal with the matter. He first approached the Ministry of Religions which was in charge of a large section of the area and suggested that it participate in the task of planning an integrated design for the

Wall. The Minister, Dr. Zerah Warhaftig, was inclined to accept the proposal. He indicated his acceptance orally but because of internal ministry pressures, his acceptance was never committed to writing. The mayor of Jerusalem, Teddy Kollek, gladly ordered all relevant city agencies to cooperate on the project. The Company for the Rehabilitation and Development of the Jewish Quarter was eager to see a design that would connect the piazza at the Wall, including the archaeological site, with the buildings it was planning on the slopes leading down from the Jewish Quarter. The archaeological expedition, which had instigated the project, was, of course, delighted.

When agreement was reached between all these bodies, Mr. Safdie and his associates set to work. After many months of studying the area in all its various aspects, a proposal which later was commonly called "Moshe Safdie's plan for the Western Wall", was presented. It was a master plan which spelled out the design's objectives in general terms, and it never reached the detailed pre-execution stages since many of its components depend on information which will only be available when archaeological excavations are completed.

After consideration in the government and the Ministerial Committee for Jerusalem, then headed by the minister of justice, Hayyim Zadok, it was decided to appoint a committee of experts to examine the proposal and make recommendations to the government. In its mandate, the committee was told that it could accept the proposal as it was, reject it *in toto*, or accept it with changes. The members of the committee were: Irvin Shimron, lawyer: Chair-

The model of the Safdie proposal from the southeast.

man. At that time he was the chairman of the board for the Company for the Rehabilitation and Development of the Jewish Quarter; Messrs. A. Sharon, J. Rechter, and Y. Yaski, architects representing the Union of Architects in Israel; Meir Ben-Dov, archaeologist, representing the archaeological expedition; Mr. M. Benvenisti, the mayor's aide for East Jerusalem, representing the city council; David Cassuto, architect, the minister of religion's consultant for the Western Wall, representing the Ministry of Religions.

After a while, Mr. A. Yaski resigned because the minister of religions had appointed a committee of his own to examine the halakhic and architectural problems at the Wall and, although the chairman of the Ministerial Committee for Jerusalem made it clear that the above described committee was the only one whose decision could commit the government, Mr. Yaski was not persuaded. His place on the committee was not filled.

Mr. D. Zifroni was appointed secretary and coordinator to the committee. At that time he served as the deputy general manager of the Company for the Rehabilitation and Development of the Jewish Quarter. After a while, Rabbi Isaiah Hadari, the head of Yeshivat Ha-Kotel in the Jewish Quarter, was appointed to the committee as its expert on Jewish religious law. He never attended any of the committee's meetings; he told this author that his appointment had not been given to him in a suitable manner.

The committee informed the public, in all the communications media, that it was starting its deliberations and invited members of the public to make their ideas on the design proposal

The model from the Jewish Quarter.

known to the committee in writing or by personal appearance before it. To this end, the plans together with a model and photographs were exhibited. Some fifteen thousand persons visited the exhibition which was held in the Jewish Quarter and remained open for six months. The committee's meetings were held at least once a month over a period of two years and each meeting lasted a full day. In all, one hundred public figures, including architects, archaeologists and rabbis, appeared before the committee. Some two hundred and fifty reactions to the plan were received in writing. The committee also gave a presentation of the plan before the two chief rabbis and the Chief Rabbinate Council.

Most of the testimony given before the committee orally was generally positive. Here and there criticism was voiced about one detail or another but the critics did not present any counter proposals for the details with which they disagreed. One exception to this rule was Mr. Pereg, a Haifa interior-architect, who brought sketches with him to illustrate his plan for the piazza. His main idea, which incorporated a large number of historical symbols, did not win the committee's support. The general view of the committee was that architectural solutions had to be found for the problems the area presented and that the principles on which the design was based must be simple.

Most of the letters received also praised the proposal in general terms, pointing out details which, in the opinion of the writers, should be changed. As was to be expected, terms such as "dwarfing the Wall" and "the relationship between the Temple and the Wall" cropped up quite frequently. These are emotional value judgements and it is impossible to establish their weight when dealing with a practical proposal. Attitudes to the Western Wall are, primarily, emotional and not attitudes to a wall with intrinsic value, be it a beautiful wall, or giant wall or the opposite. An examination of the accounts of Jewish visitors to the Western Wall (such as those contained in Chapter III of this volume) reveals quite clearly the storm of Jewish emotions that is aroused by this memorial to the Temple in contrast to the Christian reactions to the same Wall. Added to this general Jewish emotionality with regard to the Wall, is the nostalgia of those who remember the Wall as a gigantic monument dominating the narrow alley of pre-1967 days. For them, the enormous dimensions of the piazza had reduced the size of the Wall. One well known architect argued before the committee that a great deal of time must pass before an architect would be able to design the Wall area: "The time has not yet come; we have not yet disgested the subject. A generation or two must pass before anyone can deal with this subject." This view was rejected by the committee, for who can guarantee that in a generation or two the architect who will deal with the matter will be better than the present architect? Will his ideas be riper? Jerusalem has been reunited in this generation and it is this generation that must contend with the challenge. "It is for our generation to find the solution and solve the problems presented by the Wall as best it can",was the committee's opinion.

Finally after many meetings, the committee adopted Safdie's proposal by a majority as a general master plan. In the committee's opinion it would be possible to decide on final details only after the archaeological excavations had been completed and the preparatory work started. The committee recommended that an architect examine the matter of the rock outcropping on the edge of the Jewish Quarter opposite the Wall and find a way to integrate it into the general plan. This clause was, in fact, an expression of the thoughts of many critics who saw the outcropping as a competitor to the Wall for the visitors' attention. The representative of the Ministry of Religions did not join the committee's recommendations. His main arguments were of a formal nature, i.e., he objected to the manner in which the plan had been commissioned and particularly to the fact that all the various bodies had been party to it whereas he felt that the right to commission a plan belonged to his ministry and his ministry

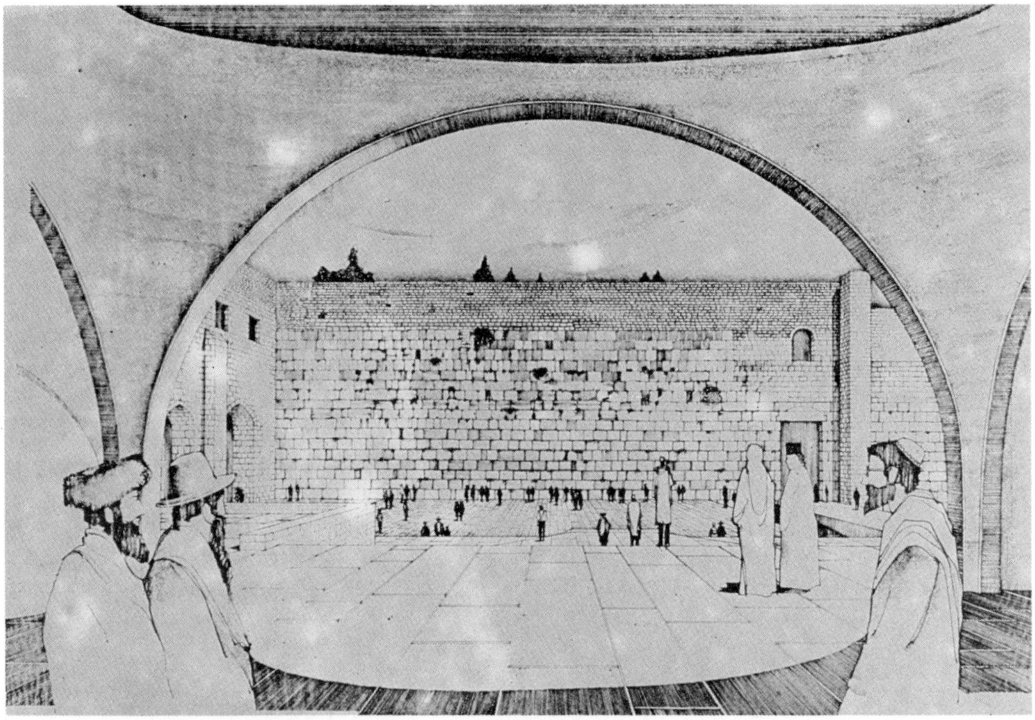

A projection; the view in the direction of the Wall from the Shalshelet St. point of access.

A projection; from the roofed-in road northwards.

alone. This argument had been rejected by the government of Israel when it was first made and naturally the committee of experts did not accept it.

Planning the Piazza at the Wall in the Light of Safdie's Proposal

Close to Independence Day, 1977, the committee of experts submitted its recommendations to the ministerial committee for Jerusalem. Whether or not these recommendations will be accepted and implemented, the Safdie proposal serves as an excellent medium to examine the problems presented by the project, since it is easier to discuss problems to which practical solutions have been offered than it is to discuss them theoretically. It should be noted, that for a limited number of problems the proposed Safdie solutions were not purely architectural but were governed by political considerations without which better solutions would have been available. It must also be remembered that the special emotions, religious or nationalistic, that the Wall arouses, as well as the behavioural norms at the Wall, are substantive to the Wall itself and should not be connected to the essence of the architectural solution offered. Generally speaking, there are a number of basic problems involved in designing the piazza at the Wall, as well as dozens of specific smaller ones. The following sections will discuss a number of basic elements, which in the way they are treated, will substantially establish the design of the area. These elements are:

1. The piazza: its shape and dimensions.
2. The slopes of the Jewish Quarter bordering on the piazza.
3. Passage through the piazza.
4. Public services in the area.
5. Entrance to the Temple Mount.
6. Archaeology and the exhibition of the finds.
7. Additional religious content in the area.
8. Execution of the design without disturbing prayer at the Wall.

The Piazza: Its Shape and Dimensions.

The space in front of the Western Wall which was created by the demolition of the Magreb Quarter in 1967 is of enormous dimensions and it will become even larger when the earthen ramp separating it from the archaeological excavations to the south is removed. Only in extraordinary public meetings and demonstrations, once a year or once every two years, is it likely that tens of thousands of people come together and even if a hundred thousand were to gather in the area in fron of the Wall, there would still be empty spaces. For most of the year, human traffic in the piazza is relatively sparse; even including groups of tourists there are rarely more than a few thousand people at the Wall at any one time. On festivals or at demonstrations, this number can be multiplied three or fourfold but even then, only the lower level prayer area and the edge of the upper level are filled. The truth is that in its present dimensions the piazza is too large, no matter how it is designed, and when the archaeological site is added, the area will be double its present size. These enormous dimensions are the main reason for "the reduction in size" of the Wall from a visual point of view.

The solution to this problem in the Safdie proposal is based on two points. The first is lowering the level of the piazza and the second is dividing the piazza into three terraced

Buildings of the Jewish Quarter to the west of the Wall according to the Safdie proposal.

piazzas each one higher than the next. Archaeology has revealed that for the full length of the southern section from Wilson's Arch a road was laid in Second Temple times. This road is eight metres below the present level of the prayer area. It is paved with large stones precisely placed and its western edge is thirteen metres from the Wall. That western edge is marked off with a kerbstone twenty centimetres high.

If this road area is uncovered, it will provide an ideal place for prayer filling the needs of the worshippers at the Wall, for they will be standing on a road laid in Temple times more than two thousand years ago. The authenticity of such prayer on a pavement from that period, with all its religious and nationalistic symbolism, would be substantive. The southern part of that road in the present archaeological site would also be uncovered and cleared of remains from later periods. Only the stones from the Western Wall which were hurled down by the Roman soldiers when they destroyed the Temple will remain there. This will constitute a "memorial to the destruction" in a concrete form and this adjacent to the section where people are praying for the rebuilding of the temple and the coming of the Messiah.

Creating a prayer area at the level of the Second Temple road will add another eight stone courses (= eight metres) to the height of the Wall. These stones, as it has been learned from the archaeological excavations, are in an excellent state of preservation and are larger than the stones above ground at present. If it is desirable to add to the "stature" of the Wall and restore some of its pre-1967 dimensions, this is the only way to do it. Beyond this first piazza, which will be of Second Temple times dimensions and on that level, another terrace will come into existence automatically and further west, above the second terrace, a third level will be created. Since we are returning to the original topography of the site, which was the slope of a hill, this third level will coincide with the westernmost hill of the ancient upper city, i.e., the slope east of the Jewish Quarter today. The three levels in the piazza are, therefore, dictated by the topographical conditions. Each of the two upper levels will serve as the roof of various underground buildings whose main function will be to preserve and exhibit archaelogical finds from the area and remains of public and private buildings that stood there before. One result of the terracing of the piazzas will be that they will be able to be used for mass rallies when huge throngs of people visit the area and want to participate in the prayers, at least visually. The terraces will also serve the tourists whose main aim is sightseeing. The lowest level will be for the worshippers and there all the norms and customs of a Jewish prayer area will prevail. Unlike today, the proposed arrangement will ensure that the worshippers are not disturbed by tourists and sightseers. Thus the size of the first piazza will be reduced and a greater majesty will be given to the Wall that towers above it and, at the same time, huge areas will be created which can be used on the special occasions when tens of thousands come to the Wall. All this is based on a return to the topography of the area as it was in its days of glory, the days of the Second Temple, when the buildings stood on the rocky slopes of the hill to the west.

The proposal seeks to solve the problem of Arabs going via the Dung Gate (opposite) and the piazza to the Old City markets.

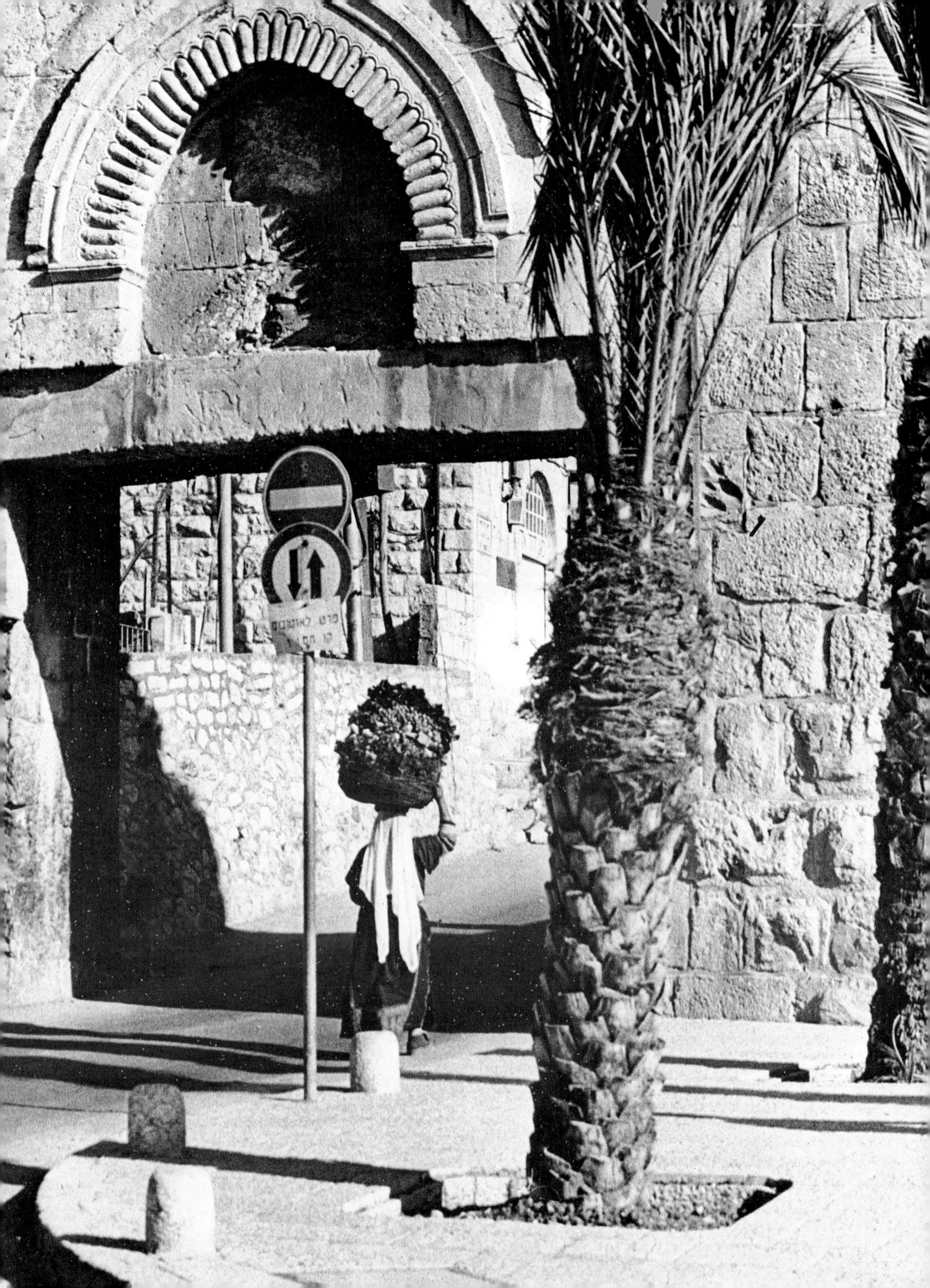

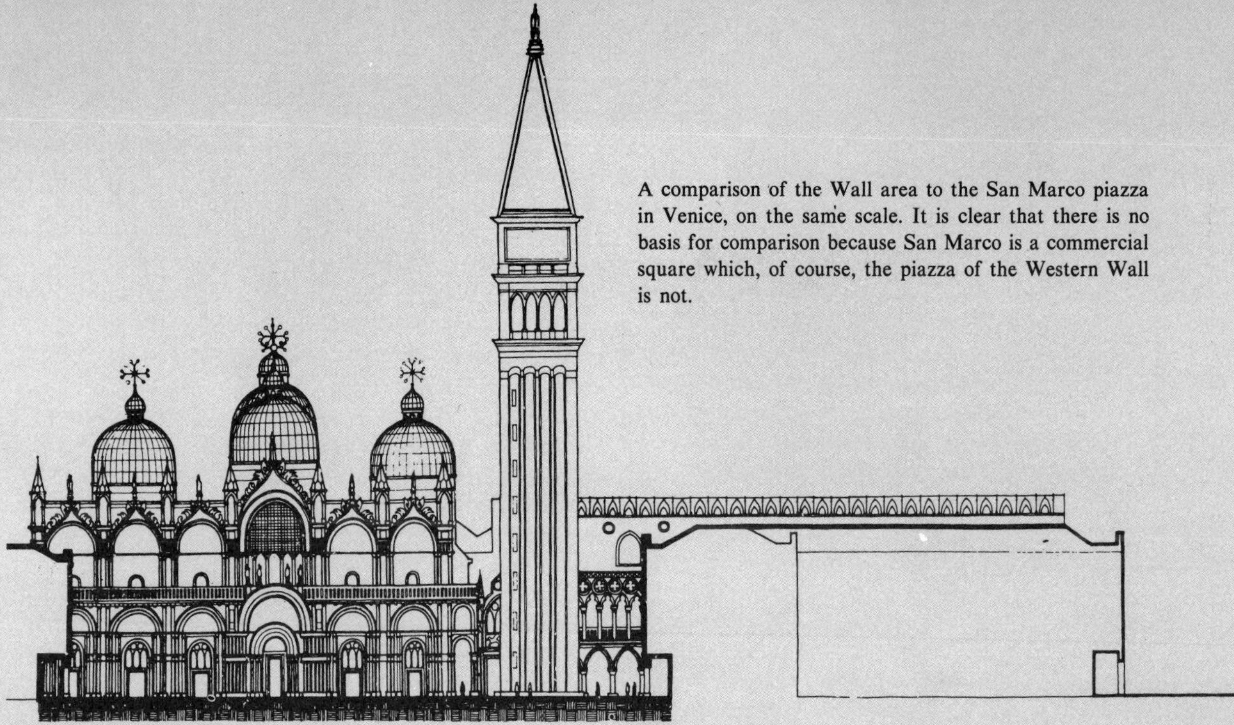

A comparison of the Wall area to the San Marco piazza in Venice, on the same scale. It is clear that there is no basis for comparison because San Marco is a commercial square which, of course, the piazza of the Western Wall is not.

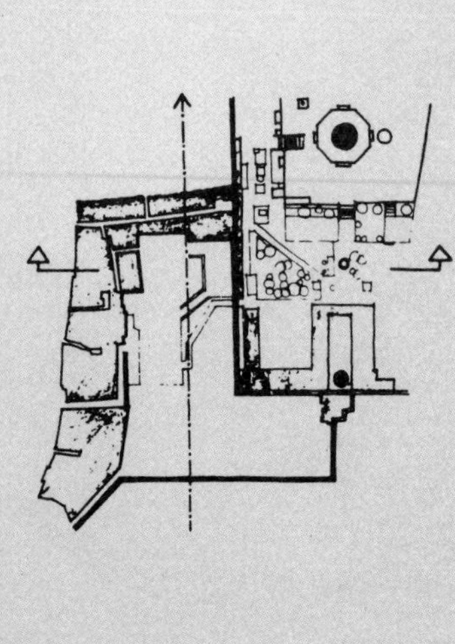

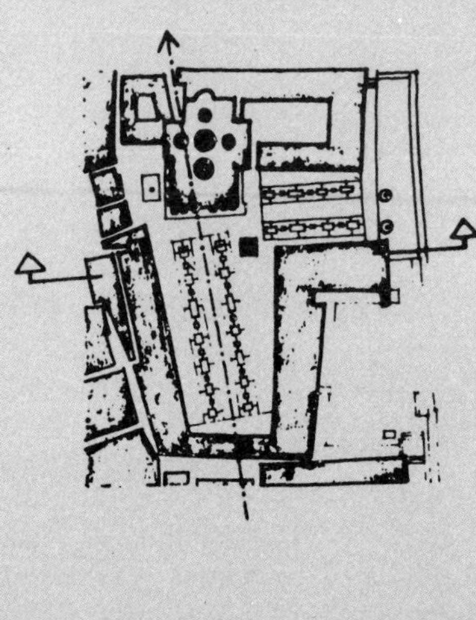

The Slopes of the Jewish Quarter Bordering on the Piazza

The three terraces-piazzas at the Western Wall will occupy only between one half and two thirds of the space available today. The remaining area is intended, according to the Safdie proposal, to be an extension of the Jewish Quarter to join it up with the piazza at the Wall. From the Second Temple period until the Six-Day War, this area was built up. Josephus, describing the area as it was in his days, records that the neighbourhood opposite the southern section of the Western Wall was built like an amphitheatre, i.e., built on rising levels or terraces like the seats in a Roman amphitheatre. In Second Temple times, the area contained several important public buildings, but without extensive excavations it is impossible to know what remains have survived. The present topography and an examination of the remains uncovered to the south of the Wall would indicate that whatever remains there are do not rise to a great height and it would seem that they could be preserved *in situ* in the bottom storey of buildings under the planned new buildings where they could become a tourist attraction.

Both the past and the present demand that there be no private buildings near the Wall. It is essential that in this area commercialisation be avoided and it is desirable that the piazzas be isolated from dwelling houses with windows, so that the privacy of the residents should not be disturbed. Therefore, this belt of land between the Jewish Quarter and the piazzas should be reserved for public religious and secular institutions.

According to the Safdie proposal, the planned buildings will have cupolas but the construction system to be utilized will be modern and modular. The general idea is to incorporate ancient visual elements into modern buildings so that they will not compete with the past but preserve something in its style. Building on terraces constitutes a return to the original topography without too much quarrying or digging and expresses, to a certain degree, elements of the buildings of Second Temple times. Within this complex of buildings, the designer was requested to pay special attention to the rock outcropping that juts out in the center of the area. This will be possible by incorporating it into a building which will be erected to store the archaeological artifacts found in the area.

Passage through the Piazza

The strip joining the three piazzas to the last buildings on the slopes of the Jewish Quarter is intended in the Safdie design to serve as a thoroughfare for the north-south traffic which at present passes through the piazza. As long as Jerusalem has existed, one of its two main lengthwise thoroughfares has always run along this line. In the Second Temple period this was the road which started at the Damascus Gate and ended at the Siloam pool. As it passed the Temple Mount, it ran along the foot of the Western Wall for its whole length. A section of this road is intended to constitute the prayer area described above. Starting from the first centuries after the destruction of the Temple, the course of this road was moved westward because of the enormous amounts of rubble that had accumulated from the devastation of the Temple Mount and the immediate surroundings. In the eleventh century under Fatimid rule, when the area protected by the city walls was reduced, the north-south road remained in this area. Afterwards its course was from the Damascus Gate in the north to the Tanners' Gate and, later, to the Dung Gate in the southern wall of the city. This road serves the traffic from the neighbourhoods to the south of the Old City to the markets in the Old City and constitutes a very important thoroughfare. It thus happens that in the piazza at the Wall as it is today, you can meet a woman from the village of Silwan with a basket of vegetables on her head on her way to sell them in the market, or villagers from Kfar Hilweh going home with their purchases after a day's shopping in the city. The piazza is also used by tourists who park their cars outside the southern city wall and walk through it to reach the Old City. According to the proposal, all this traffic will go through a roofed-in road, the western side of which will be devoted to service buildings and the eastern side, which faces the Wall, will have a number of large open arches through which it will be possible to see the Wall and its piazzas. This roofed-in road will hide the traffic going through it and reduce the "temporal" element in the area a little. It will thus contribute to the decorum and the sense of sanctity in the piazzas.

Public Services in the Area

It is only fitting that commercial activity be removed from a place endowed with sanctity and used as a place of prayer, although that was not the case in Second Temple times. In that

The unsolved problem – the Magreb Gate.

period, the lower market of Jerusalem was situated at the foot of the Temple Mount. That market was the commercial center of the city and contained hundreds of shops. The explanation for this is not hard to find. Wherever a great number of people congregate – and particularly if there are tourists among them – there is a need for the services that shops supply. However, nowadays when the focus has moved from inside the Temple Mount to outside it, to the foot of the Western Wall, it is only proper that the commercial activity be kept at a distance from the prayer area. Nevertheless, it is clear that some services are required at a major tourist and pilgrimage site notwithstanding its special character. There is a need for such services as a post office, public telephones, and a place to purchase religious accessories. Similarly, since it is a public place, there is also the need for a photography shop, a store selling mementoes and picture postcards of the place, and a facility for light refreshments, all of which items will certainly be sought by tourists. In the present situation, these services are supplied *in situ* by roving peddlars, Arab youngsters and others who offer their wares in a manner which offends the dignity of the site.

In the Safdie design it is proposed to concentrate all these services in the Western section of the roofed-in passage, which will be the connecting thoroughfare between the Dung Gate and the streets of the Old City. This will isolate the commercial activity from the prayer area, and the other piazzas, will locate them in orderly and clean premises and will add to the decorum of the place.

Other essential public services, such as a first aid station, a fire station, a police post, and toilets, will be located at the Dung Gate. A courtyard will be built around the gate to house these services as well as the project's administrative offices. This proposal exploits the available space fully and puts the commerical and other services in secluded areas and yet caters to the needs of the public since the services will be readily accessible.

Entrance to the Temple Mount

The Jewish religious prohibition against entry into the Temple Mount is today absolute. Some pious people are so sensitive about this matter that they will not come closer than fifty centimetres to the Wall itself. Fanatical members of the Neturei Karta community will not visit the Wall at all, but that is for political reasons since it was liberated by the army of the "Zionist state." Occasionally one can see a member of that community standing secretly on one of the roofs of the Jewish Quarter to at least see from afar that which his politics will not allow him to approach. At the other extreme, there are observant, religious Jews who do enter the southern section of the Temple Mount plateau near the Al Akza mosque through the Magreb Gate. They believe that the sacred part of the plaza was a square measuring five hundred by five hundred cubits at the north of the plaza where the Dome of the Rock is situated. Since the plaza after Herod's extension is larger than that square it would follow that this view is, from the point of view of Jewish religious law, the correct one and that there are no grounds for a blanket prohibition against entry into any part of the plaza.

In the wake of the Six-Day War, the keys of the Magreb Gate were handed over to the Israel Defence Forces who established a guard post there. Thus, this is the only entrance to the Temple Mount in Israeli hands and to do away with it would mean the absence of any Israeli presence on the edge of the plaza.

The Magreb Gate presents a problem in planning the piazza at the Wall. Most of the people who come to pray at the wall are religious Jews and it offends their sensibilities to see other people – and Jews among them – entering the Temple Mount plaza. Yet, it is impossible to close up the gate and abolish the Israeli presence. Attempts have been made to exchange this entrance with another, but the Moslem Religious Trust was not prepared to agree.

Any design for the area at the Wall must present a solution to the problem of the Magreb Gate. According to the Safdie plan, the rubble ramp leading up to the gate is to be removed in order to create a continuous open area in front of the Wall from its southwest corner up to the *Mahkameh* building in the north, a total of one hundred and forty metres out of the Wall's entire length of four hundred and eighty-five metres. How then will it be possible to enter the Temple Mount plaza at this spot?

Actually, there is an excellent, alternative entrance on the site under the Magreb Gate and blocked off by the rubble ramp. This gate, today known as Barclay's Gate, dates from Second Temple times and is the only entrance from that period that has been completely preserved. For that reason alone it is very special. When the rubble ramp is removed, Barclay's Gate will be revealed in all its pristine glory with its threshold on the same level as the ancient road which will then be the prayer area. There could be no better entrance into the Temple Mount than this gate since that was its exact function in the Second Temple period. However, for political reasons, Barclay's Gate will remain closed even after it is uncovered and, anyway, its opening would aggravate the problem of the religious sensibilities of the worshippers. As it is, the only entrance to the Temple Mount will remain the Magreb Gate, some seventeen metres above the ground level of the prayer area and the question is, "How will anyone get there?". This is the most difficult of the problems in planning the Western Wall.

One possible solution is a hanging bridge from the gate to the roofed-over street in the west. Another would be to repair the anchorstone of Robinson's Arch and use it as the basis for a bridge into the southern section of the Temple Mount plaza, south of the Magreb Gate or to hang a walkway from Robinson's Arch along the outside of the Wall to the Magreb Gate. Safdie's design offers a different solution. A transparent elevator shaft would be constructed from ground level to the Magreb Gate and an automatic elevator, also transparent, would operate for twenty-four hours a day. The opinion of this author is that such a structure would be foreign to the site's spirit and not befitting its status and history. A light and airy walkway from Robinson's Arch to the gate seems to be more appropriate.

Archaeology and the Exhibition of the Finds

The southern and eastern borders of the piazza at the Wall will be the walls of the Old City. Thus the area will include the entire site of the archaeological excavations and its discoveries. Furthermore, execution of the project will certainly yield a great number of additional discoveries. Some of the finds are destined to be exhibited under the piazza, the roofed-over street and the public buildings which will be erected at the western edge of the present piazza. The area from the Magreb Gate to the city wall is intended to be an open area, the main attraction of which will be the archaeological finds. Generally, the idea is to remove all the remnants of later periods and leave only those from Second Temple times, which are so impressive and numerous that there will be no difficulty in transforming the area into a most impressive attraction for visitors. In the model of the design, this aspect does not appear because it will only be executed in the course of the work. The southernmost section of the area will be devoted to finds from later periods, such as the Byzantine and the Islamic, which will preserve to some extent the historical atmosphere of Jerusalem throughout its various periods. Other artifacts will be exhibited in the basement of the service building which will be erected in this area and a visit to this site will be ended by exit through an adjacent medieval gate in the city walls.

In addition to the remains of buildings, the archaeological activities in the area have yielded a great number of various artifacts. A building to store and exhibit these items will be erected on the rock outcropping opposite the Wall on the site of the present building which houses the offices and storerooms of the archaeological expedition. There is a special importance attached to exhibiting objects close to the place where they were discovered, and the exhibition will also show plans, models, sketches and photoghraphs. Thus the visitor will be given a comprehensive historical view of the Temple Mount. This building will also contain a lecture hall and it is intended to offer regular survey-lectures to groups of visitors.

Additional Religious Content in the Area

To the north of the piazza at the Wall, the Ministry of Religions is conducting archaeological excavations, under the supervision of this author, to clean and uncover the whole length of the Western Wall as well as the beautiful vaulted spaces from various historical periods, which were built against the Wall. The piazzas at the Wall will be connected to this area by a number of entrances. The vaults near the present piazza, such as Wilson's Arch and its adjacent complex, are already being used as a prayer area, particularly in inclement weather which prevents prayer in the open piazza. The general public can also visit this area; the vaults are very attractive and are an important part of Jerusalem's history. However, a large number of the vaults further away from the piazza are unused. A proposal has been made to the Ministry of Religions that this area be turned into a museum exhibiting Jewish religious ceremonial objects of all periods and all Jewish ethnic communities. This would be an ideal place to illustrate the continuity of Jewish history through its religious symbols and would obviate the need to express such symbolism in the architectural design of the area. There could be permanent and changing exhibitions in the very appropriate setting of these magnificent vaults that are being restored and rehabilitated under the ground.

Execution of the Design without Disturbing Prayer at the Wall

The meeting of the committee of experts with the chief rabbis and the members of the Chief Rabbinate Council made it clear that the latter would insist that the execution of any design must not disturb the prayers at the Wall. There is no reason why an elevated prayer area cannot be constructed on piles which will enable prayers to continue while the archaeologists and builders work below. It should be remembered that a great deal of work is done in the area at present and that the conduct of the prayers at the Wall is always given precedence. With modern construction techniques, work systems can be created so that no disturbance will be created at all.

These, then, are the central problems involved in planning the area at the Western Wall. In order to illuminate them, we have presented the solutions that the Safdie proposal offers. Of course, the picture is made up of many small details which must all be solved in the overall plan. Whether Safdie's proposal is adopted and executed or whether another plan is adopted and executed – the time has come to restore the glory of the Western Wall.

S. RASKIN
Wailing Wall

CHAPTER IX

THE WALL IN ART AND IN CRAFTS

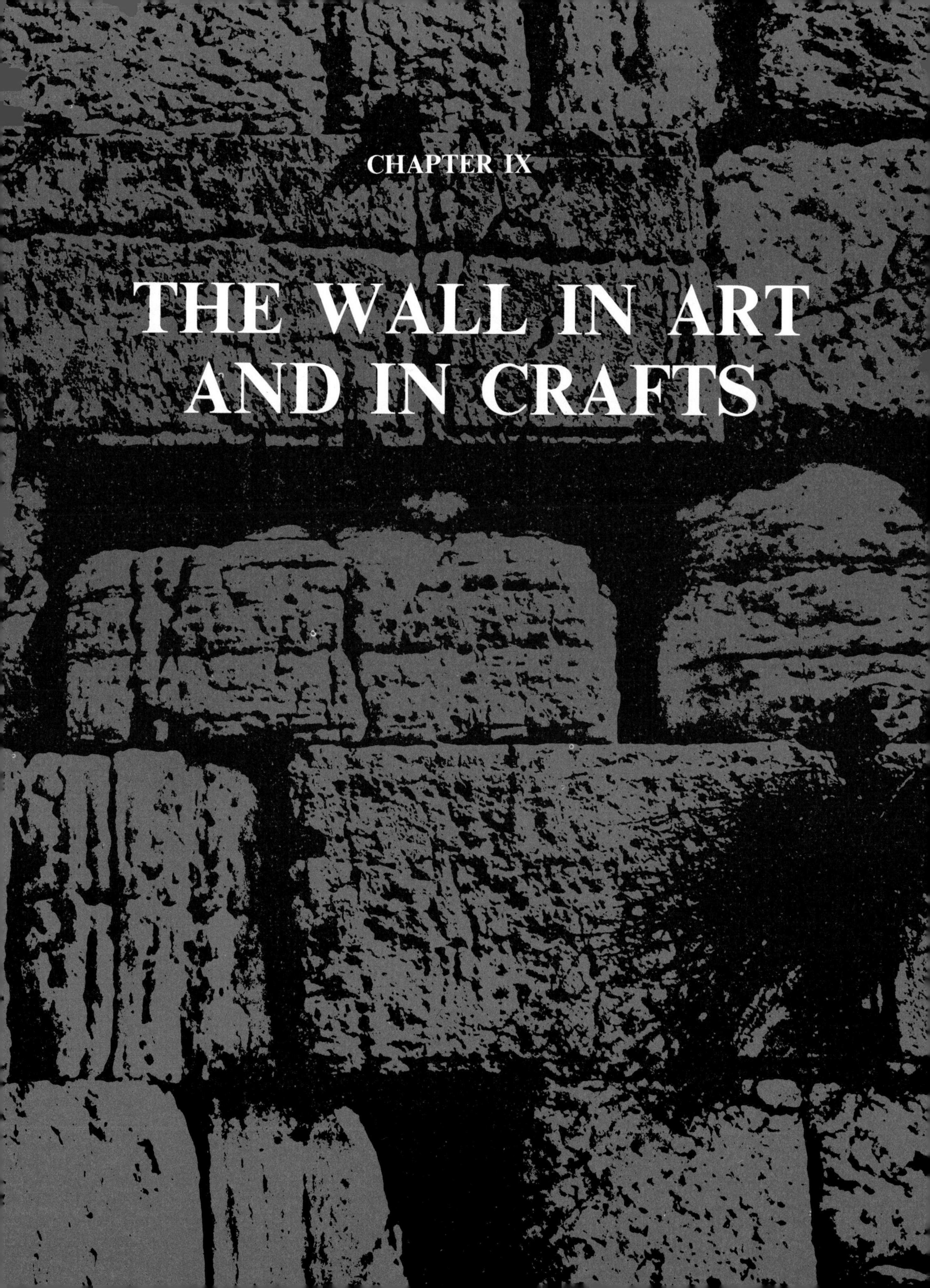

Jewish folk artists and craftsmen in Eretz Israel made great use of the Western Wall as a motif in their work. However, on examination it becomes clear that this trend only started towards the second half of the nineteenth century. This development in art and crafts is seen by some authorities as a reflection of the nationalistic awakening of the Jews which began in that century. Be that as it may, the utilization of the Wall as a motif gave the Jews – both in Eretz Israel and the Diaspora – an opportunity for national identification connected as it was with the most holy place of the Jews since ancient times.

The earliest "Jewish Art" regarding Jerusalem is mentioned by the prophet Ezekiel: "And you, son of man, take a brick and portray on it the city, Jerusalem. And lay siege against it

A coin from the Bar-Kokhba period; a photograph and a drawing of the Temple facade.

A section of the Dura Europos murals.

and build a fort against it and cast a ramp against it. And you shall set camps against it and put battering rams around it" (Ezekiel 4:1-2).

Of course, this drawing, or one like it, is not extant and indeed it may never have existed – the verses may well be allegorical. However, we do have the image of the facade of the Second Temple inscribed on a Jewish coin from the time of the Bar Kokhba revolt, from 132 C.E.

Beautiful frescoes, including perhaps the earliest drawing of the Temple and the walls of Jerusalem, were also discovered in the ruins of a third century synagogue at Dura Europos in the Syrian desert.

Christian Drawings

One of the earliest depictions of Jerusalem appears in the Medeba Map from the sixth century. This mosaic map was discovered in the ruins of an ancient church in the village of Medeba in Transjordan. The walls of Jerusalem and the gates in them are clearly visible as are other places which are all identifiable. The mosaics in the Roman cathedrals, San Giovanni in Laterano and Maria Maggiore, which also depict Jerusalem, are about a century earlier.

Since Jerusalem is also holy to Christians, there is an abundance of illustrations from later years which do a great deal to shed light on the city's appearance throughout the ages. The Western Wall only began to attract Christian travellers' and artists' attention in the nineteenth century, whereas the site of the Temple was the subject of many earlier artists.

In the nineteenth century, Eretz Israel swarmed with Christian travellers. The books they left us, illustrated as they are with spectacular drawings, present a "photograph" of Jerusalem as it was in reality. It was these travellers who first dealt with the Western Wall in detail. They drew the Wall with a draughtsman's precision, including the Jews who gathered there.

Some of these artists borrowed motifs from one another, as an examination of their work easily shows. Some actually used the first photographs of the Wall in the last century as their models – these are among the earliest photographs in existence.

Of the nineteenth-century travellers, mention should be made of: Johannes Burkhardt (1812); William Ray Wilson (1819) whose books were illustrated by A.P. Harrison; Isidore Taylor (1839) also including illustrations by Meyer; David Roberts (1838), the greatest painter of Eretz Israel in the nineteenth century; William H. Bartlett (1842,1853), whose pictures are a never ending source of ethnographic material; A.W. Schultz (1851); Sir Charles William Wilson (1864-65), the most important archaeologist of Jerusalem; and Lortha (1847,1880). Paintings and etchings of the Wall by Christian artists of the nineteenth century can be found throughout this volume.

A Fixed Depiction

Jews used Jerusalem mainly to decorate sacred objects for synagogue use and the *Haggadah* which is recited in the home at the Passover *seder* service. However, Jerusalem also appears on more mundane articles such as skullcaps, serviettes, tablecloths, boxes and pictures.

On *rimonin* (finials) and crowns for Torah Scrolls from Italy, various Temple artifacts, such as the seven-branched candelabrum, the incense shovel and the shew-bread, appear worked in gold-plated silver. Temple artifacts, embroidered in coloured threads and occasion-

The Temple; Passover *Haggadah*, Hamburg 1768.

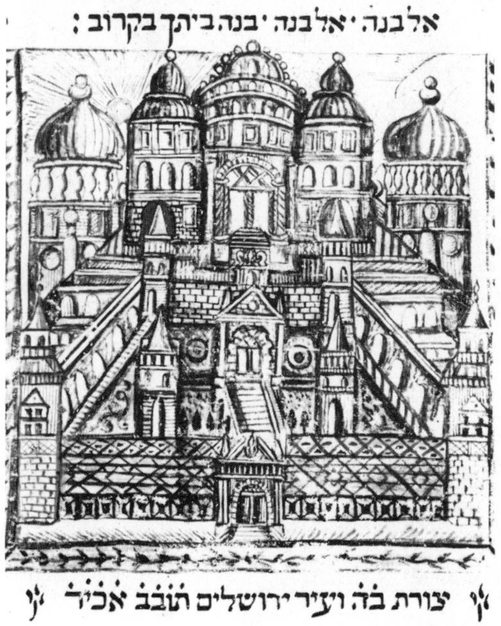

A 20th-century amulet; engraved cast brass.

The Wall and the fir trees in a 20th-century book-plate.

Marc Chagall.

Meir Gur Arie – woodcuts.

Shemuel Katz.

Ludwig Blum.

Nahum Gutman.

The Wall, the piazza and the Temple Mount – in white.

Salvador Dali.

ally with coloured stones set in, appear on the jackets of the Torah Scrolls and particularly on the curtains of the Torah Ark. The doors of such an Ark from Poland are made of wood and coloured lead and carved with the Temple utensils with an explanation and dedication to the donor.

The Temple and the Western Wall were depicted as they were in reality either from memory or according to the descriptions of Christian travellers. They were also given imaginary treatment. Among the works worthy of mention are: *Yihus Ha-Avot ve-Ha-Nevi'im* ("The Genealogy of the Patriarchs and the Prophets" 1537); *Zikaron Bi-Yerushalayim* ("Memory in Jerusalem" 1759), by Jacob Babani, in which there is a drawing of the Wall ("This is the form of the Western Wall"); *Kisaot le-Bet David* ("Thrones of the House of David" 1649), of David Mehatov; a curtain from Italy (1681). Generally, the Temple appears at the end of illustrated Passover *Haggadot* as a fortified city with a gate (in an eighteenth century *Haggadah* in the Israel Museum, the fir trees appear for the first time on the wall).

During the nineteenth century a stylized form developed for the Wall, the Dome of the Rock, and the adjacent buildings. In this depiction, with minor additions and changes, the fir trees are drawn on top of the Wall although in reality they stand behind it and can be seen from various vantage points in the city but not from near the Wall. The buildings at the side of the Wall are not in their real locations. The depiction of the Wall as it appears on most objects is schematic – straight lines, rectangles or squares – as indeed the subject, the Wall's

In this anonymous 19th-century illustration the fir trees have shrunk.

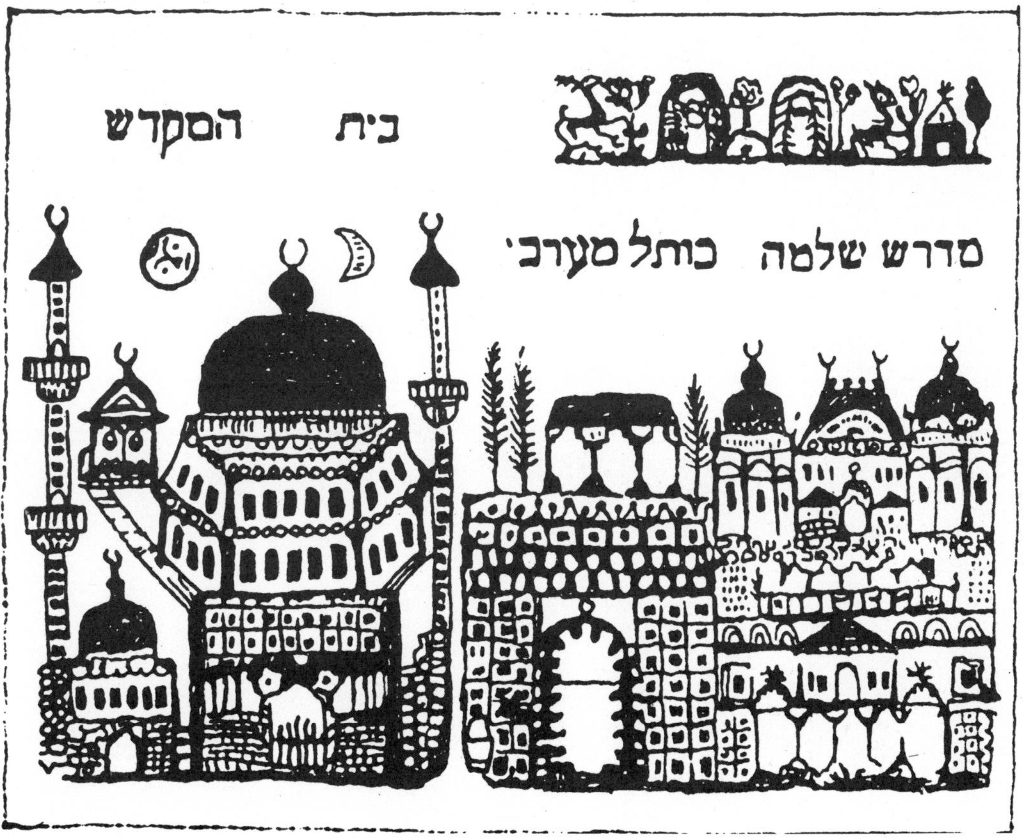

בשם ה' נעשה ונצליח

העתקת ספר

תומר דבורה

והוא מאמר נכבד מהרב המקובל האלהי כמוהר"ר

משה קורדואירו זצ"ל

בדרך ישרה שיבור לו האדם והתבוררותו ותכליתו והתבוננות דרכיו

אמר משה בסולה

ישנות משה במתנה טובה היתה גנוזה בגנזי אדוני המלך הרמ"ע
נר"ו ותתנה לי לזכות את ישראל על ידי זכות הרבים תלוי
בו בשכר זאת אל חי צורי וגואלי יזכני לחזות בנועם ה'
ולבקר בהיכלו לחבר את האהל בהר צבי קדש לעבוד
עבודתו כל ימי חיי ואבנה גם אנכי א'פ'ר
יצחק המביאו אל מכבת הדפוס ממנו
וכו' ובא לציון גואל וזאת
התורה אשר שם משה לפני בני ישראל.

מרום מראשון מקום מקדשינו

ע"י הרב המדפיס כו' כמוהר"ר **ישראל** ב"ק הי"ו

על מכבש הדפוס ונשיא **משה מונטיפיורי** הי"ו : ויהודית נשמתה בגנ"מ.

פעה"ק **ירושלים** תובב"א.

שנת **תר"ל** לפ"ק

The Wall on the title page of book published by Israel Beck, 1870.

stones, dictates. Most depictions carry an identifying legend, "The Western Wall". Usually the Wall is in the center of the composition and around it, or at its sides, are the other buildings and a view of Jerusalem. Occasionally, the Wall is shown alone and takes up the whole area of the picture.

This basic depiction was created in Eretz Israel in the nineteenth century and disseminated by way of requests for donations, seals on recommendations for emissaries who went abroad to collect funds, drawn on embroidered maps of the holy places, mementoes, etc.

On special occasions, the table was covered with a cloth embroidered with a picture of the Wall and it appeared on such things as New Year's greeting cards. In a *sukkah* (booth used for the festival of Tabernacles) from Fishach in Germany, the Wall was painted on a wooden panel between rustic German hunting scenes.

Another example of the Wall being used for decorative purposes is a special Jerusalem ***ketubbah*** (marriage document) from the nineteenth century. Here the Wall is the main decoration; the stones appear on the upper part of the sheet but are all sloping and each unit serves as the frame for a flower. On both sides of the Wall oriental-style buildings appear with a half crescent on each. The artist reworked the accepted form for his own graphic purposes and so changed the perpendicular rectangles that usually represent the stones.

Generally, the style used in depicting the Wall is folk-style or naive, fitted for the objects it was intended for and to the materials and techniques used: the Wall appears carved in simple lines on the wooden *mezzuzah* (scroll on the doorpost) holders, on blocks for printing, on boxes or on the arm-rests of Elijah's Chair (in the synagogue). On metal objects, such as plates and boxes, the depiction is usually in relief with far more delicate lines. Sometimes the depiction is converted into short, straight lines for embroidery on special paper and on others into twisting soft lines for embroidery in gold thread on velvet. When the drawing is made on paper, the treatment is much richer and variegated according to the technique used: etching, lithography, pencil or brush.

The turning point in the attitude of artists and craftsmen to the Wall was, as stated above, in the first half of the nineteenth century. Yona Fischer, the senior curator of modern art at the Israel Museum, sees the earthquake that struck Eretz Israel in 1832 as the pivot. The Jewish community in Safed was very badly hurt and most of the Ashkenazi Jews that had lived there until then moved to Jerusalem. Among the refugees was Rabbi Israel Beck, a leader of the Hasidic community, who, in 1832, had opened a printing shop in Safed. In 1841 he moved it to Jerusalem and started casting type and printing blocks. Beck and his shop had a crucial influence on the development of art in Eretz Israel from then on for several decades.

For many years, Beck claimed that he and his heirs had the exclusive right to print books in Jerusalem. After a long struggle, a trio of young Jerusalemites, Moses Salomon, Mikhal Hacohen, and Jehiel Brill, succeeded in opening a rival printing shop but, before that when they had all but given up hope, they established, from lack of choice, a lithography press (stone printing) to produce pictures and drawings. Thus, they contributed to the development of art in Jerusalem.

The Mizrah and the Wall

One of the most widespread decorative objects among Jews, both in Eretz Israel and the Diaspora, is the *Mizrah* plaque, common among Ashkenazi Jews from eastern and western Europe. The plaque was placed on the wall facing east in the house (thus the name, *Mizrah* – east) to indicate the direction of prayer – towards Eretz Israel and the Temple site. The

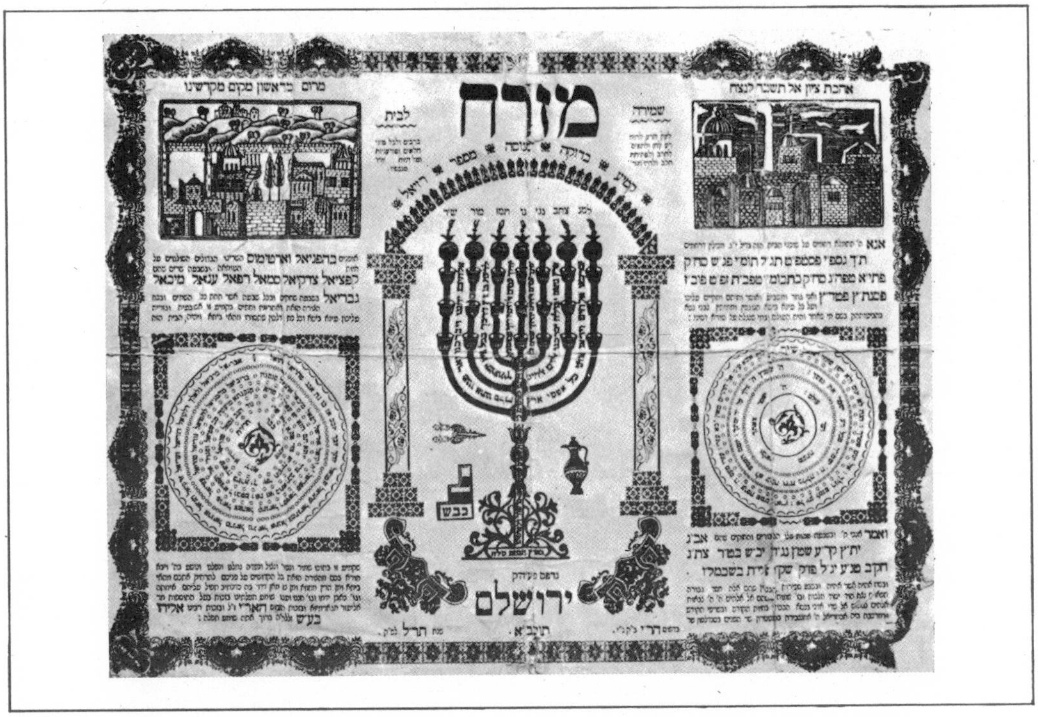

A *Mizrah* plaque.

mizrah plaque became an important art vehicle and in Eretz Israel it had a special characteristic. For the Jews there, the Temple site was not an abstract concept but a reality which they could see – so they put it in their *Mizrah* plaques. The *Mizrah* usually showed the Western Wall as well as the Dome of the Rock which stands on the Temple site.

Among the *Mizrah* plaques created in Eretz Israel, some were intended for the use of a *kollel* (communal group dependent on contributions from abroad) or other educational institution. Thus, for example, the *Mizrah* of the Hatam Sofer *yeshivah* from beginning of the twentieth century proudly bears a picture of the *yeshivah* building garlanded with roses. Above the building is a crown, representing the Crown of Torah, and beneath it, the Temple Mount with the Dome of the Rock. At the *yeshivah's* sides – the Western Wall and the holy city of Safed, to demonstrate the importance of the latter. Beneath all this is a map of the Holy Land. On each side of the *Mizrah* stands a rose-entwined column and between them the by-laws and regulations of the *yeshivah*: contributors will be listed in the *yeshivah's* memorial book; pious men will pray for their souls at the graves of Rabbis Isaac Lurie (the foremost kabbalist), Joseph Caro (the author of the accepted code of Jewish law) and Simeon bar Yohai (a famous mystic of Talmud times) etc. In order to increase *Mizrah* sales, its amulet qualities were stressed. On a *Mizrah* published by Beck in 1870, the following slogan is printed at the top: "A guard for the house. This is an amulet against the evil eye, evil spirits, . . . against being sent to prison, against the sword, for the opening of the heart (for study), and for the propagation of Torah among the public, and against all kinds of diseases and troubles and against losing one's wealth." Who would not buy such a *Mizrah*?

Isaac Einhorn, an authority and collector, researched the *Mizrah* subject and also dealt with the *Shiviti*. Whereas the *Mizrah* was intended for home use, the *Shiviti* was meant for

Elijah's Cup; carved bitumen by Yanover.

Jerusalem, the Wall and other holy places; Yehoseph Schwarz.

A *Mizrah* plaque by Mizrahi; a painting on glass.

the synagogue where it was placed on the cantor's lectern. Thus the text, "I have put (*shiviti*) the Lord in front of me always," to remind the cantor to concentrate on his prayers and be aware of to whom he was praying. Einhorn points out that the *Shiviti* plaques of Jerusalem were decorated with drawings of the holy places including the Western Wall.*

This leads us to everyday objects in life in Eretz Israel in which the Western Wall motif was incorporated. Ita Yellin in her memoirs tells of "the handicrafts of the Ashkenazi girls" which were "embroidering decorations on tule which had small holes in it . . . They would draw the Western Wall, Rachel's Tomb, Absalom's Monument and such like places on the material and afterwards they would go over the drawings with woolen thread of all colours. They would send their work to relatives as presents and to benefactors abroad to solicit donations."

These motifs also appeared on bags to hold the *tallit* (prayer shawl) and *tefillin* (phylacteries) and on tablecloths for Sabbath use. Two pictures in the Israel Museum collection show two such bags which must surely have been made by brides for their prospective grooms. The

* This citation, as well as those following, is taken from *Art and Crafts in Eretz Israel in the 19th Century*, published by the Israel Museum.

Wall, which appears in the center, is flanked by the Solomon's *Midrash* on its right and by the Temple site on its left; neither of the two mosques, the Dome of the Rock or Al Akza appear.

Five Artists

Many Jewish artists in Eretz Israel in the course of the nineteenth century used the Western Wall motif. The first among them was Yehoseph Schwarz, a geographer and artist. Havivah Peled writes about him and his work:

"The Israel Museum collections contain a lithograph showing the holy places in Jerusalem. It is rectangular; its upper section is a map of the city and beneath it are five drawings. The Temple Mount and the Western Wall appear in the centre and beyond them the Mount of Olives, the various sites on which are numbered 1 to 10 with their identification appearing below . . . At the bottom of the sheet appears the following legend: "A loving gift sent to my brethren in exile who seek (the welfare of) Zion and Jerusalem. Made in Jerusalem, the holy city, may it speedily be rebuilt, in the year 5597. Made by the insignificant young man, Yehoseph Schwarz, distributed throughout the People of Israel by my dear brother, Rabbi Hayyim Schwarz, may God keep him, of Hirben." The date, 1837, fixes it as the first dated work showing scenes of the city in this format. The depiction of the Western Wall and the Temple Mount which appears in this work served all branches of craftsmanship in the second half of the nineteenth century . . ."

Yehoseph Schwarz was born in 1804 in Floss, Bavaria. In 1833 he emigrated to Eretz Israel and settled in Jerusalem where he married Rebecca Luria. He began his geographical researches immediately on arrival and made many place identifications, many of which were very successful. For example, he succeeded in locating and identifying the site of the Ramban Synagogue in Jerusalem which was named after the medieval scholar, Nahmanides, who settled there. He published his researches in four volumes, the most important of which, for our purposes, is *Tevuot Ha-Aretz* ("The Produce of the Land") which appeared in 1845 and is devoted entirely to the geography and history of Eretz Israel. The book was translated into English and a map of the country and many drawings were added for that edition. A German edition appeared in 1851 including a map of the country, the locations of the holy places and a portrait of the author. Yehoseph Schwarz died in Jerusalem in 1865.

The second craftsman is Moses ben Isaac Mizrahi-Shah. He was born in Teheran in approximately 1870 and, some twenty years later, he came to Eretz Israel where he changed his name to Mizrahi, as was customary among Persian Jews. Moses Shah-Mizrahi was a tall man and always wore a turban. He lived near the Damascus Gate and worked as a scribe writing Torah Scrolls, phylacteries and *mezzuzot*. In order to supplement his income, he opened a shop for picture frames and mirrors in the spice market in the Old City. Moses Mizrahi was the most prolific craftsman in Eretz Israel at the end of the Ottoman period. A considerable number of Mizrahi's pieces are extant although they were executed on glass, a highly breakable material. He worked in his shop and most of his orders, at least at the beginning, were for items of a religious character. *Shiviti* plaques which he made are still in use in Jerusalem synagogues but most of them, like his other pieces, are not signed. Their origin has been established by oral testimony and on the basis of comparison with his known works. Mizrahi also created *Mizrah* plaques on glass. The fact that they do not bear the word *Mizrah* on them indicates that they were made for the local market and not for export to western countries. These plaques usually have as their central feature the Dome of the Rock, more beauti-

The Wall on a silver snuff-box; Eretz Israel, 19th century.

ful than it is in reality, surrounded by architectural floral designs. Occasionally, the fir trees, a Star of David (with or without the word Zion) and lions also appear. Only one of his extant *Mizrah* plaques depicts the site of the Temple in the traditional manner – the Western Wall with fir trees on top, the Al Akza mosque to the right and the Dome of the Rock to its left.

The city of Safed also played a role in the subject under discussion. The craftsman, Samuel Shulman, arrived in Eretz Israel in 1850 and settled in Safed. For most of his life he was active in attempts to expand Jewish settlement in the country. For example, he participated, together with Simon Berman, in establishing a company called "The Settlement of the Holy Land" in Tiberias, and was appointed its secretary. Later, he became the secretary of a company formed in Jaffa in 1882 called "The Pioneer Committee, Yesod Ha-Ma'alah." Shulman, who like Moses Mizrahi was a traditional scribe, died in 1900. Havivah Peled evaluated his artistic work:

"Samuel Shulman used his scribal skills to attain his objective. He sent micrographic lithographs to donors to get them to support his ideas. Some of them are extant. In a micrographic work, 'The Love of Zion', in the Einhorn collection, the holy places in Jerusalem are depicted in the manner established by Yehoseph Schwarz. The legend runs: 'This picture presents: 1. Zion and David's City; 2. Two Arabs with the harps and other musical instruments that the exiled Jews hung on themselves when they sat by the rivers of Babylon when they remembered Zion. The first part (of the micrography) is made up of all the scriptural verses about Zion and David; the second part is made up of the Books of Ezra and Nehemia. I made this as a memorial of the Love of Zion. Samuel Shulman . . .' "

Ephraim Lilien's famous etching.

Jews at the Wall; a charcoal drawing by Nahum Gutman.

Another Jerusalem artist, perhaps the most important of this group, was Simhah Diskin known as Yaniver or Yanover. He was born in Grodno in 1846 and came to Eretz Israel with his family in 1853. Pinhas Grayevsky, who wrote a history of the old Jewish community of Jerusalem, devoted several articles to Diskin and called him "a master." He worked in copper, brass, zinc, marble and other materials. Two bitumen stone *Kiddush* goblets of his have survived. The one in the Israel Museum collection is roughly engraved with an inscription and pictures among which is the Western Wall; the one in the Wolfson Museum is engraved, on one side, with the Wall and on the other with the word Jerusalem. Diskin was not only a carver and engraver; among his other appelations he was also known as "The Painter." Ladies of Jerusalem have recalled that they used to order designs from him to embroider *tefillin* bags, Sabbath aprons and tablecloths, and *Mizrah* mirrors. When the "canvas style" arrived in Jerusalem he used to sketch pictures of the Wall on that material for the young ladies to embroider and hang in their homes.

Meir Rozin, who arrived in Jerusalem in 1891, owned a souvenir shop near David's Tower and was an excellent wood carver. He also prepared a booklet of embroidery designs which was printed by the Monzon Press for a girls' school in Jerusalem. On the title page the following appears: "Embroidery designs of paintings of the Holy City, may it speedily be rebuilt, one of the handicrafts that are taught to the girls in Bet Hinnukh Yeladim in Jerusalem, may it be rebuilt." In 1913 Meir Rozin opened a small museum to exhibit his work. He died in 1917.

The Wall in Modern Art

When did the Western Wall become a motif in Jewish painting? There can be no doubt that that happened in the second half of the nineteenth and the beginning of the twentieth centuries. One of the outstanding artists who painted the Wall in that period was Ephraim Lillien. In its early days, he was a teacher in the Bezalel Art School for a short period (1905-1907). He painted in the fashion of the "Jugendstil" which was nearing the end of its popularity. In 1905 he made an etching of the Wall in which he departed from the style which utilized twisting lines. The narrow alley in front of the Wall – so different from today's great piazza – is given clear expression, and the figure of an old man on the left side of the composition starkly closes off the narrow prayer area. At the bottom of the sheet is a scene which has no connection to the subject – ploughing as it was done thousands of years ago. In another etching executed five years later in 1913 the alley is given no expression; there the whole weight is on the Wall itself. The artist endows the Wall and the worshippers by it with great power. Various inscriptions appear on the stones and among them the artist's own full Hebrew name proudly indicating that he is a *kohen*, of priestly descent.

The Wall motif appeared frequently in works executed in the Bezalel school, on candelabra for the Hanukkah festival and engraved on casings of artillery shells among other items. Meir Gur-Arie, a pupil and later a teacher at Bezalel, depicts the Wall as a great wall with the worshippers in the alley, very small, out of all real proportion. He also produced several coloured prints of the various types among the worshippers. The Wall also appears in the work of Joseph Budko, who was the director of the "New Bezalel" from his arrival in Eretz Israel in 1933 until his death in 1940. Herman Struck, who was of German origin, also painted and etched the Wall among the other holy places. He visited Eretz Israel in 1903 but was not a teacher at Bezalel.

Slowly, the Wall began to disappear from the works of the Bezalel students and their colleagues who studied and painted under the influence of the "Paris School." A rare painting of Jerusalem is that of Nahum Gutman, one of the students who rebelled against the artistic method that Bezalel tried to instill in its pupils. This painting shows Jerusalem and the Western Wall but it is an exception which proves the rule that the Wall had ceased to be a motif for paintings. It is possible that this was a reaction to what Bezalel was preaching but it is also possible that the artists stopped painting the Wall because it was too closely identified with the work of craftsmen who worked in metal, embroidery, copper relief, etc., and had become stylized and commercial.

Later, the severance of access to the Wall contributed to its absence from Israeli art. The Wall's appearance in the work of artists – Jewish and non-Jewish – such as Chagall, Baskin, Macabbee and Dali only emphasizes Israeli artists' neglect of it. The first signs of renewed interest in the Wall can be seen in the Knesset (Parliament) building in Jerusalem, completed in 1966. Alfred Bernheim's photographs of the Wall's stones were greatly enlarged and exhibited in one of the halls. The wall of hewn stones in the main hall designed by Dani Karavan can also be seen as a modern version of the Western Wall.

After the Six-Say War, the Wall reappears as a motif, directly expressed or hinted at. In a print of Mordecai Ardon of a wall of giant stones (1967), the latter is the case as it may be in the blue spot in a silk screen print of Alima, which appears above forms evocative of hills and which may represent the echo of the Wall. The subject appears explicitly in a series of lithographs by Menashe Kaddishman, which are based on photographs of the Wall to which splashes of colour have been added.

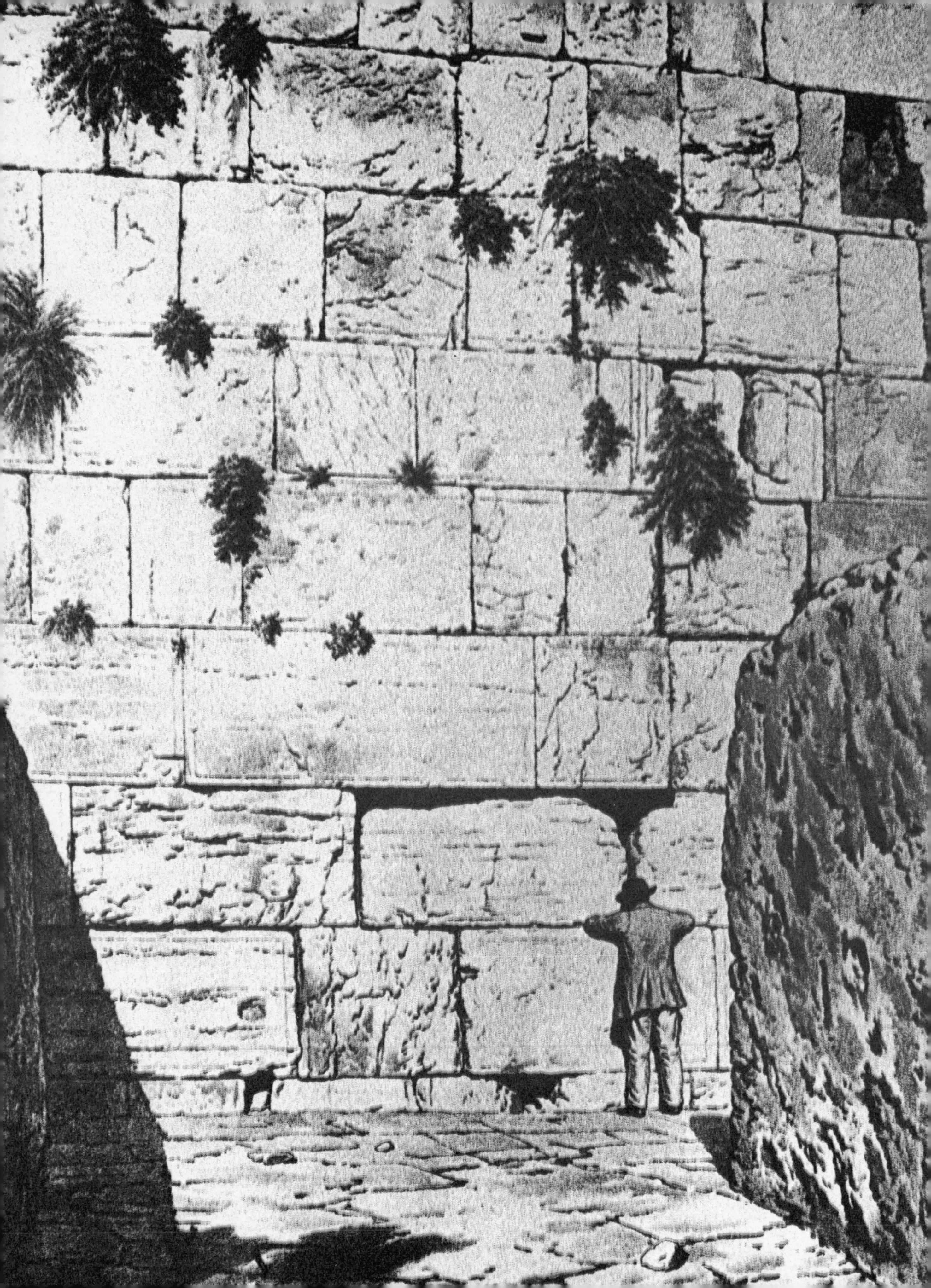

CHAPTER X

FLORA AND FAUNA AT THE WALL

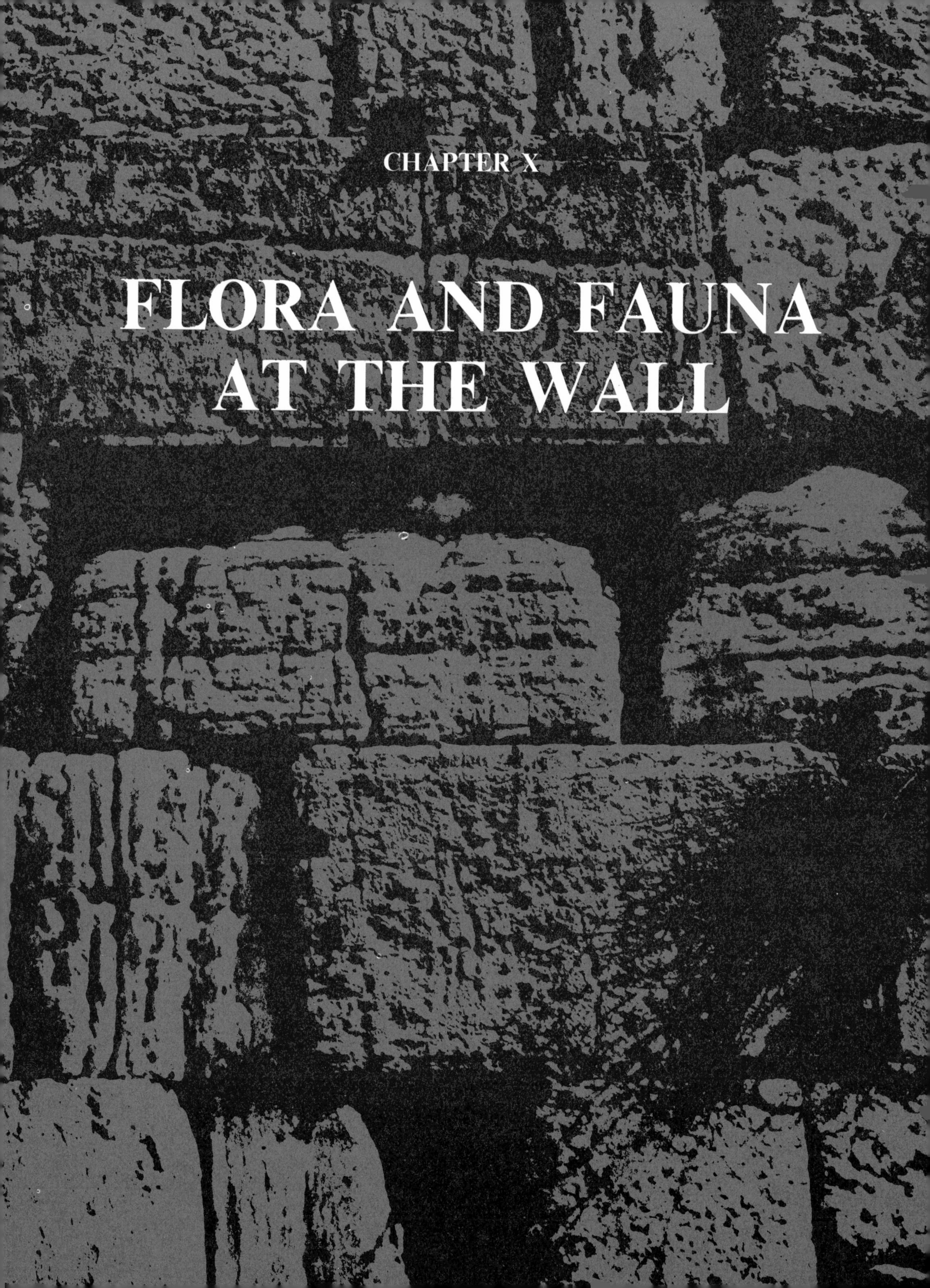

Frequently, when one stands before the ancient glory of the only vestige remaining of the Temple, one's attention is drawn by the plants growing out of the cracks between the stones, reminiscent of "the hyssop that springs out of the wall" (I Kings 5:13). The ancient rabbis considered the thorny caper (*Capparis spinosa*) which grows between the Western Wall's stones to be "the fiercest of trees" like Israel which is "the fiercest of nations" (Bezah 25a). They knew the fact that the caper takes root anywhere and is thus very difficult to uproot. Even if it is cut down to the roots, in spring it will sprout again and blossom and bear fruit and spread its seed to other places. Thus the allegory of the People of Israel that manages to survive in even the hardest exiles and when it is expelled from one country, it takes hold in another.

Where do the Wall's plants find their water? There are several answers to this question: 1. Winter rains penetrate the cracks and the water is absorbed by the soil that has accumulated there. From there it is drawn by capillary attraction into the limestone which can absorb water more than 10% of its own mass, and the plants reach it by penetrating the stones with their roots. 2. The Western Wall which faces into the rains receives more rain water than the other walls of the Temple Mount and thus its plant life is richer. This is particularly true with regards to the southern wall in which only one plant, the thorny caper, takes hold. 3. Most wall plants are equipped with mechanisms which minimize evaporation. Some of them have hairy or felt-like stalks and leaves. The hairs minimize the evaporation because the air between them, which is a bad heat conductor, acts as an insulating layer between the plant and its environment. 4. Some of the plants have a thick epidermis (cuticle) which limits evaporation, others emit an ethereal, fragrant oil which, as it evaporates, cools the plant's leaves and reduces the evaporation rate of the water in them.

The Common Ephedra (1)

This plant, *Ephedra campylopoda*, grows in the center of the Wall and is the most dense and developed of its plants. It is unique in Israel's flora; it belongs to the class Gymnospermae

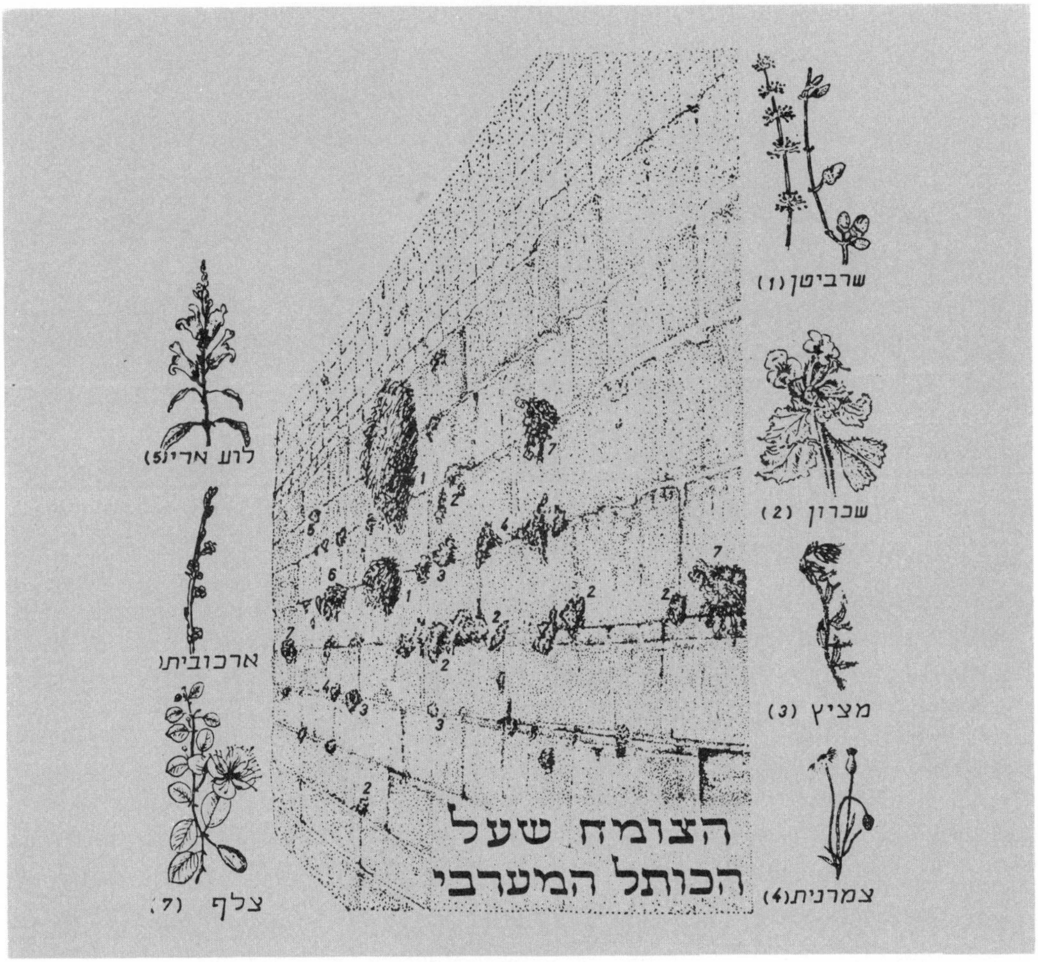

The plants on the Wall; drawn by J. Gavish, described by Y. Feliks.

(like the coniferous trees), whereas most Israeli plants are angiospermous. The ephedra has almost no leaves; its thin branches are arranged around its main sprout. The plant is dioecious, i.e., one is male and the other female. The female plant develops red fruits which are eaten by birds. The plant's long shoots climb on rocks and trees and hang down from them. The ephedra can be found on the hedges of the orange groves of the coastal plain. The plant is the source of ephedrin, a drug used in the treatment of bronchial diseases. There are also a few smaller examples of the ephedra on the Western Wall.

The Golden Henbane (2)

The most common plant on the Wall is the golden henbane (*Hyoscyamus aureus*) which can be identified by its relatively large leaves. It is completely enveloped in glandular hairs; its flowers are yellow and their pharynx is deep purple. After ripening, its fruits, which are in hard calyxes with five points, protrude. This plant received the first morphological description in ancient Jewish literature; Josephus (Antiquities 3,7) describes it in detail. He compares its calyx to the tiara of the highpriest. The Hebrew name for the plant, *shikaron* (a form of the word for drunkenness), derives from the poisonous, intoxicating substance it contains.

The Syrian Podosnoma (3)

The henbane's main competitor at the Wall is the Syrian podosnoma *(Podosnoma syriacum)*; its leaves are dark and smaller than the henbane's. The whole plant is enveloped in dense, sticky bristles. Its flowers have pale blue and white corollas with the lobes turned backwards. The podosnoma is a typical rock plant and is able to penetrate the stone with its roots and so draw out the water.

The Rock Phagnalon (4)

Here and there on the Wall one can see the white stalks of the rock phagnalon (*Phagnalon rupestre*). On the heads of the stalks are spherical growths which are the skulls of the tiny flowers out of which develop the fringed seeds which the wind scatters afar.

The Sicilian Snapdragon (5)

In the higher courses of the Wall there are a few examples of the Sicilian snapdragon (*Antirrhinum siculum*) with their yellow flowers. This plant belongs to the family of the common garden snapdragon, an ornamental flower of many beautiful colours. It grows wild on the rocks of the Upper Galilee. The fruit contains thousands of tiny seeds which are scattered by the wind and take root in the cracks between stones in walls and fences.

The old and the new; ancient plants and a modern tree.

The plants on the Wall.

The Horsetail Knotgrass (6)

This plant (*Polygonum aquisetiformae*) sits in splendid isolation to the left of the ephedra at the centre of the Wall. Like its neighbour, it too has long shoots that hang downwards and between its small leaves long inflorescences break out bearing dozens of small white-pink flowers. The Mishnah (Shabbat 14:13) mentions that an antidote for snake bite was prepared from this plant.

The Thorny Caper (7)

This plant (*Capparis spinosa*) can hardly be seen in winter but when spring comes, there emerge from its roots long shoots, oval leaves with distorted thorns at their sides, and flower buds which, in ancient times, served as a spice after marination. Every day some of the buds open and develop into white flowers out of which develop fruits, like tiny cucumbers. One of the rabbis used this plant as the basis for his remark that when the Messiah comes, trees will bear fruit every day (Shabbat 30b). There are several specimens of the caper on the Wall and it is the only plant which grows on the southern wall.

The Birds which Nest at the Wall

Several species of birds nest in the cracks between the stones of the Wall. In spring flocks of the swift (*Apus Apus*) black swallows pass through the area. These make calls which sound like, "sis, sis" and thus their Hebrew name *sis*; they build their nests in the cracks in the Wall. Here and there one can find at the Wall the most common of Israel's birds, the house-sparrow (*Passer domesticus biblicus*), which also nests in the cracks. Scripture (Psalms 84:4) has it that in ancient times this bird used to nest between the stones of the Temple itself. Doves also nest at the Wall and occasionally one hears "tzit, tzit", a sound made by the house-lizard (*Hemidactylus turcicus, in Hebrew: semamit*) (cf. Proverbs 30:28).

The stones of the Western Wall, apparently so silent, are in fact a large habitat for plants, among them some, which give forth real life. This process has not stopped even for a second during more than two thousand years of the Wall's existence.

CHAPTER XI

FOUR STONES

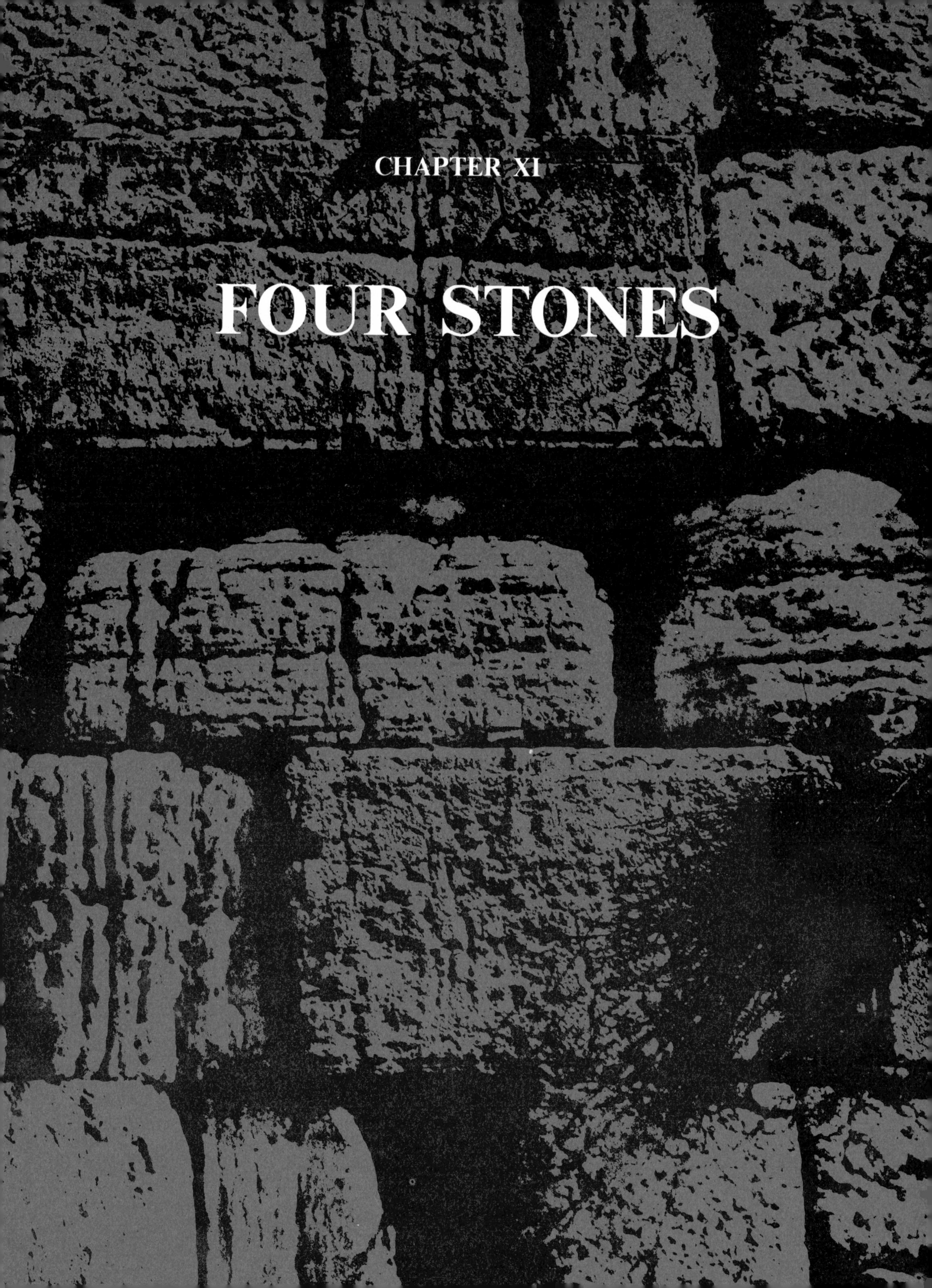

A Stone Weighing Four Hundred Tons

Anybody who examines the courses of stones in the Western Wall from the Second Temple period cannot fail to be impressed by the size of the stones. They are 1 metre high and from 1 to 4 metres long. The larger ones weigh more than 10 tons each, and some reach as much as 15 tons. Josephus reports that there are stones in the Temple Mount walls which are longer than 20 cubits (i.e., more than 10 metres) and some longer than 40 cubits. Scholars ridiculed this assertion and dismissed Josephus as an ancient Baron Munchausen. They admitted that there are large stones in the Wall, but stones of the size Josephus reported just do not exist. However, the excavations at the foot of the Temple Mount and the Western Wall have revealed stones which come close to the sizes described by the ancient historian. At the corner, where the Western Wall meets the southern wall, there are a number of stones which are each more than 10 metres. long; these weigh approximately 70 tons each. A little to the north of Wilson's Arch even larger stones have been uncovered. They are more than 3 metres high and one is 12 metres long, which brings us very close to Josephus' maximum figures. In order to work out the weight of this massive stone, it is necessary to establish its thickness, i.e., its depth into the Temple Mount and fortunately a hewn hole was discovered in the stone which extends its whole thickness which is 4 metres. With all the necessary data, 12 x 3 x 4 metres, it is possible to establish its weight – more than 400 tons!

The question which almost asks itself is: How were such huge stones quarried, transported, lifted, and placed in the construction? Before attempting to answer, it must be pointed out that the matter is not theoretical; after all the stones are there – so it must have been done! Another difficult question is: Why was it done? The answer that it was done to impress the public is unacceptable. The effort and investment required were far too great for that to be the reason. The question becomes more acute when one considers that in the rest of the world in that period no less impressive buildings were constructed using small bricks or rough unhewn stones. As far as the technicalities of the construction are concerned, there are no mysteries; most of the information is readily available in contemporary books of architecture. Vitruvius, a Roman architect in the first century C.E., established a school of engineering of architecture and prepared a textbook, titled *Architecture*, which describes precisely the available solutions to problems of quarrying, transportation, lifting and construction. Derricks, wheels and the way to calculate the center of gravity were already well-known in those times and with skill and exact calculations it was possible to solve all technical problems. The crux of the task lay in working out the calculations and the technical skill, not in the size of the work-force although large numbers of laborers were available and indeed utilized.

There were two motives for the choice of this massive construction method. First of all, the planners and executors wanted to build walls that would stand forever. That is why they sunk the foundations of the walls down to the bed-rock. But they were not satisfied with that measure alone and chose to use huge stones. As indicated above, they could have achieved the desired stability with smaller stones or bricks but that method of construction requires some sort of material to join the stones or bricks to each other. Nowadays, cement is used for that purpose. The amount of cement needed to bond the stones together and to solidify the filling of small stones in the thickness of the walls would have been enormous and have amounted to one half of the actual volume of the walls themselves! The "cement" of ancient times was a mixture of sand (wadi or sea) and plaster. In order to create the plaster, limestone had to be burned in kilns continuously for a period of 24-48 hours. This process required huge amounts of fuel which, in those times, was mainly wood. Wood was the chief raw material for industry; it was used to manufacture tools, doors, roofs and furniture etc., and agriculture depended on

Stones several metres long in the courses revealed by the excavations.

it for handles for implements, for ploughs and for threshing boards among other uses. Eretz Israel is a country poor in forests and to provide the amount of fuel to create the necessary amounts of plaster, tens of thousands of acres of forest-land would have had to be stripped. This would have had a major effect on the whole economy and would certainly have led to a drop in the standard of living. When the country was ruled by outsiders, forest-land was often denuded without consideration, but when the country enjoyed sovereignty, the government always took steps to preserve and develop the forested areas. The decision to build the walls of large stones which do not need cement – "dry construction" – saved a large part of one of the country's main natural resources. The drawback in the use of huge stones was that it required a high level of technical skill in stone-dressing but this was far outweighed by the economy of the method.

Another reason for choosing large stones was speed. When Herod started rebuilding the Temple Mount area, he did not know whether the Romans would agree. Although he was a sovereign monarch, he depended very heavily on the grace and goodwill of Rome and was apprehensive lest the Romans see his rebuilding as the creation of a stronghold in Jerusalem which would be used – as indeed it later was – in a revolt against Rome. An echo of Herod's dilemma can be heard in the Talmudic legend which has him consulting with an old sage named Bava, who advised him to start building and then ask. If he was to present the Romans with a *fait accompli*, speed was of the utmost importance. Public building usually takes a

The quarry above Zedekiah's Cave, the source of the Wall's stones.

long time because of the need to raise the necessary funds. In the case of the Temple Mount, however, Herod's political considerations moved things along very quickly.

As strange as it may seem, the use of monumental stones reduces the time needed for building on condition that the construction teams have been well trained and are skilled in operating the mechanical equipment. The laying of a 12-metre stone, for example, completes, in one action, 12 metres of construction. This consideration also applies, of course, to its height and its depth and so one such stone takes care of approximately 150 cubic metres of the building. All the walls of the Temple Mount took only three years to construct and it is estimated that, had small stones or bricks been used, the project would have taken twice that time.

The huge stones gave the walls a most impressive appearance but it must be pointed out that aesthetics were, at best, only a secondary consideration. This is clear from the fact that the foundations, which were also built of huge stones, were covered with earth and indeed, the first three courses of monumental stones which were above the ground were hidden from view by the shops built against them. And those shops were part of the original master-plan for the area.

Stones for the Presidential Palace and Why Lead?

A few weeks after the archaeological excavations at the Western Wall began, a number of large, beautiful stones were uncovered in the rubble near the southwest corner. These stones had originally been part of the upper sections of the Western Wall and had been thrown down in the seventh century. This was when the Byzantine Christians, led by Emperor Heraclius, reconquered the city from the Persians and, as an act of revenge for what the Persians and

A stone which was thrown down from the plateau. Three such stones were taken to the presidential palace.

their Jewish allies had done to Christian churches and as punishment for Jewish support of the Persians, set about the systematic destruction of the Temple Mount. The Western Wall, which at that time still rose to a great height, was severely damaged; many stones from its upper sections were thrown down to the foot of the Temple Mount where they were uncovered by the archaeologists. When the find became known, the architect who was then (1968) designing the gardens of the new presidential palace visited the archaeological site. He wanted to incorporate stones from the Wall in the garden and when he saw what had been discovered, he asked for three stones which he planned to put one on top of the other. The archaeological expedition saw no reason to refuse, and the three stones were taken to the president's garden.

Now it was necessary to place the stones without using cement – "dry construction" – and the engineers were not quite sure how to do it. They placed two stones side-by-side and wanted to put the third stone on top of them. This is usually done by placing a small mass – generally a stone the size of a clenched fist – under the stone to be placed as a prop. This enables the stone to be maneuvered with relative ease to the exact position desired. Then the stone is levered up with a heavy crow-bar, the prop-stone removed and the stone falls into its exact place. However, because of the great weight of the stone it was feared that a drop of even as little as 10-15 centimetres might damage the corners of the stones and the engineers, understandably, wanted to preserve the beauty of the stones' dressing. They came back to the archaeologists for advice – did they know how the ancients used to do it? The archaeologists were, at that time, far too occupied with their excavations to have considered the technical problems of how the Wall was built, so they sent the engineers to the above-mentioned Vitruvius' textbook on architecture.

That ancient architect instructed the modern engineers. He records that in order not to damage the edges of massive stones, they were to be placed on lumps of lead instead of stones. The weight of the stone slowly crushes the lead and in a few minutes the stone descends to its exact place. Thus, using Roman technology at least two thousand years old, the engineers working at the presidential palace succeeded in placing the stones.

The incident of "the president's stones" also cleared up another mystery. Josephus, who had actually seen the destroyed upper sections of the wall, mentions that the massive stones were stuck together with lead! Apparently, what he had seen was the remains of the pieces of lead used in placing the stones. Ignorant as he was of building techniques, Josephus naturally thought that the lead was used to bond the stones together. An exact observation but the wrong conclusion! Later on, bodies of compressed lead were observed between stones and always near the extremities.

Later on, when the matter became public knowledge, a Jewish dignitary from New York arrived in Jerusalem on a visit. As a sign of appreciation for his activities on behalf of Israel, the official in charge of the holy places in the Ministry of Religions and the mayor of Jerusalem agreed to let this man have a stone from the Wall to incorporate in a new synagogue that was being built in New York. The idea was to put the stone near the Holy Ark in which the Torah Scrolls are kept. The gentleman visited the archaeological site accompanied by the Mayor and the official and had himself photographed standing over "his" stone. The photograph was published in the press on the following day and only by reading the photograph's legend did the archaeologists realize why their visitor had wanted to be photographed with a stone that had fallen from the Wall!

When some of Jerusalem's rabbis read this news item, they were shocked. How can a stone from the Western Wall be taken into exile!? "If people want to emigrate to New York," they said, "let them. A stone from the Wall – God forbid"! The official in charge of the holy places argued that three stones had been transferred to the president's garden and that he did not see the difference. When this argument was published, the president, Zalman Shazar, immediately had the stones returned to the site of the excavations. The only ones who benefitted from this entire incident were the archaeologists – they still had the stones and they had had a comprehensive and practical lesson in ancient building techniques.

A Corner Headstone and an Inscription

In the course of the archaeological excavations at the southwest corner a stone with very unusual dressing was discovered lying on the stone pavement of the road from Second Temple times. This stone had been dislodged from its place and thrown down by Titus' legionnaires when they conquered the Temple on Av 10, 70 C.E. The stones of the Wall are generally finely dressed on the side facing outwards and those at the corners, which have two such sides, are dressed on both of them. In most of the stones the dressed face had been smoothened very finely and a border, about two centimetres deep, chiselled out on all four sides. The width of the border is not uniform to all the stones and occasionally varies in one stone itself. It is these borders that give the Wall its special appearance.

The stone which was discovered in the street had been the top stone on the corner and its dressing was distinctive. In addition to the normal dressing on the two sides which faced outwards, a ridge had been chiselled out along the upper section of the face. This relief ridge, which looks like a coarse rope, continued along all the top stones and added a decorative element to the Wall. In the language of the masons in that period such a stone was called, in

The engraved inscription – more than 2000 years old.

Hebrew, *even rosh pinah*, "the corner head stone" and its setting marked the completion of the building. In modern Hebrew the term *rosh pinah* has taken on the opposite meaning and is used for the foundation stone. Logic, however, is on the side of the ancients. It is clearly more sensible to hold the ceremonies and celebrations when the building is finished than it is to hold them before it has even been started. This is particularly true with regards to public buildings which often stand half-completed for years after the *even ha-pinah* celebration have taken place!

Our corner headstone has an inscription engraved on it in fine letters which reads: *le-beit ha-teki'ah lehakh...* – "For the house of sounding..." The corner stone was broken and so the inscription is only a fragment; it should, apparently, be completed: *le-hakhriz* – "to announce." But there must have been more. From the various sources it is clear that at the southwest corner of the Temple Mount plaza stood a tower at the top of which was a structure (possibly a platform) from which one of the priests on duty sounded a trumpet to indicate the beginning of the Sabbath and its termination. For this purpose, the southwest corner was ideal since at its foot lay the crossroads of the lower market of Jerusalem, where throngs of pilgrims and local residents congregated to conduct their purchases and other business. We know of this tower from Josephus who only mentions it in passing. He gives an account of the fortifications built on the Temple Mount by the zealot faction led by Simeon bar Giora. The rival zealot faction, led by Johanan of Gush Halav, established itself in the upper city, in the area of today's Jewish Quarter. From these positions the two factions waged war against each other. Simeon bar Giora had a catapult firing-post set up in the southwest tower. In order to identify that tower exactly, Josephus described it as the tower from which they sounded trumpets to announce the Sabbath.

What, however, is the significance of the inscription and why was it engraved on the corner headstone? Any inscription starting with the Hebrew letter *le* could have been a sign-post, i.e., it indicated the direction to go in order to get to the "sounding post." This makes sense because the Temple was operated and maintained by twenty-four "watches" of priests who each worked for two weeks a year. Priests coming in from the country would not be familiar with the geography of the Temple Mount and would need sign-posts. However, the inscription was on the stone at the top of the tower, and when the priest got there he had no need for direction!

There is another possible explanation. The Hebrew *le* also indicates "belonging", i.e., this stone belongs to the "sounding post." It must be remembered that preparations for the rebuilding of the Temple Mount took some eight years, during which period stones were quarried, dressed and brought to the site. Clearly, the important stones had to be marked so that the masons would know where they belonged and it is possible that our inscription is, in effect, such a marking. The objection to this theory is twofold. Firstly, the masons usually marked their stones with abbreviated signs and not with full sentences. Why would they take the time to make such a fine engraving? Secondly, what is the meaning of the broken word *le-hakh...*? That was certainly not necessary if the inscription's purpose was to identify the stone.

The inscription must, therefore, be understood as a dedicatory inscription. Although great wealth had accumulated in the Temple treasury from which the project was financed, great additional sums were still needed. A part of this was raised by contributions from the public; people would donate the price of a stone, half a stone, etc. A rabbinic legend tells of one pious man who suffered dire poverty but wanted to contribute his portion. A miracle occurred and he carried a huge stone on his back from the desert. Of course, there were wealthy contributors who donated the funds for entire sections and, as is the practice today, they had their generosity perpetuated by having the section named after them, with a dedicatory inscription (instead of today's ubiquitous plaque). This was the custom in temples throughout the world and it was adopted in synagogues in Eretz Israel where many such inscriptions have been discovered. The inscription should, therefore, be reconstructed to read: "For the house of sounding to announce [the Sabbath], donated by so-and-so."

"And You Will See and Your Heart Will Rejoice"

Six metres above the paved road from Second Temple times, under Robinson's Arch, is a stone with an inscription. The inscription is incomplete, not because it is a fragment but because the engraver did not finish it. The engraving is not very deep but it can be deciphered. The verse the engraver chose is from the Book of Isaiah and the inscription reads: "And you will see and your heart will rejoice and their bones like an herb. . ."

The prophecies of consolation in the last chapter of Isaiah dwell on the "end of days", on the resurrection, and on the good times that Israel will enjoy in its own land. The text, to which our inscription belongs, reads: "Rejoice with Jerusalem and be glad in her, all that love her. Rejoice a rejoicing with her, all that have mourned for her. So that you may suck and be satisfied from the breast of her consolations; so that you may suck and be delighted from the nipple of her glory. For thus says the Lord: I will extend peace to her like a river and the respect of the nations like a flowing stream; you shall suck, you shall be lifted on [her] side and dandled on [her] knees. Like a man whose mother comforts him, so will I comfort you and in Jerusalem shall you be comforted. And you will see and your heart will rejoice, and your bones like an herb will flourish. . ." (Isaiah 66:10-14).

So prophesied the prophet. After the years of anguish and wrath, better days will come to Jerusalem. In the first few centuries after the destruction of the Temple, this prophecy occupied the minds of many and esoteric commentaries were written to it describing how Jerusalem would return to its days of greatness and glory and how the Temple would rise again and be a shining beacon in the city. This is the background to Isaiah 66 and to the inscription on the stone in the Wall.

When, then, was it engraved and by whom? Firstly, it should be noted that there is a slight discrepancy between the inscription and the traditional text of Isaiah. The traditional text reads: "And you will see and your heart will rejoice and *your* bones like an herb will flourish," whereas the inscription reads: "and *their* bones like an herb." It would seem that the inscription is more logical than the accepted Biblical text because when the reference is to living present persons it is possible to say "you will see and your heart will rejoice," but the

"And you shall see and your heart will rejoice. . ."

reference to bones is to the dead who are not present and they should be addressed in the third person. Is it possible that the inscription preserves an earlier and more exact text of Isaiah than our Bible?

Another theory to explain the discrepancy is that when a scriptural verse is copied for mundane purposes it should be slightly changed so as not to mix the sacred with the profane and so our engraver changed "your bones" into "their bones" to honor this practice and, at the same time give a more logical reading.

Whichever is the true explanation, there can be no doubt that the engraver was not just practicing but that something had happened with regards to Jerusalem and the Temple that inspired him to engrave this verse. As indicated, the inscription is on a stone six metres above the level of the road from Second Temple times at the foot of the Wall and the letters are not in the style of the Second Temple Period. On the other hand, in the Fatimid and Crusader periods, i.e., the eleventh and twelfth centuries, the stone with the inscription was already covered with rubble and so it could not have been engraved then or after.

There are several inscriptions on the Wall and all except one are from the Middle Ages; the exception is from the Byzantine period. The shape of their letters is quite different from those in our inscription and their contents are also very different. All the other inscriptions consist of names of people, occasionally accompanied by self-invoked blessings and good wishes. Our inscription is unique in that it is anonymous and consists of a scriptural quotation.

There are three possibilities with regards to the background events that might have motivated this inscription and, thus, to its date. The first is that the inscription was made in the fourth century – or to be more exact, close to the year 360. This was in the reign of the Byzantine emperor, Julian, who is known as "the Apostate." Julian rejected Christianity, which had recently been declared the state religion, and wanted to revive ancient paganism and emperor-worship. Any enemy of Christianity was Julian's ally and so he wanted to reach a *modus vivendi* with the Jews. He was also motivated by political considerations in that he was preparing a campaign against the Persians in the east and he wanted to enlist the support of the large strong Jewish communities there. He turned to the Jews and encouraged them to restore the Temple Mount and rebuild their Temple. Clearly, such a decision raised Messianic hopes in the Jewish breast and some saw it as the beginning of religious and political freedom for Israel as well as a victory over Christianity. Actual practical preparations were started for the rebuilding of the Temple and it is possible that in the excitement and ecstasy somebody inscribed the verse from Isaiah on the Wall as an expression of joy at the imminent coming of the "end of days" and the arrival of the Messiah. However, Julian was murdered shortly after his elevation to the throne and Christianity reassumed its position as the official religion of the Byzantine empire. The Jews were rudely awakened from their dream of rebuilding the Temple and triumphant Christianity destroyed whatever work had already been done and burned the Temple Mount storehouses in which the necessary material had been collected. The act of arson was described by the Christians as the hand of God.

Another possible period for our inscription is the beginning of the seventh century. In 614, the Persians, with Jewish help, conquered Jerusalem after they invaded the Byzantine empire. In return for their past help and in order to ensure their future cooperation, Khosroe II, king of Persia, entered into a covenant with the Jews and gave them permission to rehabilitate the Temple Mount and rebuild the Temple, with all the implications of religious – and perhaps political – independence. The treaty was honored by the Persians for three years (614-617) during which period the Jewish settlement in Jerusalem was increased and work started on the repair of the Temple Mount. It is possible that some Jerusalemite at that time engraved the verse from Isaiah to celebrate the redemption which was so close.

However, the end of this affair was evil and bitter. The Persians abrogated their treaty with the Jews in order to cooperate with the Byzantines, their avowed foes! They wanted to redraw the political map of the area and sought Byzantine agreement to their new borders. The Byzantines returned to Jerusalem, took cruel vengeance on the Jews and did their best to obliterate the Temple Mount.

The third possibility for the background to our inscription is the end of the seventh century when the Ommayad Caliphate started major building activities on and around the Temple Mount. At that time the Dome of the Rock was built almost on the site of the destroyed Temple and the Al Akza mosque was erected to its south. In order to do this, the Temple Mount support walls, including the Western Wall, had to be repaired. Around the Temple Mount an enormous complex was built and at its center stood the caliph's palace. A considerable number of Jews were employed as builders and service workers for the mosques. In contemporary sources these are called *Al-Hames* ("The Fifth") because the Moslems used to conscript one fifth of the local population for public works. The Jews were important because of their special skills in cloth-finishing and dyeing; the cloth was needed for carpets and drapes in the mosques. In addition to the available literary evidence, the archaeologist's pick has uncovered silent testimony to the Jewish presence. On the walls and plaster of simple stone buildings from the end of the Byzantine period, engravings of the seven-branched candelabrum of the Temple have been discovered. Furthermore, in many of the doorposts the archaeologists found small hewn-out recesses to hold the *mezzuzah* parchment scroll. All these are clear indications of the presence of Jewish workers who were billetted in these quarters.

It can very well be that one of those Jewish builders who worked on the Wall carved out our inscription. Watching the two beautiful mosques rising, his act was a prayer to God and perhaps something of a reproach – where are the good times You promised us, when our Temple will be rebuilt? Our inscriber may have been interrupted by one of his Arab overseers and so did not finish his prayer.

These are the three theories that have been suggested to explain the unfinished inscription on the Wall. Perhaps there are others. But one thing is almost beyond doubt: that inscription was carved sometime between the fourth and the eighth centuries.

CHAPTER XII

THE WALL HAS A THOUSAND FACES

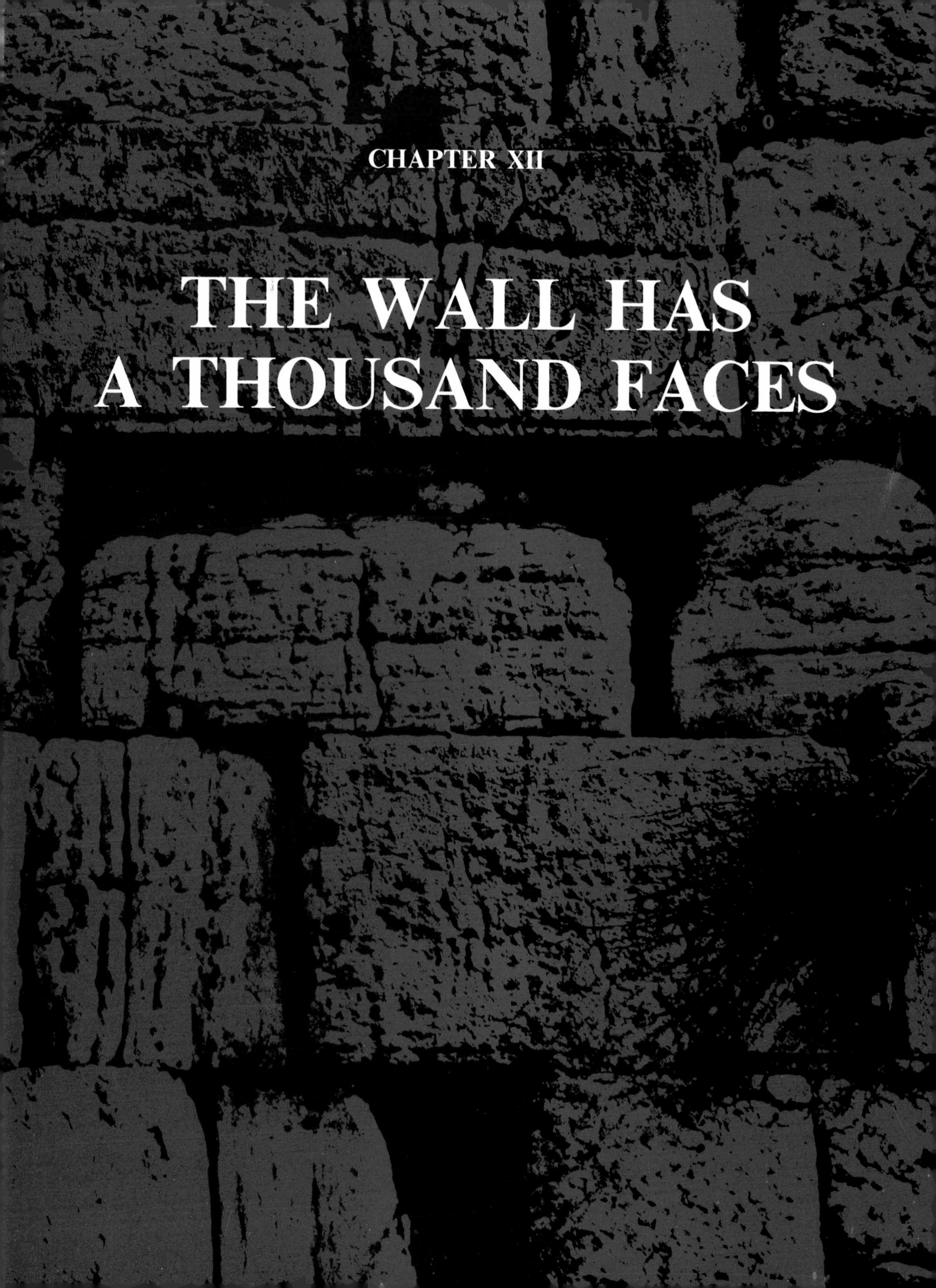

One Wall – many petitions.

The great piazza on weekdays.

Women to the right,
men to the left, at high noon.

Four mothers.

The faithful – even in the snow.

An ancient hand
on an ancient
stone.

Three worshippers and an infant.

Once there was a Hasidic lad...

A scene at the Wall – two boys from abroad are *bar-mitzvah*.

A prayer shawl and a paper skullcap.

Putting on phylacteries at the Wall.

Members of a Japanese religious sect in prayer at the Wall.

Moments – contemplation and joy.

SONNENFELD
Chief Rabbi of the Ashkenasic Community Jerusalem
A I KOOK
Chief Rabbi of Erets-Israel Jerusalem

A SELECT BIBLIOGRAPHY

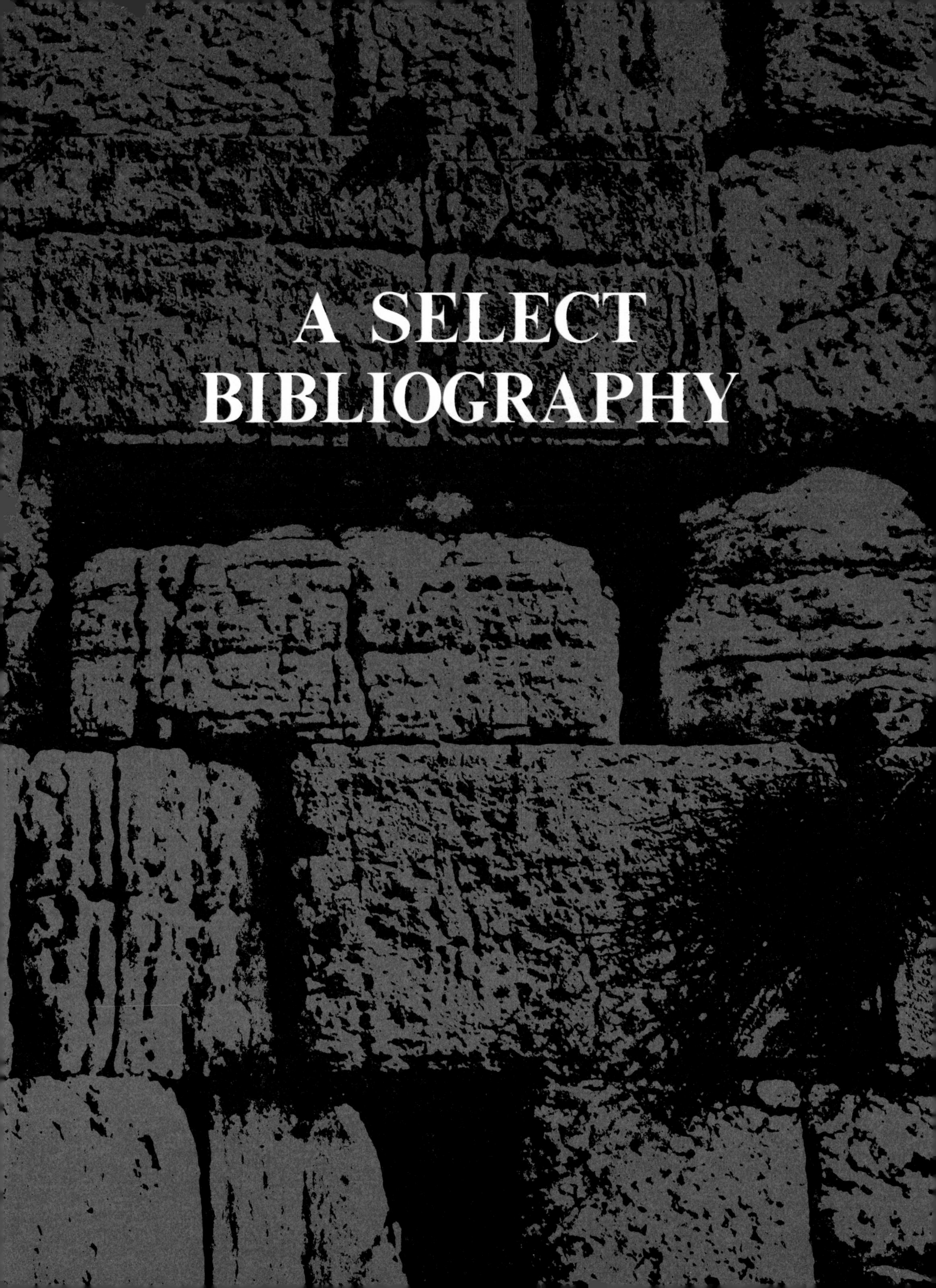

This bibliography lists books, monographs and articles in the English language. A comprehensive bibliography listing 460 items can be found in the original Hebrew edition of this volume, *Ha-Kotel* (Tel Aviv, 1981).

General

1 J. Auerbach, 'Western Wall', *Encyclopaedia Judaica*, XVI. Jerusalem 1971, pp. 467-472.

2 M. Benvenisti, 'The Western Wall and the Jewish Quarter', *Jerusalem The Torn City*, Jerusalem, Isratypeset, 1976, pp. 305-322.

3 J. Comay, 'The Western Wall', *The Temple of Jerusalem*, London, Weidenfeld & Nicolson, 1975, pp. 235-255.

4 G. Cornfeld, 'The Western Wall', *The Mystery of the Temple Mount*, Tel Aviv, etc., Bazak, 1972, pp. 68-87.

5 J. Fergusson, 'History of the Temple after the Destruction of Jerusalem', *The Temples of the Jews*, London, J. Murray, 1887, pp. 182 ff.

6 C. Geikie, 'The Wailing Place' *The Holy Land and the Bible*, London etc., Cassell, [n.d.], pp. 480-482.

7 J. Gray, *A History of Jerusalem*, London, R. Hale, 1969, pp.336; illus.

8 J.H. Hertz, *The History and Significance of the Western Wall*, London [n.d.], p.4.

9 M. Har-El, 'The Western Wall', *This is Jerusalem*, Jerusalem, Canaan Publishing House, 1977, pp. 258-269.

10 C. Hollis & R. Brownrigg, 'The Jewish Holy Places', *Holy Places*, London, Weidenfeld and Nicolson, 1969, pp. 13-73.

11 A. Holtz (ed.). *The Holy City – Jews on Jerusalem*, New York, W.W. Norton, 1971, pp. 187.

12 L. Hutton, 'The Wailing Wall of the Jews...', *Literary Landmarks* of *Jerusalem*, New York, Harper, 1895, pp. 19-23.

13 F.H. Kisch, *Palestine Diary*, London, Victor Gollanez. 1938, pp. 478.

14 J. Klausner, 'Jerusalem the Universal City'. *Palestine & Near East Economic Magazine*, II, 5-6, Tel Aviv 1927, pp. 139-140.

15 M.C. & H.A. Klein, *Temple beyond Time*, New York, Van Nostrand Reinhold, 1970, pp. 191; illus.

16 C.Z. Klotzel, *The Way to the Wailing Wall*, Jerusalem, 1935 [unpaged].

17 P. Loti, 'Wailing Place', *Jerusalem*, translated from the French by W.P. Baines, London. T. Werner Laurie, 1894-1895?, pp. 115-119.

18 B.Z. Lurie, *The Western Wall*, Jerusalem, World Zionist Organization, 1969, pp. 48.

19 B. Meistermann, 'Wailing Place', *Guide to the Holy Land*, London, B. Oates and Washbourne, 1923, p. 212.

20 J.M. Oesterreicher & A. Sinai (eds.), *Jerusalem*, New York, John Day, 1974, pp. xvi, 302.

21 G.F. Owen, 'The Wailing Wall', *Jerusalem*, Kansas City, Beacon Hill Press, 1972, pp. 106-111.

22 R. Patai, (ed.), 'Western Wall', *Encyclopedia of Zionism and Israel*, II, New York, Herzl Press, 1971, pp. 1215-1217.

23 J.L. Porter, 'The Place of Wailing', *Jerusalem Bethany and Bethlehem*, London, Thomas Nelson, 1887, pp. 39-43.

24 S. Schaffer, *Israel's Temple Mount... An Illustrated Compendium on the Holy Temples... and Walls... based on Jewish Sources...* Jerusalem, 1975, pp. xv. 299.

25 E. Schiller (ed.), *Jerusalem in Old Engravings and Illustrations*, Jerusalem, Ariel Publishing House, 1977, pp. 195; illus.

26 S.H. Steckoll, *The Temple Mount – An Illustrated History of Mount Moriah in Jerusalem*, London. Tom Stacey, 1972, pp. 96.

27 Z. Vilnay, 'The Wailing Wall', *The Holy Land in Old Prints and Maps*, Jerusalem, R. Mass, 1965, pp. 94-99.

28 Idem, 'The Western Wall', *Jerusalem Eternal*, edited by A. Eisenberg, New York, Board of Jewish Education, 1971, pp. 106-111.

29 Idem, 'Wailing Wall', *The Guide to Israel*, Jerusalem, 1977, pp. 136-138.

30 'Wailing Wall', *The Universal Jewish Encyclopedia*, X, New York 1943, pp. 441-442.

31 '...The Wailing Wall...', *Jerusalem – A History*, foreword by E.O. James, London, P. Hamlyn, 1967, pp. 258-259.

32 C.W. Wilson, '...The Wailing Place', *Ordnance Survey of Jerusalem*, London, H.M. Treasury, 1865, pp. 26-27, and Photographs, pp. 14-16.

33 C.W. Wilson & C. Warren, 'West Wall', *The Recovery of Jerusalem*, London. R. Bentley, 1871, pp. 76ff.

Travellers' Accounts

34 W.H. Bartlett, 'Jews' Place of Wailing', *Walks about the City and Environs of Jerusalem, Summer 1842*, Jerusalem, Canaan Publishing House, 1974, pp. 140-142.

35 Benjamin of Tudela, *The Itinerary of Benjamin of Tudela*, Critical text, translation and commentary by M.N. Adler, London, H. Frowde, 1907, pp. xvi, 94.

36 (Idem), *The Itinerary of Rabbi Benjamin of Tudela*, Translated and edited by A. Asher, New York, Hakesheth [n.d.], 2 vols.

37 I.J. Benjamin, 'The Temple', *Eight Years in Asia and Africa from 1846 to 1855*, Hanover 1859, pp. 13-19; Hanover 1863, pp. 19ff.

38 C. Biggs, '... Wailing Place of Jews', *Six Months in Jerusalem*, Oxford etc., Mowbray, 1896, pp. 165-168.

39 The Bordeaux Pilgrim, '... Jews' Wailing Place', *Itinerary from Bordeaux to Jerusalem*, translated by A. Stewart, London, Palestine Pilgrims' Text Society, 1896, I. p. 22.

40 I. Cohen, '...Western Wall', *The Journal of a Jewish Traveller*, London, Bodley Head, 1925, pp. 13-14.

41 M. Ehrenpreis, 'Kotel Maarawi', *The Soul of the East*, New York, Viking Press 1927, pp. 112-116.

42 Idem, 'At Wailing Wall', *A Book of Jewish Thoughts*, selected and arranged by ...J.H. Hertz, London, Office of the Chief Rabbi, 1943, p. 105.
D. Frischman, 'At the Wailing Wall', *Jerusalem Eternal*, edited by A. Eisenberg, New York, Board of Jewish Education, 1971, pp. 113-116.

43 S.S. Gafni, 'The Western Wall', *The Glory of Jerusalem – An Explorer's Guide*, Jerusalem. Steimatzky, 1978, pp. 28-31.

44 J.E. Hanauer, '... The Jews' Wailing Place', *Walks about Jerusalem*, London, London Society for Promoting Christianity amongst the Jews, 1890, pp. 100-105.

45 J. Kean, '...The Jews' Wailing Place', *Among the Holy Places*, London, T. Fisher Unwin [n.d.], p. 36-37.

46 Lievin de Hamme, 'Tears of the Jews', *Guide to the Holy Places*, Ghent, 1875, pp. 196-201.

47 M. Montefiore, '...The Western Wall'. *A Narrative of a Forty Days' Sojourn in the Holy Land*, London, Wertheimer, 1875, p. 134.

48 'The Prince of Wales and the Jews at Jerusalem', *The Jewish Chronicle and The Hebrew Observer*, 385, London 1862, p. 5.

Archaeology

49 B. Mazar, 'The Excavations south and west of the Temple Mount', *Ariel*, XXVII, Jerusalem 1970, pp. 11-19.

50 Idem, 'The Excavations in the Old City of Jerusalem near the Temple Mount – Preliminary Report of the Second and Third Seasons, 1969-1970', Jerusalem, Hebrew University etc., 1971, pp. 44; illus.

51 Idem, 'The Outer Walls and Gates of the Temple Mount – the Western Wall Section Formerly Called the Wailing Wall', *The Mountain of the Lord*, New York, Doubleday, 1975, pp. 131-138.

52 C. Warren, 'The Wailing Place', *Underground Jerusalem*, London, R. Bentley, 1876, pp. 355-379.

Rabbinic Material and Legend

53 R. Charif & S. Raz (eds.), 'The Western Wall', *Jerusalem the Eternal Bond*, Tel Aviv, Don, 1977, pp. 31-38.

54 M.M. Kasher, *The Western Wall – Its Meaning in the Thought of the Sages*, translated by Charles Wengrov, New York, Judaica Press, 1972, pp. 171.

55 'Midnight Prayers', *Jerusalem Eternal*, edited by A. Eisenberg, New York, Board of Jewish Education, 1971, pp. 117-121.

56 L.I. Rabinowitz, 'Misuse of Halacha', *The Jerusalem Post*, xlvii, no. 14002, Jerusalem 1977, p. 10.

57 Z. Vilnay, 'The Wailing Wall of the Jews'. *Legends of Palestine*, Philadelphia, Jewish Publication Society of America, 1932, pp. 59-73.

58 Idem, 'Kotel Ha-Maaravi – The Wailing Wall', *Legends of Jerusalem*, Philadelphia, Jewish Publication Society of America. 1973, pp. 159-181.

The Political Struggle for the Wall

59 N. Bentwich, 'The Crisis of the Western (Wailing) Wall, 1928-1928-1930', *England in Palestine*, London, Kegan Paul, Trench, Trubner, 1932, pp. 170-210.

60 H.E. Bocis, The *Jerusalem Question*, 1917-1968, California, Hoover Institution Press, Stanford University, 1971, pp. xii, 175.

61 ESCO Foundation for Palestine '. . .Wailing Wall Issue. . .', *Palestine – A Study of Jewish, Arab, and British Policies*, New Haven, Yale University Press, 1947, I, pp. 424-426.

62 Idem, 'The Wailing Wall Controversy and the Course of the Disturbances', *Palestine – A Study of Jewish, Arab, and British Policies*, New Haven, Yale University Press, 1970, II, pp. 597-635.

63 *Great Britain and Palestine 1915-1945 – Information Papers*, no. 20, London, Royal Institute of International Affairs, 1946, pp. xii, 177.

64 Y. Porath, 'The Conflict over the Wailing Wall and its Repercussions'. *The Emergence of the Palestinian – Arab National Movement*, 1918-1929, London, Frank Cass, 1974, pp. 258-273.

65 *The Rights and Claims of Moslems and Jews in Connection with the Wailing Wall at Jerusalem*, Beirut, Institute for Palestine Studies, 1966, pp. 93.

66 H. Sidebotham, 'The Wailing Wall, *Great Britain and Palestine*', London, Macmillan, 1937, pp. 158-175.

67 J. Klausner, 'Love or Hatred – Choose!' *The Palestine Weekly*, Jerusalem 9.8.1929, pp. 116-118.

68 Palestine – Petition Concerning the Incident at the Wailing Wall, Jerusalem (September 24th, 1928), *League of Nations Permanent Mandates Commission, Minutes of the Fourteenth Session. . . October 26th to November 13th, 1928*, Geneva 1928, pp. 205-207.

69 'The Wailing Wall "Atrocities" ', *The Palestine Weekly*, Jerusalem, 9.8.1929, pp. 114-115.

70 I. Ben-Avi, 'J'accuse! A sequel to "The Wailing Wall Atrocities", *The Palestine Weekly*, Jerusalem, 23.8.1929, pp. 136-139.

71 *The Western or Wailing Wall in Jerusalem*, Memorandum by the Secretary of State for the Colonies, Presented by the Secretary of State for the Colonies to Parliament by Command of His Majesty, November, 1928, London HMSO, 1928, pp. 6.

72 J.H. Kann, *Some Observations on the Policy of the Mandatory Government of Palestine with Regard to the Arab Attacks on the Jewish Population in August 1929 and the Jewish and the Arab Sections of the Population*, Hague, M. Nijhoff, 1930, pp. 60.

73 Colonial Office, Palestine Commission on the Disturbances of August 1929, London, HMSO, 1930, 2 vols. + Index.

74 *Report of the Commission on the Palestine Disturbances of August, 1929*, Presented by the Secretary of State for the Colonies to Parliament by Command of His Majesty, March, 1930, London, HMSO, 1930, pp. 202.

75 H.B. Samuel, *Beneath the Whitewash (A Critical Analysis of the Report of the Commission on the Palestine Disturbances of August, 1929)*, London, Hogarth Press, 1930, pp. 50.

76 L. Stein, *Memorandum on the 'Report of the Commission on the Palestine Disturbances of August 1929'*, London, Jewish Agency for Palestine, 1930, pp. 111.

77 H. Schneiderman, 'Review of the Year 5689', *AJYB* XXXI (1929), pp. 70-79.

78 C. Sykes '. . . Wailing Wall. . .', *Crossroads to Israel*, Cleveland and New York, World Publishing Co., 1965, pp. 100-102, 108-111, 112-114.

79 C. Adler, *Memorandum on the Western Wall*, Submitted to the Special Commission of the League of Nations on Behalf of the Rabbinate, the Jewish Agency for Palestine, the Jewish Community of Palestine (Knesseth Israel) and the Central Agudath Israel of Palestine, Jerusalem 1930, pp. 76.

80 *Report of the Commission Appointed by His Majesty's Government. . .to Determine the Rights and Claims of Moslems and Jews in Connection with the Western or Wailing Wall at Jerusalem, December 1930*, London, HMSO, 1931, pp. 75.

81 Jewish Agency for Palestine, *Memorandum on the 'Report of the Commission on the Palestine Disturbances of August 1929'*, Submitted. . . to the Secretary-General of the League of Nations, for the Information of the Permanent Mandates Commission, May, 1930, London 1930, pp. 110.

82 'Holy Places', *Report by His Majesty's Government in the United Kingdom of Great Britain and Northern Ireland to the Council of the League of Nations on the Administration of Palestine and Trans-Jordan for the Year 1930*, London, HMSO, 1931, pp. 76-77.

83 H. Schneiderman, 'Review of the Year 5690' *AJYB*, XXXII (1930), pp. 129-139.

84 'Palestine (Western or Wailing Wall) Order in Council, 1931, At the court at Buckingham Palace, the 19th Day of May, 1931', *Official Gazette of the Government of Palestine 1931*, Jerusalem 1931, pp. 464-468.

85 'The Palestine (Western or Wailing Wall) Order in Council, 1931', *The Laws of Palestine*, Revised edition... by R.H. Drayton, ILL, London 1933, pp. 2635-2639.

86 'Palestine (Western or Wailing Wall) Order in Council, 1931. At the Court at Buckingham Palace, the 19th Day of May, 1931', *Laws of Palestine 1926-1931...*, edited by M. Doukhan, IV, Tel-Aviv, 1933, pp. 1484-1487.

87 F.H. Kisch, 'The Wailing Wall', *Letter... to the Chairman Political Commission, XVII Zionist Congress..*:, Jerusalem 1931, p. 30.

88 Y. Porath, 'The Resolution of the Wailing Wall Problem', *The Palestinian Arab National Movement*, II, London, Frank Cass, 1977, pp. 6-8.

89 A. Revusky, 'The Wailing Wall', *Jews in Palestine*, New York, Bloch, 1945, pp. 17-28.

90 H. Schneiderman, 'Review of the Year 5691', *AJYB*, XXXIII (1931), pp. 99-109.

91 'The Jewish Claim in Regard to Jerusalem', *Palestine Partition Commission Report*, Presented by the Secretary of State for the Colonies to Parliament by Command of His Majesty, October, 1938, London, HMSO, 1938, pp. 73-80.

92 'Wailing Wall', *A Survey of Palestine*, Prepared in December 1945 and January 1946 for the Information of the Anglo-American Committee of Inquiry, 2 vols., Palestine Government Printer, 1946, pp. 26 923.

93 'Neturei Karta Seek Consent to pray at Wall – from Hussein', *The Jerusalem Post*, xlviii, No. 14213 (Jerusalem 9.1.1978), p. 3.

The War of Independence and the Six-Day War

94 P. de Azcarate, 'The Surrender of the Jewish Quarter of Jerusalem', *Mission in Palestine 1948-1952*, Washington, The Middle East Institute, 1966, pp. 64-79.

95 R.S. & W.S. Churchill, 'Jerusalem and the West Bank', *The Six Day War*; London, Heinemann, 1967, pp. 123-142.

96 D. Joseph, *The Faithful City – The Siege of Jerusalem, 1948*. New York, Simon and Schuster, 1960, pp. 356; illus.

97 E. Landau, 'The Wall', *Jerusalem the Eternal*, Tel-Aviv, Otpaz, 1968, pp. 166-168.

98 A. Rabinovich, 'The Temple Mount', *The Battle for Jerusalem, June 5-7, 1967*, Philadelphia, Jewish Publication Society of America. 1972, pp. 409-439.

99 W. Stevenson, 'The Wailing Wall', *Strike Zion*! New York, Bantam Books, 1967, pp. 61-72; illus.

Planning the Piazza at the Wall

100 *Plan for the Western Wall Precinct – Preliminary Submission*, Prepared for the Municipality of Jerusalem and the Corporation for the Development of the Jewish Quarter, Jerusalem, Moshe Safdie Architect Ltd., 1974, pp. 21, 17; illus. [In Hebrew and English; duplicated].

101 'Haifa Architect Offers Plan for Western Wall', *The Jerusalem Post*, xlvi, no. 13614 (Jerusalem, 1976), p.2.

102 D. Kroyanker, 'The Various Plans for the Square in front of the Western Wall', *Developing Jerusalem, 1967-1975*, Jerusalem, Jerusalem Committee, 1975, pp. 118-123.

103 A. Rabinovich, 'New Proposal for Western Wall Area', *The Jerusalem Post*, xlviii, no. 14296 (Jerusalem, 1978), p.3.

The Wall in Literature

104 I.J. Benjamin, '... The Western Wall', *Eight Years in Asia and Africa from 1846 to 1855*, Hanover 1863, p. 20.

105 Scholem Aleichem. 'The Wailing Wall' *Jerusalem Eternal*, edited by A. Eisenberg, New York, Board of Education, 1971, p. 112.

The Wall in Islamic Tradition

106 C.D. Matthews, 'The Wailing Wall and Al-Buraq – Is the "Wailing Wall" in Jerusalem the "Wall of Al-Buraq" of Moslem Tradition?" *The Moslem World* XXII, New York 1932, pp. 331-339.

ACKNOWLEDGEMENTS

The authors and the Publishing House of the Israel Ministry of Defence wish to acknowledge the help they have received in making this book from individuals, bodies and institutions. This help manifested itself in advice, suggestions and research and in making available to us written material, photographs and illustrations. Our particular thanks are extended to:

"Masada" publishing house for its permission to use material from *Ha-Kotel Ha-Ma'aravi*, by Rabbi Mordechai Ha-Kohen; Prof. Dov Noy for his monograph, *Sippurei Am Al Ha-Kotel Ha-Ma'aravi* ("Folk-tales about the Western Wall"); Prof. Yehuda Feliks for his article *Ha-Zimhiyah ve-Ha-Hai she-al Ha-Kotel* ("Flora and Fauna on the Wall"); "Yad Ben Zvi" for permission to use Ruth P. Goldschmidt-Lehman's comprehensive bibliography which originally appeared in *Katedra*, No. 12; Israel Museum in Jerusalem for the great amount of material on art and crafts; Tel Aviv Museum which allowed us to photograph Marc Chagall's painting; the Rosenfeld Gallery in Tel Aviv for its help regarding the photographs of Shemuel Katz's paintings; Mrs. Dora Gutman who helped us locate Nahum Gutman's paintings and drawings of the Wall; Mrs. Hermon for her permission to reproduce her father's, Ludwig Blum, painting; Mr. Nahman Ran who supplied the colour separation of David Roberts' etching; Hayyah Benjamin, Iran Levitt and Judith Heller of the Israel Museum; Dr. Micha Levin who helped in the chapter on art and crafts; Ya'acov Lehman of Jerusalem who made his great collection of post-cards available; Rabbi Israel Low whose advice at the beginning of the project was so valuable; the author, Hayyim Beer who read the manuscript and made important suggestions.

A book of the nature of this volume, based as it is on hundreds of photographs and old illustrations, could not possibly be made without the active cooperation of libraries and archives and particularly their staffs: The Israel National Library in Jerusalem; the library of "Yad Yitzhak Ben-Zvi;" the library of Tel Aviv University; the Keren Ha-Yesod Archive; the Jewish National Fund Archive; the Central Zionist Archives; the IDF Archives; the Government Press Office; the editorial board of Ba-Mahaneh.

Dozens of photographs of past generations and the present are represented in this volume. Many of the new photographs are the work of Meir Ben-Dov and Moshe Eitan, a photographer and laboratory technician of the Publishing House of the Israel Ministry of Defence, who also helped a great deal in "rejuvenating" some of the old illustrations and photographs. Our special thanks are extended to Micha Bar-Am, who, in addition to his own photographs, made available a number of photographs from the beginnings of the art in Eretz Israel.

This list would be incomplete without mentioning the debt we owe to the many technicians who were involved in all the multifaceted stages in the production of this book. Our thanks to all of them.

Finally, in a list of acknowledgements as long as this errors and omissions are likely to be made. Our gratitude and apologies are extended to all who helped us and whose names were omitted from this list.

הכותל

מאיר בן-דב, מרדכי נאור
זאב ענר

עיצוב גרפי: יואב בן-צור
יואב גרפיקה בע"מ

משרד הבטחון - ההוצאה לאור

1983